INDIANA *A History*

INDIANA *A History*

By WILLIAM E. WILSON

INDIANA UNIVERSITY PRESS · *Bloomington and London*

First paperback edition 1977

Copyright © 1966 by William E. Wilson

All rights reserved

Published in Canada by Fitzhenry & Whiteside Limited, Don Mills, Ontario

Manufactured in the United States of America

Library of Congress Catalog Card Number 66–22445
cl. ISBN 0–253–14150–8   pa. ISBN 0–253–28305–1

For Gordon and Ellen Katherine

ACKNOWLEDGMENTS

The friendship of many people in Indiana has been of help to me while I was writing this book. I am grateful to all of them. I wish to acknowledge specifically the aid and comfort of the following:

Mr. Edwin H. Cady, Mrs. Dorothy C. Collins, Mr. Philip B. Daghlian, Miss Caroline Dunn, Mrs. Hazel Hopper, Mr. Alexander L. Leich, Dr. Charles F. Leich, Mr. William Merimee, Mr. Lynne L. Merritt, Jr., Mr. Robert W. Mitchner, Mrs. Thomas J. Morton, Jr., Mr. Norman J.G. Pounds, Mr. David A. Randall, Miss Jane Rodman, Mr. David Rogers, Mrs. Beverly Strong, Mr. Gordon Bish Thompson, Miss Emma Lou Thornbrough, Miss Gayle Thornbrough, Mrs. Milburn Truitt, Miss Marcia Wheeler, Mr. Douglas C. Wilson, and my wife Ellen.

I wish also to express my thanks for a grant for research assistance from the Graduate Research Division of Indiana University.

W. E. W.

Contents

☆

Illustrations

(between pages 116–117)

Maps

INDIANA *A History*

Chapter One

☆

The Hoosier State

THE STATE of Indiana points southward 276 miles from the lower end of Lake Michigan toward the Gulf of Mexico and so stands athwart one third of the path that any east-west traveler must take on an overland journey across the United States. Because the fastest east-west interstate highways and the majority of railway trunk lines pass through the northern and central portions of Indiana and because modern tourists are intent mainly upon arriving anywhere other than where they are, and in the greatest possible hurry, the impression of Indiana left in the minds of such east-west transients is often incomplete and not altogether accurate. A flat land is what most of them remember, a flat land of rectangular fields planted mostly in corn, a flat land ornamented occasionally by small lakes and tree-shaded villages and scarred in one or two places by unprepossessing industrial areas.

Fewer travelers from outside the state cross Indiana in a north-south direction than those who make the east-west journey. One reason is that fewer direct highways run north and south through Indiana; another is that there are fewer places to come from or go to in a hurry on such routes. If there were more of these north-south tourists, the image of Indiana in outsiders' minds would be considerably altered. Corn would remain among the travelers' principal impressions; corn is everywhere in Indiana; but added to the flat land and the lakes and villages and industrial areas would be hills and ravines, caves and deep woodlands, and winding rivers.

3

Two thirds of the distance from Lake Michigan to the state's southernmost tip—or as far down as Terre Haute on the western border and Lawrenceburg on the eastern side—Indiana is monotonously 145 miles wide, even where it invades the southern loop of Michigan's waters and boldly approaches Chicago's lakefront. The state is thus straight-sided from the waist up because lawmakers and surveyors corseted it along meridian lines when Illinois was separated from Indiana Territory in 1809, with slight alterations in 1816 when Indiana became a state. Below the waistline—from Terre Haute and Lawrenceburg down to the tip of Posey County, where the Wabash River joins the Ohio—the width of the state varies with the temperamental meanders of these two rivers.

Every Hoosier schoolboy learns to say that Indiana is bounded on the north by Michigan, on the south by Kentucky, on the west by Illinois, and on the east by Ohio. In the main this is so, but a close look at a map shows that Kentucky bounds some of the east of Indiana as well as the south. The Wabash River definitely forms the western boundary of the state below Terre Haute, but the Ohio River, commonly called the southern boundary, is more eastern than southern along one third of its edging of Indiana. Most people, including most Hoosiers, forget that the Ohio flows in a sharp southwesterly direction and that when Hoosiers cross it to leave the state in many places above Jeffersonville they are headed east, not south.

The reason for such different views of Indiana as those of the east-west and the north-south travelers across the state is that Indiana is two distinct regions instead of one. Geologists like to think of it as three, but Hoosiers generally see their state divided by the Old National Road, now U.S. Route 40, and are likely to say, if asked where they are from, either "Northern Indiana" or "Southern Indiana." Within Indiana's boundaries, the Old National Road, surveyed by a Quaker named Jonathan Knight and cleared of outcropping geodes for its first traffic by 1832, is only a few miles longer than the state's width, entering Indiana from the east just below the 40th Parallel at Richmond, passing through the heart of Indianapolis, and departing for Illinois a short distance west of Terre Haute and the Wabash River.

Above this highway, Indiana is indeed a far-horizoned land, if not altogether flat. Here the great prairie begins its gradual upward tilt toward the Rockies a thousand miles away, and here, hardly distinguishable among lakes and marshes, is the watershed between the systems of the St. Lawrence and the Mississippi. This land is fabulously fertile for the growing of corn, wheat, oats, soy beans, and tomatoes, except in the Calumet area near Chicago, where a Colossus of comparatively recent industrial development stands astride a stretch of singing sand dunes along the shore of Lake Michigan.

The Calumet takes its name from the river Calumet, christened by the early French as the Chalumeau, which means a hollow reed of the sort that pipestems can be made of. It includes Gary, Hammond, East Chicago, and Whiting, each one contiguous to another and with a combined population close to half a million. Outside the Calumet there are two other large cities in the north, South Bend and Fort Wayne, each with metropolitan populations above 200,000; and there are a half-dozen smaller cities of 40,000 or more north of the Old National Road: Anderson, Elkhart, Kokomo, Lafayette, Marion, and Muncie.

Below the Old National Road, the scenery of Indiana changes to hills, smaller farms, smaller towns, and fewer cities. Large manmade reservoirs are beginning to dot this area, but it is not naturally lake country. Here in the south, however, are most of Indiana's major rivers, among them the two-forked White and the two-forked Whitewater, the Blue, and the lower Wabash, and many rambling creeks. They flow toward all points of the compass, but eventually each fingers its way southward and in time its waters join those of the Ohio. Some of these rivers and creeks provide rich bottomlands in the Ohio Valley, and on the good land of the south corn, soy beans, and tomatoes prosper, but not in such great abundance as in the north. The southwestern corner of the state, known as "The Pocket," is famous for its melons as well as these other crops.

Here, on the Ohio, is the region's largest city, Evansville, a community of ups and downs in its growth throughout its century and a half of history, but with a metropolitan population in 1960 of

200,000. The only other large urban concentration in the south is the New Albany–Jeffersonville area on the Ohio, across from Louisville, Kentucky, with about 60,000 people in 1960. Vincennes, the state's oldest town continuously inhabited by white men, is in southern Indiana, as is Corydon, the first state capital. The population of Vincennes was less than 20,000 in 1960; Corydon is a village of a few thousand people.

Geology explains, in part, the difference between the two halves of Hoosierland. After the receding of the pre-Cambrian Sea, which once covered the whole area, three glaciers invaded what is now the state of Indiana. The first, called the Illinoian, moved down as far as the Ohio River and beyond it, except for one north-south strip that runs through the central part of the state and is known as the Crawford Upland. The second, called the Early Wisconsin, stopped about two thirds of the way down the state at a line that is sometimes almost visible in the abrupt change of scenery that one witnesses as one drives along a north-south highway. The last, the Late Wisconsin, came only halfway down the state.

The result of the triple invasion of ice in the north was the leveling of hills and their crumbling into fine glacial subsoil, which in some of the farm land is many feet deep. In the once-glaciated and the unglaciated sections of the south, on the other hand, the hills remain tall and sometimes steep, and the land is not so fertile. Where there was no glaciation at all, there is almost no subsoil, and the bedrock is eroded into deep canyons and sharp ridges.

This unglaciated area, the Crawford Upland, which extends in a band down from Parke and Putnam counties to the Ohio River, is the most scenic of the state. It is the location of Marengo and Wyandotte caves—Wyandotte is the third largest in the United States—and of "Jug Rock" and "The Pinnacle" near Shoals, and its geological history accounts for the beauties of Shades, Turkey Run, McCormick's Creek, and Spring Mill, four of Indiana's score of state parks. In this unglaciated strip, as in the rest of southern Indiana, the hills generally run east and west, and streams and rivers have a difficult time wending their way south. Across the entire southern half of the state, there are seven bands of alternating upland and lowland, three such combinations occurring in southeastern Indiana, three in south-central Indiana, and one in the southwest.

Indiana's climate is mild and does not vary greatly from north to south, the widest difference in mean temperatures in the extremes of the two regions being only ten degrees in January and five in July and the altitudes above sea level ranging only from 313 feet in Vanderburgh County to 1,285 feet in Randolph County. Nevertheless winter temperatures can, and do, drop well below zero in the north, and a day or two when the thermometer reaches 100 can be expected almost every summer in the south. These figures are of course Fahrenheit.

The high humidity of Indiana comes from the Gulf of Mexico, the prevailing wind in the mid-latitudes being from the southwest. An average of seven tornadoes a year strike the state, but five within a few hours on April 11, 1965, created the worst disaster the state has ever known, killing 140 people, injuring more than a thousand, and causing about one hundred and seventy-five millions of dollars of damage to property in two bands across the north and central regions of the state. The north, especially in a snow-pocket around South Bend, is subject to annual blizzards. But even including such dramatic exceptions as these, the average wind velocity in Indiana is only eight miles an hour and only one fifteenth of the average annual precipitation of 40 inches is snow. In spite of increasing efforts at flood control, floods ravage the valleys of the White, Wabash, and Ohio rivers in early spring, but seldom disastrously, and droughts, especially in the southern hill country, cause hardship from time to time.

Because the climate of Indiana from north to south does not vary widely, indigenous animal and plant life is almost uniform throughout the state. The persimmon, the black gum, the cypress, and certain oaks of the south do not commonly grow in the north, and the tamaracks and bog willows of the north are not seen in the south; but the beech, the sycamore, hickories, the common fruit trees, and the yellow poplar or tulip tree, which is the state tree, are almost ubiquitous. The elderberry is the commonest shrub and the violet the commonest wildflower; however, anyone familiar with the Hoosier countryside, north and south, associates with it also the wild roses, trumpet vines, ox-eyed daisies, and Queen Anne's lace of summer and the sumac, goldenrod, asters, and sunflowers of autumn. Trailing arbutus, one of the earliest of spring flowers, grows only in Monroe County and in the Lake Michigan dunes. Apricots do not flourish north of the Old National Road, and the Golden Rain Tree, sometimes thought of as synonymous with Indiana but actually an import from China via Mexico, has a hard time where winters are excessively cold.

Throughout Indiana there is a glut of bird song in the air in spring and summer, a phenomenon immediately noted by visitors and new residents, and Hoosiers are often inveterate birdwatchers. The cardinal is the state bird, but equally characteristic of the state are meadowlarks, orioles, robins, flickers, grackles and redwinged blackbirds, phoebes, wrens, finches, and many varieties of singing sparrows. In some sections the melodious and friendly mockingbird stays all winter, among juncoes, chickadees, titmice, and cardinals. Warblers pass through the state in spring and fall in great profusion, and in winter evening grosbeaks are sometimes seen as far south as the Old National Road and below it. Common also in the background music of the Hoosier setting is the coo of mourning doves, which are not regarded as game birds in the state as they are in some places. Quail, partridge, ducks, and pheasants of course are protected by limited hunting seasons.

Hardly a native Hoosier lives who has not at one time or another in his life caught a catfish or sunfish and who does not recognize pike, pickerel, and bass. Fewer Hoosiers have killed rattlesnakes and copperheads, although these reptiles are encountered occasionally, along with many that are nonpoisonous, in the hills of the south especially. Although wildcats and bears have left the state, most Hoosiers have been brought up on stories about them. Gone too is the wolf, or at least reduced almost to extinction, leaving the red fox, the gray fox, and a few coyotes as the only remaining carnivorous wild animals. There are deer in Indiana woods and beaver along the streams, and perhaps it was as much to divert hunters from them as to replenish a scarcity that the state's Department of Conservation imported rabbits from Missouri in the 1950's, with the result today that it is not uncommon to see

Peter and his relatives lippety-lip across city streets as well as country roads. Hoosier suburban gardeners regard Mr. MacGregor's problem as nothing compared with their own in the growing of unfenced flower and vegetable plots. Raccoon, opossum, muskrat, woodchuck, squirrel, and skunk still thrive in Indiana, as do the smaller mole, shrew, fieldmouse, and chipmunk.

Indiana's farmers raise horses, beef and dairy cattle, and some sheep, although from pioneer days to the present mutton and lamb have never been widely popular in the Hoosier diet. But the four-legged creature that dominates the Indiana farm scene is the hog. In pioneer times, hogs were seldom fenced and were allowed to roam the woods and feast on mast. Later, with improved fencing, their diet changed to corn. By 1860 there were two hogs for every person in the state. Today, with roughly 60 per cent of Indiana urban and less than 40 per cent rural, hogs and human beings populate the state in about equal numbers, but Indiana still stands third in the nation in hog raising, outclassed in that endeavor only by Iowa and Illinois. A few years ago, Logan Esarey, an Indiana historian, nominated the hog as monarch of the state. "We may sing the praises of all the heroes of Indiana from La Salle or George Rogers Clark to the present," wrote Professor Esarey eloquently, "but the prosperity of our state . . . has depended on Mr. Hog. In fat years and lean years . . . he has come up with his part, even though he does grunt about it considerably."

There are others, however, who argue that corn, and not the hog, is king in Indiana. After all, corn predates the hog in the state, and now that the supply of mast is depleted, the growing of corn must precede the raising of hogs. Corn was a staple of the Hopewellian mound builders' diet in prehistoric times before hogs were domesticated, and of the later Indians' diet before the white men came, and corn was always the first crop the white men planted after they arrived and settled. Although the land area of Indiana is comparatively small—36,291 square miles, less than two thirds of that of Iowa or of Illinois—Indiana ranks with Iowa and Illinois among the three top producers of corn as well as hogs in the United States.

Certainly it is corn that every visitor to Indiana remembers, whether his path takes him across the great corn-producing counties of the north or the less fertile hill country of the south. In the late 1940's, an author at the Indiana University Writers' Conference, fresh from New York City and probably never before strayed from its sidewalks, was taken on the customary tour of Brown County near Bloomington and came back so impressed by the cornfields of that region, noted for its hills but certainly not for its farmland, that he was heard muttering throughout the rest of his stay in Indiana: "All that corn! There's lots of bourbon in them-thar hills!"

The prevalence of corn in the diet has had its effect upon the Hoosier as well as his hog, if we can rely upon the statistics and the logic of a member of the United States Sanitary Commission who once undertook a study of human height and came up with the conclusion that because Indianans ate corn they were at one time the tallest people in the world. The statistician's reasoning ran something like this: in the 1860's natives of the United States were "the tallest of all civilized countries"; in the Civil War Indiana men were "the tallest of the United States"; the grains of the North Central states are the richest in the world in proteids and heat units; prior to the Civil War Indianans ate more corn than anything else; *ergo.* . . . Such a statistician might be able to demonstrate that corn still makes the Hoosier the tallest civilized man in the world if statistics are available to prove the apparent preponderance of Hoosiers among the nation's finest basketball players.

In spite of a certain uniformity of climate, flora, fauna, and farm life, and a universal predilection for corn, not only in diet but sometimes also, alas, in humor, music, literature, politics, education, and even religion, the two halves of Indiana are different, as has been stated above, and the reason for the difference is not altogether geological. There is a noticeable disparity that derives from the origins in America of the people who live on either side of the Old National Road. While the majority of Indianans are of English, Scottish, Irish, and German descent, the southern half of the state was settled mainly by pioneers moving up via Kentucky from Virginia and the Carolinas, while the northern half drew some of its early population from New England and New York State via Ohio. Furthermore, the people of the south have been in the state, on the whole, a generation or two longer than those of the north.

Evidence of this difference offers itself in the architecture, the social habits, and even, in some degree, in the speech of the two regions. Old houses in the south, especially along the Ohio River, are high-ceilinged, sometimes columned or galleried, and often casually rambling and gracious as such houses are in the South, whereas in the upper counties of the state there is often a certain shipshape austerity in both architecture and landscape that suggests the more restrained elegance of the East. Life in southern Indiana moves at a slower pace, food is of the Southern variety and cooked in the Southern manner, and the people there tend to drawl and distort their vowels as they do in the South; in northern Indiana, manners and speech, while certainly not Eastern, are hardly distinguishable from those of northern Ohioans and the Michigan people who live nearby.

There are, of course, many exceptions to these generalizations, for no generalization is consistently tenable and the Hoosier is not a person who can be simply explained or easily catalogued. For example, the Quakers who settled the upper Whitewater Valley, though they came from the Carolinas and Virginia, have made a distinct impression upon this southeastern region of Indiana that is not altogether Southern; in the southwest, around Jasper, Huntingburg, and St. Meinrad, where a sudden view from State Road 62 of the spires of St. Meinrad Abbey gives the traveler a sense of being translated to the Old World, the culture is predominantly German; and in the north the Calumet stands definitely apart from its surroundings. Gary, in the Calumet, is the only major city in the United States besides Washington, D.C., in which the nonwhite population outnumbers the white.

The Calumet might indeed be called a third region of Indiana. Within the twentieth century it has mushroomed from a few small villages with a total population of only 19,000 in 1905, before the founding of Gary, to its present metropolitan size and density. This rapid growth came about largely through the immigration of people with more recent and more widely varied European origins than those of the rest of the state. The result is the development of a different culture, with many folkways preserved from the Old World and with attitudes and concerns common to American city dwellers everywhere.

In spite of Indiana's divisions and its variety, Indianans are homogeneous in at least one respect. All natives and inhabitants of Indiana exhibit a strong and sometimes egotistical pride in their state. Indeed if we may interpret a remark by an Indian chief as an expression of regional pride, it could be argued that hubris in Indiana predates the white man. According to Jacob Piatt Dunn, another of the state's historians, when The Little Turtle was told that his Indians probably descended from Asians, he asked how anyone could be sure that the Asians had not descended from the Indians. Had The Little Turtle known the word, he would probably have called himself a Hoosier, as do all Indianans today, northerners, southerners, and residents of the Calumet alike.

Where this nickname came from is still a matter of debate, even among the Hoosiers themselves. Some say the word is one way of spelling the pioneer's greeting to strangers at his cabin door: "Who is yer?" or maybe "Who's yere (here)?" Others trace the word to a company of hussars who once made a nuisance of themselves in Kentucky by their hard drinking and rowdyism with the result that the term "hussar" or "hoosier" was applied to any objectionable outsider in Kentucky, especially the frontiersmen of Indiana from across the river. "Dirty person, tramp . . . a native or inhabitant of Indiana," is the definition of *Hoosier* arrived at by the editors of *Webster's New World Dictionary of the American Language,* among whom, incidentally, were several Hoosier professors. Other authorities, including the aforementioned Jacob Piatt Dunn, contend that the word originally came from England where "hoose" is still a common name for a disease of calves, known otherwise as *strongylus micrurius,* or roundworms, which "causes their hair to turn back and gives them a wild, staring look." Such, we may suppose, was the condition of the Hoosier frontiersman's hair and eyes after he had worn a coonskin cap all winter and had not seen a fellow human being in the wilderness for a coon's age. *Indiana: A Guide to the Hoosier State,* compiled by the Work Projects Administration in 1941, offers a more flattering answer to the question of the word's origin. In 1825, say its editors, there was a contractor on the Ohio Falls Canal at Louisville named Samuel Hoosier who preferred Indiana men as laborers on his project because they were more reliable than the other workmen available in the vicinity. Hoosier's employees were known as "Hoosier men" and later simply as "Hoosiers." If such matters could be decided by referendum, no doubt the people of Indiana would settle for this last explanation, because they regard the sobriquet "Hoosier" as a great honor and distinction.

Prehistoric mound-building Indians were the first inhabitants of Indiana, and after them and descended from them were tribes of Shawnees, Miamis, Potawatomis, Piankashaws, Delawares, and other Indians. Before any white men actually settled in the region, French *coureurs de bois* came down singly from Canada and lived and traded among the Indians. The first permanent settlement of Europeans in the Wabash Valley was that of the French at Vincennes. They were probably there as early as 1727; they had built a fort by 1732. Vincennes was taken from the French by the British and was later captured by George Rogers Clark during the American Revolution. In 1800 it became the seat of government of Indiana Territory.

Indiana was admitted to the Union in 1816, and Jonathan Jennings became its first Governor. In that same year, Abraham Lincoln, a boy of seven, came to Indiana with his parents and sister and lived in Spencer County for fourteen years before moving on to Illinois. Lincoln's mother, Nancy Hanks Lincoln, died in Spencer County and is buried there. In 1820, a commission of the General Assembly selected a site in the wilderness at the center of the state as the future capital, and the town of Indianapolis was laid out the next year.

In the period of early settlement, the Indiana country was the scene of numerous Indian wars. The Little Turtle, a Miami chief born near Fort Wayne, won two engagements with the United States Army near Fort Wayne in 1790 and 1791 before he was finally defeated at Fallen Timbers in Ohio. In 1811, General William Henry Harrison, governor of Indiana Territory, surprised and overwhelmed the followers of Tecumseh at Tippecanoe. Tecumseh himself was not present at this battle, having left his people in the care of his brother, The Prophet, while he traveled through the South to recruit Indian allies. When Tecumseh returned, he found his Indian federation in ruins. By the middle of the nineteenth century there were very few Indians left in the state that had been named for them. Today, of the 700,000 Indians in North America only about 4,000 persons of Indian ancestry live in Indiana.

The only other battles fought on Indiana soil were the skirmishes between Home Guards and the Confederate cavalry of General John Hunt Morgan when Morgan crossed the Ohio at Mauckport in the summer of 1863 and raided across the southeastern corner of the state. Although Indiana was believed to be the stronghold of secret Copperhead societies in the Civil War, Morgan's Raid failed to rally any Southern sympathizers among the Hoosiers. In fact, Indiana was strong in its support of the Union during the war. About 200,000 Hoosiers served in the Federal army, and of that number 25,000 lost their lives in the conflict.

Since the Civil War, the history of Indiana has been largely the story of its gradual development from an agrarian to an industrial state. As the Calumet grew, steel became one of the major products of the state and in recent years, like corn and hogs, placed Indiana third in the nation in its output. Eighty per cent of the nation's building limestone comes from Indiana as does 12 per cent of its household furniture. Indiana is seventh in the United States in the production of fire clay and is one of the country's major sources of bituminous coal. Once a center of the manufacture of agricultural implements, carriages and wagons and, later, the heart of the automobile industry, Indiana's principal products now, in addition to those previously mentioned, are electrical machinery, pharmaceuticals, chemicals, communications equipment, prefabricated buildings, musical instruments, and phonograph records.

In the last one hundred years, Indiana has been more often Republican than Democratic in its politics, but from an outsider's view it has not always been easy to tell which party was in power, for both of them tend toward conservatism. Because of the remoteness of the state from the coasts, the interest of its people concentrates upon domestic problems more often than international affairs, and as a consequence some of the strongest isolationist sentiment in the nation has emanated from Indiana's politicians. In varying degrees of stridency the voice of "one-hundred-per-cent Americanism" has appealed to Indiana voters for the past fifty years. At the same time, the state has produced Eugene V. Debs, the most noted leader of the Socialist Party in American history, and men with broad international views of American destiny such as Albert J. Beveridge and Wendell L. Willkie. Since 1962, the governor and both senators have been Democrats. Seven presidential candidates have been either natives or, for considerable numbers of years, residents of Indiana, and three of them—Lincoln and the two Harrisons—were elected. Of eight candidates for the vice presidency, Colfax, Hendricks, Fairbanks, and Marshall were elected.

A few crusading Hoosiers from the beginning supported public education, and the once backward state now has one of the highest literacy rates in the nation. As early as 1825 Robert Owen was experimenting with new educational theories in his Utopian colony at New Harmony; soon thereafter, William Maclure established in that town the first trade school in the country; Evansville opened the first public high school in the West for both boys and girls in 1854; and for many of the early years of the present century the public school system of Gary was a subject of observation and study among American and foreign educators. There are four state-supported institutions of higher learning in Indiana: Indiana University at Bloomington, Purdue University at West Lafayette, Ball State University at Muncie, and Indiana State University at Terre Haute. These public universities are supplemented by branches, or "centers," throughout the state and by thirty-five privately supported colleges and universities, including such nationally recognized institutions as DePauw, Wabash, Earlham, Butler, Hanover, and Notre Dame, which is the largest Catholic university for men in the United States.

This long tradition of emphasis on education may account, in part at least, for the third major preoccupation of Hoosiers after politics and schools; that is, literature. Since the publication of *The Hoosier School-Master* in 1871, Indianans have maintained a steady flow of books from the nation's publishers, not the least of which is the firm of Bobbs-Merrill at Indianapolis, now a subsidiary of Howard W. Sams and Company. The list of Indiana authors includes such widely varied talents and interests as those of Lew Wallace, James Whitcomb Riley, Booth Tarkington, Meredith Nicholson, Theodore Dreiser, George Ade, George Jean Nathan, Elmer Davis, and Eli Lilly. Riley is probably the only poet who ever became a millionaire by writing verse; Lilly is one of very few millionaires who ever became a writer with a genuine literary style.

Today the literary flood flows unabated in Indiana, although its so-called "Golden Age," when Riley, Tarkington, and Company were in their heyday, has passed. Each year Hoosier writers are honored with awards at an Indiana Authors' Day banquet, and in 1965 the Indiana Author's Day Committee had to consider 158 books published in the previous year by 135 natives and residents of the state. That means that about one out of every 20,000 adult Hoosiers got his name on the title page of a book in 1964; it is safe to guess that most of the other 19,999 will keep on trying.

Some Hoosiers who have made a place for themselves in the nation's history by following other avenues than politics, education, and literature are: James B. Eads, builder of the Eads Bridge across the Mississippi; Richard J. Gatling, inventor of the prototype of the machine gun; Elwood Haynes, a pioneer in the making of automobiles; Wilbur Wright, Virgil Grissom, and Frank Borman, pioneers in air and space; Alva Roebuck, co-founder of Sears, Roebuck; Bernard Gimbel, president of Gimbel Brothers; John T. McCutcheon, *Chicago Tribune* cartoonist; Hoagy Carmichael and Cole Porter, popular composers; Knute Rockne, Wilbur Shaw, Don Lash, and Mordecai (Three-Finger) Brown, of the sports world; Generals Burnside and Hershey, of the Civil War and World War Two; and George W. Whistler, civil engineer, the husband of "Whistler's Mother."

The Hoosier then, what is he? His character is not easy to describe, for he is a compound of many contradictory qualities. He is both sentimental and shrewd, provincial and sophisticated, suspicious and generous, nosey and self-contained, quick-tempered and kind, self-righteous and tolerant, egotistical and unpretentious. In another book about Indiana, I once wrote:

> The Hoosier's friendliness and hospitality are universally recognizable. He is easy to meet and quite ready to talk about himself. His eagerness to share his possessions as well as his private life sometimes appears naïve to the outsider accustomed to the self-protective reticence and suspicion of more thickly populated regions. But the Hoosier is not naïve. He inherits his tradition of cordiality from lonely pioneer days when every stranger was at once a welcome friend and a helpless supplicant; yet from those same early days, he inherits a talent for quick and accurate appraisal of character. You may think that the Hoosier lays himself wide open on short acquaintance; but the chances are that he knows all there is to know about you long before he tells you a single thing about himself.

An adopted Hoosier, Irving Leibowitz, has said the same thing of Hoosiers more recently and more succinctly: "They are country smart and their kids are university educated."

Of late, the Hoosier has broadened his view of the world considerably by travel, by education, and by both adversity and success; but the foregoing quotations still define something basic and immutable in his character.

Chapter Two

☆

The Indians

INGENUOUS and beguiling as it was, The Little Turtle's rebuttal to the white man's explanation of his origins was unscientific. Anthropologists and archaeologists are convinced that the first inhabitants of Indiana originated in Asia, and although their hypothesis may never be proved beyond the shadows of such chauvinistic doubts as those of The Little Turtle, who preferred to reverse the genealogical order, they adduce arguments that seem incontrovertible.

If man evolved from the earlier primates, as is now generally believed, then man must have originated in the Old World, for remains of the earlier primates have been found there in great abundance in contrast to an absence of proof that they ever existed in the Americas. Obviously primitive man could have come to America only from those regions of the Old World that lie close enough to the New World for him to have crossed the intervening waters in the crude vessels that he was capable of building, and only four regions of the Old World suggest themselves as near enough to the American continents to permit the limited navigation of prehistoric times. They are the Polynesian Islands, northwestern Europe, the western coast of northern Africa, and northeastern Asia. Of these four the Polynesian Islands may be immediately dismissed as the original home of the American aborigine because those islands were uninhabited prior to the habitation of the Americas.

There could have been some migration to North America from

northwestern Europe, and indeed some of the Indians of the eastern and southeastern United States have a European look. The distance of northwestern Europe from North America, however, is so great and the difficulties of the sea voyage between the two continents would have been so nearly insurmountable in prehistoric times that any such migration could have been only sporadic and no more than a trickle of a few adventurous individuals, certainly insufficient to populate the two American continents to the degree in which they were populated when white men discovered them. Northwestern Europe may have been the scene of genesis of some of our American Indians, but only a few.

The western coast of northern Africa is geographically a more likely place of origin, because the distance from that continent to South America is within the range of prehistoric sea travel, although it would have been difficult. But the differences between Negroes and Indians make an African origin of the American aborigine seem unlikely. For one thing, the American Indian's physique is entirely different from that of the Negro, much slighter and weaker. Indeed, the Indian, who would have to be descended from the very hardiest of African tribes, is vulnerable to the diseases of climates such as Africa's.

For northeastern Asia a much better case can be made than for any of the other Old World regions near enough for prehistoric migration, and not the least of arguments in its favor is its very nearness. At their closest point, Asia's mainland and North America's are separated by only thirty miles of water. This point is the Bering Strait, which is frozen in winter and passable to determined men on foot. Another short route between the two continents is by way of St. Lawrence Island. Although this water passage is now longer than the Bering Strait, in ancient times St. Lawrence Island was part of a redwood forest belt extending from the present California coast to Asia and may well have been of the same mainland. Finally, the first migrants to America could have come in short stages via the Aleutian Islands without too much difficulty.

The resemblance of the American Indian to the Asian is almost in itself conclusive. The two races have similar coloring, the same kind of hair in both quality and distribution, the same prominent cheekbones and slanted brown eyes, and similar nomadic behavior. They also resemble each other in their religious beliefs and practices and in their use of the sinew-backed bow and slatted armor. Since skeletons of Pleistocene animals, which Asians must have hunted, are common in Alaska but rare in eastern Canada, it would appear that prehistoric men followed such game across the Bering Strait. Alongside the mastodon, the louse also bears testimony to the relationship between American Indians and Asians, according to Hans Zinsser, an authority on that minuscule creature. Lice found in the hair of prehistoric American mummies in southwestern United States and in Peru are of the same family as those that still inhabit the heads of Eskimos and Chinese of the Aleutian Islands.

In his *Prehistoric Antiquities of Indiana,* Eli Lilly has presented the case for Asia effectively, but even so, when he published that book in 1937, he was still some ten years away from his later intensive study of the *Walam Olum,* which adds further proof to his arguments. The *Walam Olum* is the migration legend of the Lenni Lenape, or Delaware Indians. In 1820, some of it came into the possession of an eccentric naturalist named Constantine Rafinesque at Transylvania University in Lexington, Kentucky, through the kindness of a man whom Rafinesque identified only as "the late Dr. Ward of Indiana." The record of the Lenni Lenape was painted on sticks, preserved in bundles, and kept from generation to generation. Indians on the White River in Indiana probably entrusted it to "Dr. Ward," who later gave it to Rafinesque.

Linguists, anthropologists, and archaeologists, including Mr. Lilly, working together on the pictographs and the story of the *Walam Olum,* have recently devised from the narrative a probable route of the Lenni Lenape, suggesting that they crossed the Bering Strait in 366 A.D., moved down through Alaska and British Columbia, reached the Missouri River in what is now Montana in 808, crossed the Mississippi River in the year 1000, lived in southern Indiana in the twelfth and thirteenth centuries, and reached the Tidewater of Delaware in 1396, where in 1498 they saw "persons . . . floating in from the north and the south: the Whites . . .

friendly people with great possessions: who are they?" They could have been the company who made the voyage for the English under John Cabot.

The Lenni Lenape were comparatively late arrivals in America, for there is a strong presumption that man first appeared on this continent long before that time. These earliest of immigrants were the first inhabitants of Indiana, entering what is now the Hoosier state many centuries before the Lenni Lenape came but also long after their ancestors had crossed the Bering Strait. It was not until after the withdrawal of the glaciers that they roamed the state, and then only in the southern half.

The era of the first of prehistoric Hoosiers is known as the Paleo-Indian Period, and its people are identified by the large projectile points they left behind in their wanderings. Obviously they were hunters of big game that is now extinct, and they had no knowledge of agriculture. They probably came from the West, driven eastward by the radical changes of climate that followed the glacier period, and they finally moved on when the climate of the Indiana region became unendurable and the kind of game they hunted diminished to a point where it was too scarce for their survival in the forests of spruce and pine that covered the land at that time.

Following the Paleo-Indian Period is one that the archaeologists call the Archaic Period, dating from about 4000 B.C. to 500 B.C. Still hunters primarily, prehistoric men in this period discovered that the mussels abounding at the shoals of the Wabash and Ohio rivers were edible. Although migratory like their predecessors, they settled sporadically and temporarily and left mounds of mussel shells in their wake. One of the most famous of these mounds is at the Falls of the Ohio, near New Albany, Indiana. The Archaic people, who probably came from the South, were big-game hunters like the Paleo-Indians, and they still used spears instead of bows and arrows, although they could make grooved axes as well. But they had learned to roast and boil food, which their predecessors could not do, and they fashioned stone pestles which they used for grinding roots and seeds. They made no pottery, however, and because their vessels were of wood or bark or skin they could not set them over a fire. To bring such inflammable utensils to cooking temperature they heated rocks and dropped them into their contents. Many scorched rocks have been found at the shell mounds of the Archaic people along with their buried dead. In spite of their primitive attempts at cooking, there is no evidence that they raised any of their own food.

The Woodland Period of prehistory that followed the Archaic began about 800 B.C., overlapping the end of the Archaic, and lasted until it blended into history with the coming of the white man into the Mississippi Valley in the Sixteenth Century. It is entirely different from the two preceding periods, for its people could make pottery, had some knowledge of agriculture, used the bow and arrow, grew tobacco and smoked pipes, erected mounds over their dead, whom they revered, and lived a much more sedentary life than their predecessors. For convenience, archaeologists have divided the Woodland Period into three major eras: Early, Middle, and Late Woodland, the latter finally merging into the culture of the American Indian as we know him in history.

The earliest of the Early Woodlanders, called the Adena peoples, date from 800 B.C. to 200 or 300 A.D., and appeared in the Whitewater Valley in Indiana toward the end of that era. They derive their name from the name of the estate of Thomas Worthington, an early governor of Ohio, near Chillicothe, where archaeologists' diggings first identified them. In Indiana, their remains have been found at Winchester, Brookville, Lawrenceburg, and New Castle, although identification in the last-named place is not definitely established. They built earthworks as well as burial mounds, but there is no evidence that they engaged in extensive warfare. A smallish people with broad faces, they probably came from the South, like the Archaic Indians.

Some three hundred years after the arrival of the Adena peoples, the Hopewellian culture of the Middle Woodland Period began to make its imprint upon Indiana. Hopewell was the name of the owner of the estate near Chillicothe where the first Hopewellian mound was excavated. In Indiana, Hopewellian remains have been found mainly in Posey County. The Hopewellians are known to have grown corn, and apparently they traveled widely or else had contacts with other regions, for they used copper from northern Michigan, obsidian and grizzly bear teeth from the Rockies, mica from North Carolina, and shells from the Gulf of Mexico.

Woodland culture reached its peak in the Late Period that followed, comprising Middle Mississippi and Fort Ancient societies. The Fort Ancient people date from 1400 A.D., the Middle Mississippi from about two centuries earlier. The Fort Ancients are named for Fort Ancient on the Little Miami River in Ohio, where they built large fortifications. In Indiana, their artifacts have been found in Dearborn, Ohio, and Switzerland counties, whereas the Middle Mississippi culture seems to have flourished most extensively in this state in Posey, Vanderburgh, Spencer, and Warrick counties. The most notable dwelling site of all in this latter culture is the Angel Site, once a farm owned by a family named Angel near Evansville. Angel Site was apparently a kind of Middle Mississippi capital for the region, although Murphy Site and Bone Bank on the Lower Wabash are also impressive. The Middle Mississippi people were organized in some degree in their politics, economy, and religion and were somewhat more advanced than the Fort Ancients. Glass beads have been found in both Middle Mississippi and Forth Ancient diggings, proving that their sites were used by later Indians until the coming of the white man.

It was during the Late Woodland Period that the Lenni Lenape arrived in southern Indiana sometime between 1100 and 1300 A.D. In Book Five of the *Walam Olum,* Verses One and Two read: "Long ago all kept peace with each other there in the Talega country. Road Man was chief there along the middle reaches of the White River." This "Talega country" is assumed to be the country of the Late Woodland people and "the White River" the middle reaches of the Ohio. Apparently the Lenni Lenape lived in peace side by side or even among the Hopewellian, Middle Mississippi, and Fort Ancient cultures, and their addition to the numbers of the Hopewellians, Middle Mississippis, and Fort Ancients may account for the Adena fortifications not far away, built by a culture in its decline which was not by normal practice warlike.

As time passed, the Lenni Lenape moved on toward the east, and the cultures they left behind in southern Indiana scattered and became disorganized, marking the deterioration of the Woodland Period. By the time the French arrived, these Woodland people were living lives similar to those of the Indians of northern Indiana, a migratory hunting people, stern and gloomy, in constant fear of their environment. They had long heads and narrow faces, ate nuts, roots, berries, seed, game, and fish, raised no food crops, had no pottery, and inhabited movable camps. With the arrival of the French, these people ceased to be prehistoric, or as Glenn A. Black, one of Indiana's most distinguished archaeologists, has written: "When the Indian maintained contact with whites for very long, he ceased to live an aboriginal life . . . and the records of the European, in written form, are the province of the historian and not the archaeologist."

Studious and scholarly interest in the mound-building Indians came late to Indiana, as may already be evident in the fact that the names of the early cultures derive mostly from sites in Ohio. No genuinely scientific exploration of prehistoric mounds was undertaken in Indiana until 1926, when J. Arthur MacLean began diggings in Sullivan County. Fort Azatlan, near Merom in Sullivan County, remains today one of the most interesting sites in the state. But it is to Glenn A. Black that Indiana owes the largest debt among archaeologists for his pioneering in the excavation and preservation of prehistoric remains before the earthen monuments of the mound builders had been completely leveled or demolished by the plow and the bulldozer or ravaged beyond repair by souvenir hunters. The most impressive of all Black's labors took place at the Angel Site, near Evansville, on the Ohio River.

After the Ohio River flood of 1937, a levee round the city of Evansville was in prospect, with the construction of protective earthworks beginning near the mounds on the Angel farm. This place was overlooked during and after the period of La Salle, while it may have been still inhabited; it was not mentioned by the man who made the Congressional survey of the region in 1806; and it was mentioned only in passing by the state geologist who made a survey in 1875. No one interested in archaeology ever examined it seriously until two amateurs, Charles Artes and Dr. Floyd Stinson of Evansville, took artifacts from it in 1876. In the

1880's Cyrus Thomas gave a very good description of it, and again in 1896 Albert H. Purdue described it. In 1937, to the threat of the levee near the Angel farm was added the rapid growth of Evansville in the direction of the mound site, which made the available earth in the mounds a temptation to builders who might need filldirt for their projects. In 1938, the Indiana Historical Society purchased land that surrounded and included the Angel Site, and with the assistance of the Federal Works Projects Administration and government money to supplement the funds available to the society, Mr. Black began an archaeological study at once and conducted a field school from 1946 to 1962. After 1948, the site belonged to the Indiana Department of Conservation, with the Indiana Historical Society retaining the digging rights; it now belongs to Indiana University.

There were 456 acres in the original purchase, which included numerous mounds, the largest of them 644 feet long, 335 feet wide, and 44 feet high at its greatest elevation. The site stands on the river, but was, and still is, hidden from the main waterway by an island about three miles in length. Between the island and the mainland flows a channel, which local residents call a "chute." It affords a good harbor for small craft and is still famous, in spite of modern river pollution, for the size of its fish. Surrounding the site on the east, north, and west is a protecting slough. Mr. Black believed that the original settlers of the Angel Site chose it not only for its terrain but because the flora, fauna, and climate of the region reminded them of the deep South from which they had come.

Black laid out the area in 100-foot squares before any digging was done, and then some squares were divided into ten-foot blocks and excavated individually and with great care. Because earth that has been removed can never be replaced exactly as nature originally arranged it, a skilled archaeologist can discern scars as small as postholes centuries after they were made, and for this reason structures of prehistoric men, though built of perishable materials, can be reconstructed with remarkable accuracy. Ultimately revealed at Angel Site were evidences of a village that must have housed at one time about 1,500 inhabitants. With the largest mound and a public square as an axis, the village spread out toward the slough and was protected on its vulnerable sides by a wattled palisade with bastions at approximately 120-foot intervals. The highest mound was probably the location of the chief's home. Another was a temple mound. Still others were probably for burials. From the site archaeologists have taken literally millions of sherds and artifacts, cataloged and preserved them, and thus illuminated the culture that existed in southwestern Indiana before the white men came.

These artifacts, made from chipped and polished stone, bone, and shells, include not only the arrowheads that the layman associates with Indian sites but also handaxes, blades, drills, hoes, mortars, pestles, gorgets that were worn as ornaments on the throat or chest, birds and boats, as well as discoidals for games, tubes and pipes and effigies, one of which, the figure of a seated man, was beautifully carved from yellow fluorspar. Along with these artifacts and the urn burials that have been unearthed and quantities of cobs, beans, and squash and melon seeds, the discoveries at Angel Site suggest that the Middle Mississippi people who lived there were intelligent and devout, craftsmen and horticulturists, organized into a political and economic body that encompassed the surrounding countryside, and unified in religious beliefs that involved worship of both the sun and their own dead.

Local belief is that Choctaws lived in the village for a while after the prehistoric men of the Angel Site, although white men apparently never saw the place while it was occupied. At least, they never recorded such a discovery. The Choctaws have a tradition that their ancestors came out of a hole in the ground, not just a single ancestor walking forth from the earth but the whole Choctaw nation; and since one theory about the disappearance of the mound builders is that the arrival of the white men along the Ohio River drove them into hiding in the caves of Kentucky and Tennessee, it could be that the Choctaws eventually followed them. But if the Choctaws did play a role in the story of early Indiana, it was a very small one. The tribes principally associated with the state that was named for the red men were the Miamis, Delawares, Potawatomis, Piankashaws, Kickapoos, Weas, and Shawnees.

When, in the seventeenth century, white men began to arrive in increasing numbers, Indiana actually had a very small Indian population, and those Indians who made their home in the state were largely Algonquian-speaking refugees from the depradations of the powerful Iroquois of the East. Although it is believed that the Iroquois never had more than a few thousand braves on the warpath at one time, they were well disciplined and had been well armed by the Dutch in the East, and the terror they spread among their weaker neighbors extended far beyond the perimeter of their raiding. In the late seventeenth century, white men found Miamis living a semisedentary life on the St. Joseph River and near what is now Chicago, Weas at Ouiatanon near what is now Lafayette, and Piankashaws near the mouth of the Vermilion River. But that was all, except for roving hunters.

Delawares and Kickapoos did not move into the state until nearly a century later, when the Delaware Indians, who had been migrant residents of the region some five hundred years earlier, according to the *Walam Olum,* received permission from the Miamis to settle in the country between the White and Ohio rivers, and when the Kickapoos established themselves along the Wabash in spite of Miami opposition. About the same time, Nanticokes and Mohegans moved from the East and made their home on the White River, but they remained less than forty years and were gone by 1818. In the late eighteenth and early nineteenth centuries, the Shawnees used Indiana as a hunting ground, and from time to time the wigwams of Shawnee women studded the shores of the Wabash where these squaws settled seasonally to raise corn. The Shawnees strongly influenced the policies of the Kickapoos of the Wabash Valley and also the activities of the Potawatomis, who were the last tribe to migrate in large numbers into what is now the Hoosier state. By the time the Potawatomis came, in 1795, white settlers had already begun to claim and clear the land. The Potawatomis set themselves up in villages from the Kankakee River eastward across the state and were especially numerous around the headwaters of the Tippecanoe.

When France ceded to England in 1763 the western land that included the present state of Indiana, the Indians were dismayed

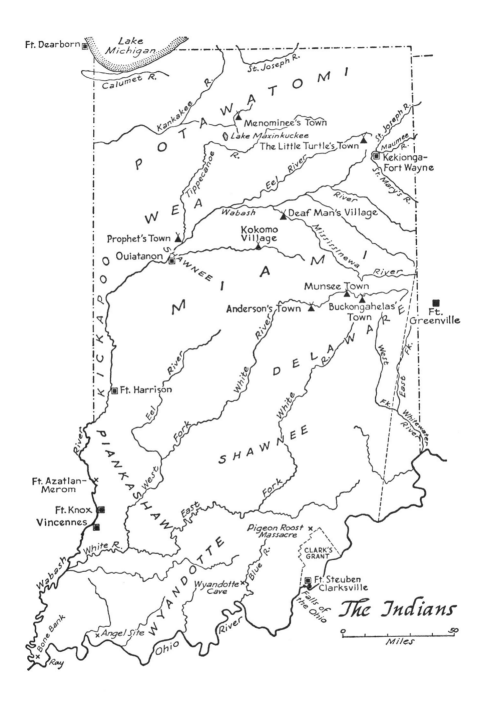

The Indians

and, in general, opposed the change. Even so, they were divided. In the middle of the century, Captain Céloron de Bienville and Major George Croghan had each traveled through the Ohio country trying to establish a monopoly in the fur trade for his own nation. While the English could pay higher prices than the French, they were arrogant and aloof, treating the Indians like children, whereas the French lived among them, often adopting Indian customs, and treated them like brothers. After 1763, especially during Pontiac's War, Indians often tried to block English investment of French posts. At Ouiatanon, the English commandant was for a time held prisoner; at Fort Miami, on the site of Fort Wayne, his equivalent was betrayed and murdered. But the English never tried to settle the country, and their policy worked to their advantage. Indeed, by proclamation, the English king ordered that the West be preserved as hunting grounds for the Indians. By the outbreak of the American Revolution, most of the Indians of the West had allied themselves with the English, recognizing that their enemies, the Americans, were a far greater threat to their own continued possession of the western land. The English then made frequent use of Indians as instruments of terror against the Americans, and one British officer, Colonel Henry Hamilton, governor of Detroit, earned for himself among American pioneers the epithet of "Hair-Buyer." Nevertheless, serious, organized, widespread "Indian trouble" did not come to the region now known as Indiana until the close of the war for American independence.

The peace treaty of 1783 divided American and British territory in the north by a line extending through the middle of Lake Erie, the Detroit River, Lake Huron, Lake Superior, Long Lake, Lake of the Woods, and thence confusedly "westward" to the Mississippi River, although the Mississippi was east of the last-named lake; but the English continued to hold many posts south of this boundary, among them Detroit, and from these forts they supplied the Indians with weapons and incited them to hostilities against the Americans. The Miamis, with headquarters at Miamitown, or Kekionga, later to become Fort Wayne, were among the principal allies of the English and were instrumental in the killing of some 1,500 men, women, and children in the Old Northwest during the seven years immediately following the close of the American Revolution. These deaths were mostly murders committed by small raiding parties and were not the casualties of open warfare. To death and torture the Miamis added the horror of cannibalism, which their braves were said to have practiced periodically in formal rites at the site of Fort Wayne.

Two famous names stand out in the cast of Indian characters in Indiana history during the hostilities that finally led to the War of 1812; they are The Little Turtle and Tecumseh. Of the two only The Little Turtle was a native of what is now Indiana. Tecumseh came from across the border in Ohio. Mystery obscures The Little Turtle's ancestry, although he is commonly called a Miami. Years after his death, his granddaughter, The Setting Sun, insisted that he was indeed a full-blooded Miami, but some students of the Indians say that his mother was a Mohegan woman while still others contend that he was the child of a Mohegan brave and an Iowa squaw who had settled among the Miamis. However that may be, The Little Turtle grew up among the Miamis and they considered him one of them and elected him a war chief of their tribe. He was born near the present city of Fort Wayne about 1751 and died in that city on July 14, 1812.

The Little Turtle first endeared himself to the British before the close of the Revolution when, in 1780, he thwarted an attempt of French settlers in the West to capture Detroit. Surprising and destroying the French expedition on what is now Aboite Creek near Fort Wayne, he delivered to the British the one survivor he captured. This victory over white men made The Little Turtle a full-fledged Miami war chief by tribal choice. Thereafter he was the master organizer of the Miamis' raids, although his admirers insist in their histories that he never advocated torture or cannibalism and protest that, in fact, he tried to prevent such barbarities. Be that as it may, he was unrelenting in his animosity toward the American pioneers, and for a decade after the ambush on Aboite Creek, the Miamis swarmed and attacked like hornets under his direction, penetrating even into Kentucky and spreading havoc and panic in white settlements throughout the Ohio country. But even as they raided, the Miamis were gradually pushed back into concentration at Kekionga, and that town soon became the headquarters of a thousand fighting men of various confederated tribes.

By 1790, it was obvious to the Americans that Kekionga was the place they must destroy if the Indian depredations were to be brought to an end, and in that year General Josiah Harmar, commander in chief of the American army, set out from Cincinnati for the Miami town with about 1,500 men. Of this number less than 400 were regulars, and of the rest many were old men and boys, undisciplined and poorly armed. It was often the practice of such volunteers to answer a call to arms only for the purpose of getting their broken guns repaired free of charge by army gunsmiths and with the intention of soon thereafter deserting. Harmar lost many of them before he reached his destination. His advance guard of 600 came upon Kekionga in mid-October, 1790, and found it deserted. They destroyed the village and burned the Indians' crops, but ten miles away, a day or two later, The Little Turtle ambushed about half of them under Colonel John Hardin and killed all save one of those who did not flee.

Meanwhile, the remainder of the advance guard of Americans was destroying other villages and more crops along the Maumee River, and when that work was done, Hardin, who had escaped The Little Turtle's ambush, attempted to make good his original failure by returning to the attack with 400 fresh troops from Harmar's main army. Once more The Little Turtle fell upon Hardin's men and routed them, forcing them to retreat up the St. Joseph River. With a total loss of nearly 200 killed and missing and many more wounded and with the remainder of his army rapidly dissolving by desertions, Harmar retired from his mission. Although the Indians had lost a great deal of property, they were jubilant and The Little Turtle was once again their hero. Victorious and confident, they recommenced the raiding of white settlements to the south and east.

In the fall of 1791, a year after Harmar's defeat, Congress authorized General Arthur St. Clair to undertake what Harmar had failed to do and, in addition, to build forts in the Indian country that would insure peace in the future. St. Clair began by establishing Fort Hamilton on the Great Miami River and then, forty miles away, Fort Jefferson. Marching through autumnal rains and, like Harmar, weakened by desertions of his militia, St. Clair finally made camp with 2,000 men on November 3 at the headwaters of the Wabash. About 1,400 Indians, mainly Miamis, Shawnees, and Delawares, had meantime gathered on the St. Mary's River not far away, the Shawnee chief Blue Jacket and the Delaware Buckongahelas having yielded the supreme command of this force to The Little Turtle. On the night of November 3, The Little Turtle moved his army down upon St. Clair's chosen position and waited watchfully through the dark hours.

At dawn, according to custom, the American forces were called up for parade, and the Indians, still watching from the surrounding woods, waited until they were dismissed; then, with a warwhoop, they charged. Taken by surprise, the disassembled soldiers scattered and bolted for the main encampment three hundred yards away, overrunning in their stampede the regulars who had been left on guard duty. By the time full daylight illuminated the scene of battle, the white men were surrounded and most of their officers were dead. Those who had survived could command no obedience until finally they gave the order for retreat. More mob then than army, the soldiers abandoned their wounded and their arms, headed for the road, gained it, and fled. It was their good fortune that the Indians pursued them only a few miles. Many of the white men did not stop for food or sleep till they reached Cincinnati.

In the end, the American loss was close to a thousand men killed or wounded and some $30,000 worth of artillery, rifles, and supplies. It has been said that General St. Clair himself escaped only because he was not wearing a uniform and the Indian marksmen could not identify him. St. Clair was back in Cincinnati by November 8.

This victory of The Little Turtle's was so overwhelming and so shattering to the white men's hopes for an end to Indian hostilities in the Old Northwest that there was sentiment in Congress thereafter to abandon the Northwest Territory to the red men, as the British had done, and make the Ohio River the northern boundary of the United States. But President Washington rejected this defeatism. He foresaw the disastrous effect that any retreat would have upon the future expansion of the nation. His answer to The Little Turtle's victory was to call back to duty a hero of the Revolution, General Anthony Wayne, and give him command of a new force, which Congress finally authorized at 5,000 men.

General Wayne moved out from Pittsburgh in the fall of 1793 and first established Fort Greenville. After that, he chose the site of St. Clair's defeat for a second post and named it Fort Recovery. Then he settled his army into these fortifications for the winter. In June of the next year, the Indian chiefs persuaded The Little Turtle against his better judgment to attack Fort Recovery. The attack failed. About a month later, General Wayne moved forward and established Fort Defiance at the junction of the Auglaize and Miami rivers. He sent an Indian prisoner out to try to persuade The Little Turtle to stop listening to the English and to make peace; but when no peace delegation had arrived at Fort Defiance by August 15, he moved westward once again, this time along the Maumee toward Kekionga. Finally the Indians met the Americans in ambush just above a fort that the English had illegally built at the foot of the rapids of the Maumee. This point of encounter, near what is now Toledo, Ohio, is known as Fallen Timbers.

Fallen Timbers got its name from the trees strewn about by a tornado in the dense forest of the region, and the Indians chose the site for an ambush because they believed the American cavalry would be helpless among the tumbled logs. They were right. But The Little Turtle had also been right just before his attack on Fort Recovery in June when he argued that General Wayne was "a chief who always sleeps with one eye open." Wayne, too, recognized the danger to mounted men among the fallen trees and sent his cavalry round both flanks of the enemy to oppose them from the rear while his foot soldiers made a frontal attack through the logs and brush. With bayonets and rifle fire at close range, the American infantry swept the Indians out of the woods, earning for their general the Miami sobriquet of "Alomseng," or The Wind. The Indians fled to the British fort at the Maumee rapids, clamoring for admittance; but the British, although they had always welcomed them before, would not let them in. Betrayed and panicked, the red warriors scattered and disappeared into the woods.

After the Battle of Fallen Timbers, Anthony Wayne marched on to Kekionga, destroying both the British and Indian property that he found in his path. After burning the Miami town, he established Fort Wayne beside the ruins. The fort, which was named by Colonel John F. Hamtramck, was completed on October 22, 1794, and Wayne then left the colonel in command of it and returned to his winter quarters at Greenville, where he invited the Indians to come to a council the following year.

Disastrously defeated and now disillusioned by his British allies, The Little Turtle undertook the role of statesman, a role that he played the rest of his life. With Buckongahelas, Blue Jacket, and other chiefs, he attended the council at Greenville in the summer of 1795 and was a party to the treaty that was signed there opening half of Ohio and a long strip of eastern Indiana to peaceful white settlement. After that, he busied himself primarily with the task of trying to persuade the whites to stop giving liquor to the red men. Before white men came to America, Indians had no knowledge of the process of distilling and consequently had neither a practice nor a tradition that prepared them for the use of strong spirits. Whiskey corrupted and demoralized them, and The Little Turtle was right when he said, "This liquor is more to be feared than the gun or the tomahawk."

The Little Turtle visited the legislatures of Kentucky and Ohio and Congress itself to bring his plea to responsible white men. While in Philadelphia as a guest of President Washington, he learned about vaccination and had himself inoculated against smallpox. On that visit, Gilbert Stuart, commissioned by George Washington, painted his portrait, and he received a sword from the President. The portrait presents the Miami in a pensive mood, with a high forehead and intelligent eyes. The sword is today among the most prized possessions of the Allen County–Fort Wayne Historical Society Museum. In Baltimore, The Little Turtle persuaded the Society of Friends of that city to set up a farm on the Wabash where Indians could be trained in agriculture. Until his death, the Miami chief preached friendship with the Americans and opposition to British influence. In 1811, he was able to prevent most of his fellow tribesmen from taking part in the Battle of Tippecanoe and kept them neutral throughout the war. When in his old age he was told that gout, the disease he was being treated for in Fort Wayne when he died, was regarded by white men as an ailment of gentlemen, he replied that he had always thought of himself as a gentleman.

A gentleman he was, at least in the later years of his life, respected by all the whites who dealt with him; but after Fallen Timbers, there was another gentleman of his own race who regarded him only with contempt. This was Tecumseh, or The Shooting Star, a Shawnee, some fifteen years younger than The Little Turtle, and in some ways a greater man. Tecumseh was an idealist who refused to exploit the inevitable and never forgave the Miami chief for his capitulation to the Americans. "The whites are not friends" was the enduring theme of all Tecumseh's thinking, and by "whites" he meant all white men, British and Americans alike. The Little Turtle's peacemaking seemed traitorous to Tecumseh.

Tecumseh was born in Ohio, near Piqua. He had his first taste of fighting with white men at the age of twelve in a skirmish on the Ohio River, and in his mid-twenties he was in command of a small band of Shawnees at Fallen Timbers. There he hardly distinguished himself as a warrior, for early in the battle he made the mistake of ramming a ball into his rifle before he put the powder in and, weaponless, had to retreat. But he became an able fighter afterward, and he was also a skilled hunter, learning to kill buffalo on the Great Plains. Tall, slender and supple, hazel-eyed and, like most Shawnees, tan of skin instead of red, Tecumseh was a commanding figure and a man of solemn dignity. Like The Little Turtle, he became a statesman as he grew older, but unlike The Little Turtle he continued to be a warrior all his life and never compromised his ideals. His dream was to build an Indian federation that would maintain independence of the white men in the Northwest, for he knew that the fatal weakness of his people was their intertribal rivalries, which the white men exploited in the ages-old strategy of dividing and conquering. Among all the tribes of the West he preached his doctrine that the whites were not friends, traveling from Canada to the American South and from his native Ohio to the Great Plains trying to persuade the Indians to unite against their common enemy.

When Tecumseh met with William Henry Harrison, governor of the Indiana Territory that had been carved out of the old Northwest Territory, he refused to sit in the chair the governor provided for him on the lawn of his fine mansion, "Grouseland," at Vincennes. "Your Great Father offers you a chair," the interpreter said; and Tecumseh replied, "This man is not my father. The sun is my father. My mother is the earth. I shall recline on her bosom." Twice at these meetings, he agreed to truces with Governor Harrison; but Governor Harrison knew that the Shawnee chief was only stalling for more time in which to consolidate his people. After their second meeting, the governor broke his promise without conscience. While Tecumseh was in the South preaching federation to the Creeks, Harrison marched with a thousand men to Tippecanoe, where Tecumseh's twin brother, The Prophet, had been left in charge of the Shawnee's braves. In an attack at dawn on November 7, 1811, Harrison and his men routed the Indians; and although the whites suffered great losses, 188 killed and wounded, the Indians' loss was even greater. Only about thirty of the three or four hundred braves at Tippecanoe were killed, but by noon of the day of the battle, nothing was left of Tecumseh's pan-Indian movement in Indiana but an abandoned Indian village and one aged abandoned Indian chief groaning in his wigwam over a broken leg that prevented him from fleeing.

Thereafter, Tecumseh did in some degree exploit the inevitable, although without deceiving himself. He mistrusted the British as much as the Americans, but for revenge he went to Canada and joined the English in their war against the United States. At the Battle of the Thames on October 5, 1813, leading a small band of Indians, he was killed by Colonel Richard M. Johnson of the American army firing at him point-blank with a pistol loaded with one bullet and three buckshot. So, at least, Johnson remembered twenty-five years later when there was a movement abroad in the

West to nominate him for President of the United States. When Tecumseh was killed, the British general, Henry Proctor, had already climbed into his gig behind the lines and fled and the British army had surrendered. But Tecumseh's braves fought on round his body long enough to prevent the Americans from taking possession of it. They carried it away and buried it in a secret grave whose location they and their descendants never revealed to anyone.

In the late summer of 1941, the bones of an Indian which many red men and some white authorities regarded as Tecumseh's were formally interred in a cairn on Walpole Island beside the St. Clair River. Just thirty years before, in Fort Wayne, some workmen making an excavation uncovered the remains of The Little Turtle, which were identified by the sword and other articles buried with him. The Miami's bones, too, had been lost for many years. Although The Little Turtle had been buried with military honors in 1812, the city of Fort Wayne had grown over his grave until all trace of it had vanished. The bones were reburied with a marker over them in the yard of the house the workmen were preparing to build. The house was razed in 1959, and since then the lot has been a small park with a boulder and plaque.

Tippecanoe and Harrison's other victories in Indiana Territory did not bring to a close the story of the Indians in the state. Although the red men's strength was destroyed, they remained as an obstacle to white settlers for another thirty years. And sometimes they were more than an impassive obstacle; they were aggressive. In September, 1812, a party of Shawnees came down across the White River and fell upon the Pigeon Roost Settlement near the present town of Scottsburg and killed three men, five women, and sixteen children, scalping and mutilating their bodies and cremating them in their homes. But the whites were not always the innocent victims; sometimes they matched the Indians' barbarity. In 1824, five white men entered a peaceful Indian hunting camp in Madison County, on the east side of Fall Creek below the falls, and, pretending to be looking for lost horses, persuaded the two Indian men in the camp to help them in their search. As soon as the braves were separated from each other in the woods, the white men shot them in the back and then returned to the camp and murdered the three unsuspecting squaws and the two little boys and two little girls who were waiting there. When the white men discovered that one of the boys had not died from a gunshot, one of them picked him up, swung him round by the legs, and beat his brains out against a tree. These white men were later apprehended and tried, and four of the five were subsequently hanged for murder. Although these executions were said to be the first in the United States for the killing of Indians, equal justice before the law came too late to save the Indians from their ultimate doom in Indiana.

That doom came in a series of treaties when the Indians surrendered to the United States the last of their lands within the state and agreed to move west of the Mississippi. Most of this land lay near Lake Maxinkuckee. All the chiefs of the region signed the treaty save a Potawatomi named Menominee. Menominee would not sign and he would not sell. The treaty of only four years before had given him title to his property "forever," and he intended that the United States should keep its promise. When, in the summer of 1838, the Indian agent appeared on Menominee's land and told Menominee he had to move out anyhow, Menominee said, "Brothers: I have not sold my lands. I will not sell them. I have not signed any treaty, and I will not sign any. I am not going to leave my lands, and I do not want to hear any more about it."

But of course Menominee did hear more about it. His lands were too valuable to escape the greed of the white settlers roundabout. On a hot Sunday morning of that summer General John Tipton, with one hundred soldiers and orders from Governor David Wallace, appeared at Menominee's village while Menominee and many of his tribe were in church. The soldiers fired a volley outside the church, as men fire guns to scare pigeons out of a belfry, and the Indians came tumbling out of the building in terror. But not Menominee. With a knife in his hand, he stood his ground with courage and dignity. Finally, the soldiers lassoed him, bound him hand and foot, and threw him into a wagon. Then they rounded up 859 Potawatomi men, women, and children and shunted them into a ragged line of march. There were wagons for some, but most of them had to proceed on foot.

The disgrace to the state's history that followed is sometimes called "The Trail of Death," for as the caravan of exiles dragged its way across the sunbeaten and fly-ridden countryside in the dry September weather, to Rochester, down through Logansport, and along the Wabash past Tippecanoe and Williamsport, Indians dropped by the wayside by the dozens and died. By the time the procession reached the border of Illinois, most of the babies were dead and many of the aged, and here a halt was ordered and a consultation held to decide whether it would be more merciful to kill a 100-year-old squaw who was dying or to march on with her. In the end, "civilization" prevailed, and the ancient woman was allowed to suffer four more days on the road before she died a "natural death." At Danville, Illinois, the exiles were turned over to a new escort who drove them onward to the reservation that awaited them in Kansas. The whole journey required about two months and took the lives of about 150 of the refugees. Today white men have acknowledged their injustice to Menominee with a monument to his memory some ten miles out of Plymouth, Indiana, at the point where he was lassoed and started on his expulsion from his native land.

A few Indians lingered on in the state after 1838, and among them was the widow of a Miami chief. Her name was Maconaquah, and her home and burial place on the Mississinewa River near Peru are also commemorated by a monument. Maconaquah, born Frances Slocum on the Susquehanna River in Pennsylvania, was kidnapped from her white parents by Indians in 1778 when she was five years old. She was adopted by a Delaware chief and later married a young Miami named Shepocanah. For years they lived in The Little Turtle's town, but they finally moved to the Mississinewa to escape the troubles between Indians and whites and established a village of their own. Because of the affliction that visited Shepocanah in his old age, the village became known as The Deaf Man's Village. Here, fifty-nine years after her kidnapping, Maconaquah was discovered by one of her white brothers from the East. He had been searching for her all his life, and their reunion in the Bearrs Hotel in Peru in 1837 is one of the happier stories of Indian-white relations in the state's history. However, Maconaquah, who spoke no English, had no desire to return to the world of white men and women, and she remained on her farm beside the Mississinewa until her death ten years later.

One reason for Maconaquah's decision to stay among her adopted people was her confidence in the counsel of a neighbor named François Godfroy. Half French and half Indian, the last of the Miami war chiefs, Godfroy in his youth had fought the whites around Fort Wayne but had finally retired from these hostilities to become a trader. At the time of Maconaquah's decision, he was a mountain of sedentary flesh weighing over three hundred pounds, and it was said of him that he possessed the largest fortune ever to be accumulated by an Indian in America up to that time. But perhaps those who said this were thinking of a fortune only as money, real estate, chattels, and goods and were unmindful of the far greater fortune of freedom and dignity that Godfroy's red ancestors lost when the white men came and dispossessed them of their heritage. From the Woodland prince greeting the sun with adoration each morning on his mound above the Ohio River to the gross half-breed sprawled in a great chair on the bank of the Mississinewa counting white men's money half a millennium later, the Indian had made a long and tragic journey.

Chapter Three

☆

The March of Empire

ALTHOUGH French Jesuits and *coureurs de bois,* or forest vagabonds, were probably the first white men to set foot on Indiana's soil, in the Dunes country, the first white man to explore any of the land now included in the state was Réné-Robert Cavelier, Sieur de la Salle, who in 1679 ascended the St. Joseph River as far as its "south bend," where the city of that name now stands, and crossed by portage to the Kankakee and descended that river to the Illinois. Ten years earlier, in the winter of 1669–70, La Salle saw Indiana for the first time when he discovered the Ohio River, and he may indeed have set foot on Indiana soil then, going ashore from his canoe. In that winter, he descended the Ohio as far as the Falls at what is now Jeffersonville, possibly as far south as the mouth of the Wabash, or even to the Ohio's conjunction with the Mississippi, depending on whether an accurate translation of *"où elle tombe de fort haut dans de vastes marais"* is "where it falls from a great height into vast marshes" or "where it empties after a long course into vast marshes."

In spite of his name, La Salle was not of the French nobility as is sometimes believed, but the son of a wealthy merchant of Rouen who took the designation de la Salle from an estate that the family owned near that city. Born in 1643, he came to Canada at the age of twenty-three after receiving his education from the Jesuits. Although he was not a member of the order, he attached himself to a corporation of priests in Montreal known as the Seminary of St. Sulpice, of whom his elder brother Jean was one. From the semi-

41

nary he received a large tract of land some eight or nine miles from Montreal above the rapids of the St. Lawrence in an area exposed to Indian attack. After he had made improvements on this land, he sold it back to the Sulpicians to finance a journey of exploration in quest of a westward passage to China. Because this dream of La Salle's was shared by very few other Frenchmen at Montreal, the place and the rapids of the St. Lawrence acquired the derisive name of "La Chine."

From the Indians La Salle had heard of a great river that flowed westward and southward and debouched into another river that led to the sea. This sea he believed was the Pacific. With twenty-four men he set out from Lachine in 1669 and paddled up the St. Lawrence into Lake Ontario. On its shores Seneca Indians tried to dissuade him from going south and refused to give him a guide, but he later ransomed a Potawatomi prisoner who was willing to show him the way to the river. The Potawatomi led him overland to a stream that flowed into the Ohio. After voyaging some distance down that great river, La Salle's men deserted him, but he ventured on to the point *"où elle tombe de fort haut dans de vastes marais"* before he turned back to Canada.

For an understanding of the difficulties that beset La Salle in this journey of exploration two circumstances must be kept in mind. Because of the hostility of the Iroquois, who were jealous of the Hurons (Wyandottes), with whom the French carried on an extensive trade at that time, the French found it necessary to probe westward through the northern country among sedentary and less warlike Indians and to avoid the country below the Great Lakes, although they claimed that land too as their territory. For this reason, La Salle's venture southward was extremely hazardous; even the Indians considered it so. The second obstacle to his exploration was an obstacle common to all explorers of the seventeenth century: men still believed, as Columbus had believed, that the globe was much smaller than it actually is and their calculations of longitude and latitude were not precise. That is why Europeans were not yet aware of the thousands of miles that lay between their outposts in the West and the Pacific Ocean and why their maps, even of country they had already explored, were often inaccurate and out of proportion. All that can be said with certainty about La Salle's achievement in the winter of 1669–70 is that he discovered the Ohio River. Just how far he descended it and whether or not he saw the Wabash or the Mississippi are questions that may never be answered with finality. The best authorities, however, set the end of La Salle's voyage at the Falls of the Ohio.

That the young Frenchman was profoundly impressed by what he saw from his canoe on the Ohio is a matter of record. Ten years later, in a memorial to his king, he wrote:

> Those lands surpass all others in everything. They are almost so beautiful and fertile, so sparsely covered with forest and so well adorned by prairies, streams, rivers, fish, game, and venison that one can find there, in abundance with very little trouble, everything necessary for the maintenance of powerful colonies.

Although not a native, because of his superlative-laden description La Salle could qualify as the first Hoosier of European origin. No perfervid Hoosier Chamber of Commerce has since excelled him in praise of the Indiana scene.

The French began systematic explorations of the New World somewhat later than the Spanish and English, because at first Francis I was too deeply involved in wars with Italy to devote attention to his countrymen's discoveries. True, the markets of Rouen were selling fish from the Newfoundland Banks almost a century and a half before La Salle was born in that city, and in 1524, ahead of any similar far-wandering English venture, Giovanni Verrazano, with the French king's authorization, had skirted "six hundred leagues and more of new land" from the Carolinas to Maine. But the French fishermen were operating as individuals and were interested only in commerce, and Verrazano's discoveries, although they had the king's seal of approval, made but little immediate impression on the nation's colonial policy. Nevertheless, it was France that eventually discovered and claimed the St. Lawrence River, when Jacques Cartier, sailing out of St. Malô, reached its mouth in 1534; and again, at the beginning of the seventeenth century, it was France's Samuel de Champlain, traveling with a copy of Cartier's journals at hand, who plied westward in several expeditions until he saw for himself the Great Lakes that the Indians talked about.

By Champlain's day, there were small French outposts in eastern Canada and a rudimentary form of colonial government. Champlain was himself Canada's first governor, and it was he who established the admirable French pattern of exploration and colonization by sending youths into the wilderness to live among Indians and learn their languages as training for their work in America. Later, La Salle followed Champlain's example. Within two or three years after his arrival in the New World, the discoverer of the Ohio River had mastered the Iroquois tongue and seven or eight other Indian languages and dialects. Desertion by his followers on the Ohio in 1670 or being lost from them in the woods, as he was for a time near the "south bend" of the St. Joseph River in 1679, could not deter him in his purposes.

Speaking the Indians' various tongues, adapting to their customs and often adopting them, uninhibited by race prejudice, more concerned with converting the red man to their faith than with subjugating him, hoping indeed to assimilate him into French culture and civilization, the French, with Jesuit priests in the vanguard, moved westward without the profuse bloodshed that was to come later. There were some inevitable casualties on both sides, especially in encounters with the warlike and independent Iroquois, but on the whole the French introduced Christianity to the Indian in the north without the brutality and oppression practiced by the fanatical Spanish in the south, and Gallic tolerance, along with Gallic shrewdness, established a peaceful fur trade with the Indians in Canada and the country north of the Ohio that English arrogance and bluntness found difficult to equal later.

Thus eventually French priests and traders reached Indiana. The Canadian government authorized the first trading post within the present boundaries of the state near the site of today's Lafayette at Ouiatanon in 1717; soon thereafter French traders were officially established at Fort St. Philippe, where Fort Wayne would be located seventy-five years later; and Vincennes came into being on the Lower Wabash about 1731. At these posts, in exchange for what they hoped would be a monopoly in the fur trade, the French offered the Indians their religion, beads and cloth, sometimes brandy, and occasionally, but very seldom, guns and powder. In this early period of the fur trade the Indians used traps almost exclusively.

During the French regime, the Indiana region was divided somewhat vaguely across its middle between Canada and Louisiana, the one definite point of the division lying athwart the Wabash at a place the French called Terre Haute when it was still the home of a band of Weas and not yet a white man's town. Fort St. Philippe and Ouiatanon were under Canadian jurisdiction, in the district commanded at Detroit; Vincennes was an outpost of Louisiana, in the District of Illinois, and governed from Fort Chartres on the Mississippi. Of the three Indiana posts Vincennes is the only one that has had an uninterrupted existence as an inhabited white man's town from its founding to the present.

Originally Vincennes was called *le poste du Ouabache,* and because the French often used the phrase *au poste,* early American settlers gave it the name "Opost." François Morgane de Vincennes was its first commandant, and although no reference to the place by his name has yet been found before the year 1752, in all probability the town was so christened several years earlier than that, not long after Chickasaws captured the Sieur de Vincennes and burned him at the stake in 1736. Three years before his death, the Sieur de Vincennes reported that five tribes of Indians lived on the Wabash and that the Illinois and Miamis were "more insolent than they have ever been"; by 1763, the last acting governor of Louisiana was reporting that "the Indians that live near the place are called Peauguichia [Piankashaws]." Apparently the Piankashaws gave trouble only when they were drunk.

For almost half a century after the establishment of the Vincennes post, the French there shared in common some 5,000 acres that the Indians had granted them, and in that small retreat from the surrounding wilderness they created for themselves and sustained a pleasant life. The more prosperous townspeople lived in white-washed houses of logs or puncheons set upright in the ground, sometimes with piazzas running round all four sides behind the high picket fences that enclosed their yards. They kept their woolly ponies, which came from Normandy and whose kind were the ancestors of the Indian pony, in "pole stables" that they could easily dismantle and reassemble when it became necessary to remove the manure. They danced and drank wine and played billiards, dressed like their Indian neighbors in leather shirts, leggings and moccasins, with buffalo robes wrapped round them in cold weather, and for the most part they let their commandant worry about their political problems and their village priest concern himself with the fates of their immortal souls. British occupation, when it came, hardly disturbed their carefree way of life, but in the American Revolution the capture of the town by the Americans, whom the French abetted, put an end to it.

Today in Vincennes there are many monuments to the past and numerous buildings survive from bygone days, but except for the old French cemetery, with the first interment dating 1741, and parish records in the old Cathedral Library that date from 1749, almost no reminders of the French period greet a visitor save the general ambience of a long-established society that is rare in the Middle West. Perhaps the only other communities in Indiana that suggest the past so immediately are New Harmony and Madison, and their origins are of course a century closer to the present. Fort Wayne, which is older than Vincennes as a site of human habitation, although not so old as a civilized community with a continuous history, cherishes its traditions as does Vincennes, but Fort Wayne's growth into a large city has hidden much of its past beneath a patina of modernity.

The war known as the Seven Years War in Europe and commonly called the French and Indian War in America began and ended earlier on the North American continent than in Europe. About three years before the outbreak of hostilities abroad, the Marquis Duquesne established a chain of forts on the Allegheny and the Upper Ohio which George Washington, then a lieutenant-colonel of colonial militia, soon challenged without success and which two years later the British general, Edward Braddock, challenged with a march through the Pennsylvania forests that ended in a historic disaster. But French Canada at this time had a population of only about 60,000 scattered farmers and fur traders as against a more concentrated population of a quarter of a million in the English colonies south of the St. Lawrence, and therefore chances of a French victory were very slight. By 1760 Quebec and Montreal had both fallen and the French surrendered their western territory to the English, although the Peace of Paris was not signed until 1763. In that treaty the French ceded all of Canada to the English and the Spanish gave them Florida, receiving as compensation from their French allies all of France's claims west of the Mississippi.

The fighting between French and English in America took place mostly in the East; the war in the West was largely commercial. The Indiana country felt only the distant waves of the shock of battles. Instead of military campaigns, the West was a stage for plots and counterplots among white men and subterfuge and deceit among the Indians. In the main the Western Indians preferred Frenchmen to Englishmen, but the English had one advantage that the Indians found hard to resist; in order to outlaw *coureurs de bois,* whom French priests regarded as immoral, the authorities at Quebec had required licenses of French fur traders and made them buy all their goods from a government monopoly, which kept prices high, whereas the English were under no such restrictions and could pay almost double the French price for furs. Moreover, the English were quite willing to give the Indians guns and ammunition, which legitimate French traders denied them. The result was a strong temptation among red men to bootleg furs to the English, whom they disliked, in spite of their agreements with the French, whom they respected and admired.

To explain to the Indians the "rights" of the French in the West and to persuade them, if he could, to do business exclusively with French traders, Pierre Joseph Céloron de Bienville traveled down the Allegheny and Ohio rivers as early as 1749, ascended the Miami and paddled along the Maumee to Lake Erie, crossing in this journey the northeast corner of what is now Indiana. In the eastern part of his expedition of good will, Céloron met with hostility among the Iroquois, but he was warmly received by the Indians of the West. Even so, after he was gone, cheaper British beads, cloth, knives, blankets, and especially British firearms spoke more eloquently than Céloron's words at the woodland council fires, and the irregular trade with the English continued.

Yet when defeat finally came to the Frenchmen the Indians had betrayed, the Indians were not soon reconciled to the shift of authority to the white men with the cheaper goods. Immediately after the close of the French and Indian War, Pontiac, an Ottawa chief, organized a rebellion against English rule. Although he failed to capture Detroit, which was his principal objective in the West, he had some success in Indiana, where his fellow conspirators took Fort Miami at the site of Fort Wayne. The Indians accomplished this feat by a ruse instead of a battle. Learning that the English commandant at Fort Miami, Ensign Robert Holmes, kept a Miami mistress who bore him no love, they induced the girl to decoy the young Englishman out of the fort by asking him to come and minister to a sick squaw in the village. From ambush they murdered Holmes at the squaw's doorway and then captured his sergeant when he came running out of the fort to learn what the shooting was about. After that, with the sergeant as a hostage, they persuaded the rest of the garrison to surrender. At Ouiatanon, they succeeded by another deceit practiced upon Lieutenant Edward Jenkins, who was held prisoner thereafter in French homes. Below Terre Haute and at Vincennes Pontiac's allies were among friends, for Louisiana, although formally surrendered to the English, was still in French hands. Toward the end of the war, in 1764, Pontiac himself traveled down the Wabash without incident, visiting among the Weas, Piankashaws, and Kickapoos and probably stopping at Vincennes for a conference with Captain Louis St. Ange de Bellerive, who was still in command there.

The next year French authorities withdrew to the west side of the Mississippi in preparation for turning that vast region over to the Spanish according to their agreement in Paris, but they were still at Vincennes in the summer of 1765 when George Croghan, an English agent, traveled down the Ohio and up the Wabash with a purpose similar to Céloron's sixteen years before. The English now needed to persuade the Indians not to bootleg furs to the French. Near Vincennes Croghan was captured by Kickapoos and taken to the post on the Wabash, where he wrote in his journal that the French inhabitants were "an idle lazy people a parcel of Renegadoes from Canada and . . . much worse than the Indians." Although Croghan was released, he believed that the French had engineered his capture. From Vincennes he moved on up the Wabash to the Eel River and crossed the portage to the Maumee, visiting Indian villages en route. He came away from his three months in the Indiana country convinced that, although England had won the war, trouble with Indians would continue so long as French traders were allowed to remain among them.

As Croghan predicted, the French did continue "Breeding Mischief and Spiriting up the Indians against the English" in Indiana, but such machinations were almost inevitable in the chaotic conditions that prevailed north of the Ohio in those years, and such conditions were in part the result of the English failure to establish any firm governmental authority on Indiana soil after they acquired it. Ouiatanon and Fort Miami were inadequately manned, and there was no garrison at Vincennes until May 26, 1777, fourteen years after the war. Five years before that date, in response to an order from the British government requiring "all who have established themselves on the banks of the Ouabache, whether at Vincennes or elsewhere, to quit those countries instantly, and without delay, and to retire, at their choice, into some one of the colonies of His Majesty," the French *habitants* of Vincennes wrote a memorial to General Thomas Gage, commander in chief of the British forces in North America.

"Let troops be sent to us," they pleaded. "You will see everything returning to order—trade reviving, and ourselves becoming useful men; and of all places this is the most necessary, although the most neglected, being the center between Detroit, Fort Pitt, and the Illinois country, the thoroughfare of the nations, and the security of the Beautiful River and the Mississippi; may we be permitted to represent to His Excellency that if His Majesty is planning to establish this region, he must always begin with the upper part, which makes for security of the lower, to which it can lend aid promptly; whereas it can receive help only after a long delay because of the difficulty of going up [against the current]."

There was logic in this appeal. When it went unheeded, quite naturally the French *habitants* did not "quit" the Indiana country as they had been ordered to do, and having no government, many of them continued "Breeding Mischief."

On the other hand, what seems at first glance like gross neglect by the British of their newly acquired territory was actually a reasoned, deliberate, and not unsound policy, defined by the English king's Proclamation of 1763, which said, in part:

> Whereas it is just and reasonable, and essential to our Interest, and the Security of our Colonies, that the several Nations or Tribes of Indians with whom We are connected, and who live under our Protection, should not be molested or disturbed in the Possession of such Parts of our Dominions and Territories as, not having been ceded to or purchased by Us, are reserved to them, or any of them, as their Hunting Grounds. We do therefore, with the Advice of our Privy Council, declare it to be our Royal Will and Pleasure, that no Governor or Commander in Chief . . . in any of our . . . Colonies or Plantations in America do presume for the present, and until our further Pleasure be known, to grant Warrants of Survey, or pass Patents for any Lands beyond the Heads or Sources of any of the Rivers which fall into the Atlantic Ocean from the West and North West, or upon any Lands whatever, which, not having been ceded to or purchased by Us as aforesaid, are reserved to the said Indians, or any of them.

Deflated from the king's English to the language of the common reader, the Proclamation of 1763 said simply that the country west of the Alleghenies would be an Indian hunting preserve until His Majesty could make up his mind what to do with it. The postponement was intended to hold the land problem of the West in abeyance until the Indians quieted down and until the government could draw up a workable program for the management and distribution of the enormous territory it suddenly found in its possession after the French and Indian War. In other words, the proclamation was an emergency measure designed to meet an unprecedented situation. Had Lord Shelburne, who inspired the proclamation, remained in office, a program of well-planned Indian services, licenses, regulations, and tariffs for fur traders, and an orderly distribution of land would have followed; but Lord Shelburne was soon forced out of office, and what began as a sound and deliberate program became, in the end, an indecisive evasion of responsibility.

In spite of its virtues, the proclamation produced two demoralizing results in America: it ostensibly divested the Thirteen Colonies of their Western land claims and thus antagonized them, and it invited greedy and irresponsible adventurers to exploit the Indians. Even so, Shelburne's plans might have set such matters aright had those plans been adopted; but the English government abandoned them and allowed the situation in the West to deteriorate by continuing the status quo overlong, and eventually it compounded its own difficulties by another measure known as the Quebec Act of 1774.

In one respect, the Quebec Act was a remarkably liberal and farseeing piece of legislation. It granted religious liberty to Catholic Canada and restored to Canadians their old familiar French systems of law and government. But it was politically shortsighted so far as the American colonies were concerned, for it annexed all the country north of the Ohio to the Province of Quebec and thus nullified with finality the western land claims of four of the Thirteen Colonies and shattered the hopes of American land companies for any profit from the area north of the Ohio.

By 1774, Great Britain was already so far along the road to war with her American colonies that the Quebec Act can hardly be regarded as a futher provocation of that inevitable conflict, although Virginia listed it among the "Intolerable Acts"; indeed it may have secured the loyalty of Canada when that conflict came. If it did accomplish such a result, there was no evidence that this benefit to the British cause extended to the French *habitants* of the West when the Americans finally appeared at western posts. In 1778, the French militia, left in charge at Kaskaskia after the withdrawal of British troops to strengthen Detroit, surrendered to George Rogers Clark without a fight, and at Vincennes Clark's advance agents, Dr. Jean Laffont and Father Pierre Gibault, easily persuaded their fellow countrymen to change allegiance to the Americans. By the time Captain Leonard Helm and one soldier arrived to "garrison" Vincennes, the French had the red-and-green flag of Virginia flying above the fort on the Wabash to welcome them.

Within four months, however, the *habitants* of Vincennes switched again and took the British oath of allegiance when Colonel Henry Hamilton, the "Hair-Buyer," came down from Detroit with 200 British and French troops, 400 Indians, and 97,000 pounds of military baggage and recaptured the town. Hamilton constructed new fortifications at Vincennes and then holed up for the winter, confident that no one could come to attack him in that cold rainy season and planning to move on to Kaskaskia and overcome Clark with his superior numbers as soon as the days were warm enough for marching and the flooded Wabash bottoms had dried out.

But Hamilton failed to appraise his enemy correctly.

"On the 4th (of February) I got everything complete and on the 5th I marched. . . ." In his memoirs, George Rogers Clark recalled, in this simple language, the beginning at Kaskaskia of one of the most momentous events in the history of the American West, the recapture of Vincennes.

In 1779, George Rogers Clark was twenty-six years old. A Virginian by birth, childhood friend of Thomas Jefferson and James Madison, before he was twenty he had turned his back upon the ease and grace of good living in Tidewater Virginia and struck out for the "Dark and Bloody Ground" of the Kentucky wilderness. There, within a few years, he became the recognized military and political leader of the new country, and in his campaign of the summer of 1778 against the Illinois and Wabash posts he had the backing of Governor Patrick Henry of Virginia. By February 4, 1779, Clark had made peace with the Indians in the Illinois country, won the steadfast loyalty of the French at Kaskaskia and Cahokia, and organized a new army of volunteers to supplement his own original troop of Kentucky woodsmen, who were known as Big Knives: He had "got everything complete." And so, on the 5th, he "marched."

To say that he "marched" is a euphemism. Two hundred and forty miles of flooded land stretched between him and his destination. He described the region as "one of the most beautiful countries in the world, but at that time in many parts flowing with water, and exceeding bad marching." At the end of his "march," in the heart of the Indiana wilderness, completely removed from any possibility of reinforcement, and beyond the reach of any American base of supplies, he hoped to defeat two hundred British and French regulars and the six or seven hundred Indiana warriors who had poured in from the Indiana forests at the British colonel's summons. Clark's own force consisted of seventy Kentucky woodsmen and sixty French allies newly pledged in their allegiance to the American cause.

But the tall, red-haired American leader was counting on something else besides the courage and loyalty of his men. He called it "an inward assurance of success." Drawing upon that inward assurance and keeping to himself the secret of their destination, Clark began the march as if it were a frolic, running ahead of his men through the mud and water, laughing and singing, urging them on, and at night, when camp was made, presiding over the evening's rations as if they were a banquet. "Thus," he wrote later, "insensibly, without a murmur, were those men led to the banks of the Little Wabash."

The Little Wabash was only the first of the rivers that lay athwart their route. A wild torrent of floodwater, choked with ugly sawyers and planters, logs that bristled upright and logs that floated, it would have stopped most armies; but by the time Clark's men reached it, they were so infected with his indomitable spirit that nothing could stop them. They built a platform on the submerged shore opposite them, ferried their goods over in dugouts, and struck out again across the flooded land, wading now in water that was never less than waist deep. It was the evening of February 15th before they were over the second fork of the Little Wabash, and there were still two more rivers to cross—the Embarrass and the Wabash itself.

At the Embarrass, Clark dispatched four scouts in a canoe to bring back any boats they could find and any intelligence they could gather about the journey that lay ahead. They returned with only the canoe in which they had set out, and the intelligence they brought was enough to destroy the young colonel's "inward assurance of success": for nine miles, between his army's position and Vincennes, there was nothing but water; the whole country was flooded. Yet, when he received the news, Clark plunged into the water shoulder-high and beckoned his men to follow. They did not know it, but he was going to take a roundabout route, setting out along the flooded shore of the Embarrass to follow it down to its juncture with the Wabash, hoping the way might be easier there. However, he was setting out to follow the course of one hopelessly "drowned" river only to learn that the other he was seeking was even more hopelessly "drowned." At daybreak on the 18th of February, just two weeks after their departure from Kaskaskia, the American army heard the British morning gun of Fort Sackville at Vincennes; and by two o'clock in the afternoon of that day they saw an avenue of treeless water winding southward through the flooded woods. It was the Wabash. But at least it was only one river to cross instead of two.

If the men rejoiced, their rejoicing could not have been long or loud, for by now they had been silenced by a new and fearful enemy: hunger. Grimly they built another canoe and sent two men up the river to steal or borrow boats from the French at Vincennes, and grimly they waited for their return. For those empty hours, as he recalled them in his report later, Clark could find but a single word: "Starving." For the empty moment when the scouts returned unsuccessful he had no words at all.

Two days longer they remained on the west shore of the submerged Wabash, waiting for the reinforcement with which they were to have rendezvoused on the Wabash, a batteau called the *Willing* carrying fifty men and several small cannon, which a wealthy St. Louis trader named Francis Vigo had outfitted and which a cousin of Clark's, John Rogers, commanded. The *Willing* had dropped down the Mississippi to the Ohio and ascended the Ohio to the mouth of the Wabash, but there the rush of floodwater had slowed its progress. It would not reach Clark's army till long after the "march" was finished.

In those two days, Clark's one hundred and thirty men had only one small deer for food, and on the third day they agreed with their commander that to delay any longer would be suicide. They must either advance or perish. In two canoes they ferried themselves across the Wabash to a little mound called the Lower Mammel and faced northward across the seven or eight miles of flooded bottoms that lay between them and Vincennes. There, scooping up river water in his hand, Clark sprinkled gunpowder on it and rubbed his hand over his face, emerging from the operation, with a warwhoop, a painted Indian. For a moment the men only stared at him dully as he plunged forward into the water. Then one of the gaunt skulls began to grin, and they followed him. The next three days they waded, without food, through water that was never below their knees, and on the 23rd of February, nineteen days after they set out from Kaskaskia, they came in sight of Vincennes.

The cannons of Fort Sackville stood eleven feet above the ground, aimed through ports so badly made that they could not be used for short-range firing. Having learned about this weakness of the fortifications in advance, Clark moved up to the fort in the night and deployed his scanty force in such a way that each of the cannon ports was covered by a group of sharpshooters. Then he opened fire, and it was not until then, by the combined miracles of chance, British military fatuity, and the French *habitants'* conspiracy of silence, that the redcoated soldiers in the fort knew that American troops were in the vicinity. The British manned their cannon, and the Americans waited. Each time a cannoneer's torch blazed at a porthole, a Kentucky Big Knife picked him off. By evening of the next day, Colonel Hamilton had had enough; deserted by his Indian and French allies and deceived into believing that he was being attacked by a superior force, he surrendered unconditionally.

George Rogers Clark's brilliant capture of Vincennes produced two large "ifs" in Indiana history. The first is the premise of a very dubious conjecture: If American forces had not been in possession of the post of the Wabash at the close of the Revolution, would the English have ceded the vast northwestern territory to this country when the peace treaty was drawn in Paris? Local pride has led some historians to contend that without Clark's campaigns in the West the northern border of the United States in that region would today be the Ohio River and Hoosiers would be Canadians. But the facts hardly support the contention, for the negotiators of the peace in Paris in 1782–83 seem not to have taken Clark's exploits into consideration; at least there was no mention of them in any of their deliberations or journals or dispatches.

The conjecture involving the second "if" lies more within the limits of possibility: If George Rogers Clark had advanced immediately to Detroit, as he considered doing, could he not have captured that dilapidated and inadequately manned fort easily? Detroit would not then have remained illegally in British hands at the close of the Revolution, and the new American West would have been spared the ensuing decade of Indian depredations that were largely of British instigation. The chain reaction goes on and on: The Little Turtle would have been on the American side from the start, there would have been no defeats for Harmar and St. Clair and no bloodshed at Fallen Timbers, the Battle of Tippecanoe might never have been fought and William Henry Harrison would not have become the ninth President of the United States, etc., *ad infinitum;* to rewrite history with the imagination is a beguiling re-creation. But the hard fact remains that Clark found himself so encumbered with prisoners at Vincennes after his victory that he decided against continuing his drive northward, and the history of Indiana and of the rest of the nation is what it is.

Immediately after the fall of Vincennes, Virginia organized all the land northwest of the Ohio River as the County of Illinois, but the organization was loose and inept, Virginia being preoccupied at the time with the American Revolution on her home front. The years that followed, setting a pattern that would endure until the War of 1812 was fought and won, were years of chaos and Indian savagery in Indiana, with the greatest damage to the interests of the French *habitants,* who had aided the Americans, and to the fur trade, which was the original reason for all the blood, sweat, and tears that had been expended in the region.

After the Revolution, Virginia rewarded George Rogers Clark for his services with a tract of 150,000 acres, known as Clark's Grant, in what is now Clark, Scott, and Floyd counties in Indiana, and for a time Clark settled on that land north of the Ohio, dividing some of it among his soldiers. He was the founder of the communities of Clarksville and Jeffersonville and also Louisville across the river, where he spent his last years. But Virginia neglected to recognize many of the notes that Clark had signed during his Illinois campaign, and by the time he was sixty, Clark, being a better soldier than businessman, was almost penniless; he was also by that time paralyzed, had suffered the amputation of a leg below the knee, and had taken to drink. When in 1813 Virginia presented him with a handsome and costly sword, he is reported to have said, "When Virginia needed a sword, I gave her one. She sends me now a toy. I need bread." But he is also reported to have repented his bitterness at once and added, more quietly, "I am too old and infirm ever to use a sword again, but I am glad that my old mother state has not entirely forgotten me and I thank her for the honor."

From the British the United States inherited the unsolved problems of the Indians and the lands of the West. The Indian problem led to the terror along the Ohio River that culminated first in the Battle of Fallen Timbers and the Treaty of Greenville in 1794 and 1795 and again, after a resurgence, in the Battle of Tippecanoe in 1811. It can hardly be said that the series of land ordinances that Congress enacted after the Revolution solved the land problem, but those ordinances did set up a framework upon which the ultimate solutions were eventually designed. The man who administered most of these solutions in Indiana was another young Virginian from the Tidewater, William Henry Harrison.

Son of Benjamin Harrison, who read the Declaration of Independence to the Continental Congress as it was adopted but who later opposed the Constitution in the Virginia Convention of 1788, William Henry Harrison was still a boy of twelve, learning to ride and hunt in the Tidewater country on his illustrious father's estate, "Berkeley," when the first land ordinance was passed in 1785. That ordinance provided for a division of the western lands into townships six miles square, each township to be divided into thirty-six sections of 640 acres, four of which were to be set aside for the United States Government and one preserved for the maintenance of public schools. When the more famous Ordinance of 1787 was passed, young William Henry Harrison was a student at Hampden-Sidney College in Virginia. This ordinance provided for the government of the Northwest, organizing it into a single district to be administered by a governor and several judges appointed by Congress. When this territory had a population of 5,000 free males of voting age, it could elect a territorial legislature, and ultimately it could be divided into no more than five nor less than three states whenever any one of them had 60,000 free inhabitants. By the time the Indians of the northwest recognized the full significance of the land ordinances and were reacting violently to the pressures of treaty makers, land companies, surveyors, and squatters, Harrison was an ensign in the United States Army, stationed at Cincinnati under the command of General Arthur St. Clair, governor of the Northwest Territory and commander in chief of the army in the West. This Northwest Territory, of course, included what is now Indiana.

Harrison arrived at Cincinnati in 1791. Just before his arrival, General Josiah Harmar and Governor St. Clair had suffered defeats by The Little Turtle in their thrusts at Kekionga. When General Anthony Wayne came to the West to do battle with the Indians, Harrison was a lieutenant, but serving in the capacity of a captain. At Fallen Timbers, Harrison distinguished himself and earned Wayne's commendation, and the next summer, as an aide-de-camp, he had the good fortune to observe an Indian conference as it was conducted by an old master at the signing of the Treaty of Greenville. There he stored away in his memory for future reference in Indiana the long elaborate ceremonial of metaphorical speeches, exchange of wampum, passing out of gifts, smoking of peace pipes, and carefully timed distribution of firewater. Three years later, the young man was secretary of the Northwest Territory at Cincinnati, and a year after that, when the territory moved into the second grade of government, he was elected as its first delegate to the Congress in Philadelphia.

William Henry Harrison had just turned twenty-seven when he received the appointment as first governor of Indiana Territory. This new division was separated from the Northwest Territory in 1800. It encompassed most of the present state of Indiana, all of

Illinois, all of Wisconsin, a large part of Michigan, and some of Minnesota. Its seat of government was Vincennes, and Harrison arrived there January 10, 1801, and served as governor for the next twelve years. By 1804, he had built a large brick house, "Grouseland," reminiscent of the Tidewater country, and there, with his wife, he entertained many famous guests. Among them, incidentally, was one whom he later found it advisable to denounce, the conspirator Aaron Burr. Harrison's territorial secretary was John Gibson, and his three judges were William Clark, Henry Vanderburgh, and John Griffin.

Among the new governor's first duties was the disentanglement of the land claims of the French settlers, who had acquired acreage first from the Indians, then by French titles, then by English, and finally by grants from the United States. His next and more difficult problem was the extinction of Indian titles and the concomitant pacification of the red men. For a while he was also in full charge of land sales to settlers, for there was no land office at Vincennes until January 1, 1805; after that his duties in that respect were only administrative. He was a busy man.

Using the knowledge of Indian ceremonies that he had acquired at Greenville, Harrison signed his first treaty with the Indians at Fort Wayne in 1803 and by it opened to settlement the land along the Vincennes Trace between Vincennes and Clark's Grant. It was not long until this region became as densely populated as the Wabash and Whitewater valleys, for unglaciated though it was, it was not yet eroded and its highlands were attractive to the pioneers because they carried less of a threat of ague and malaria than the richer river bottoms. Since 1803 all permanent land surveys in Indiana have taken their origin from a point six miles below Paoli where the baseline intersects the second principal meridian that was arbitrarily drawn through the territory; from it modern surveyors still number ranges and townships. By 1809, after several treaties with Indians, the governor had wrenched from the red man's control about one third of the state, purchasing for only $10,000 and a small annuity three million acres of land between the Wabash and White rivers. The survey of the 1809 cession produced the line running from the present town of

Montezuma to the vicinity of Brownstown known as the "Ten O'Clock Line," because the Indians demanded that it be drawn along the shadow cast by the sun at 10 A.M. on the day the treaty was signed.

Tecumseh denounced this treaty, and it was to assert his right to survey for it and to destroy Indian opposition that Harrison attacked The Prophet's village at Tippecanoe in 1811. Tecumseh, however, was not the governor's only critic. Many of Harrison's white contemporaries and some historians since have accused him of land-grabbing and mistreatment of the Indians. It is true that he was ruthless at times, but there can be no doubt that he was working under pressure from President Jefferson, who, like many men in the Federal government at that time, believed that Spain was on the verge of ceding the Louisiana Territory back to France. Aware of the old affinity between the Indians and the French, Jefferson was eager to establish as many white Americans as possible on former Indian lands before a transfer of Louisiana could take place.

More severe criticism came Harrison's way in his own time when, in 1805, with the population requirement waived, Indiana Territory passed into the second grade of government and organized a territorial legislature. The Legislative Hall, a two-story frame building constructed originally as a residence in Vincennes in 1800, is today, like "Grouseland," one of the city's most evocative landmarks of this early period. From the deliberations on the second floor of the hall Harrison at "Grouseland," not far away, often heard echoes of violent disapproval of his administration. In the beginning he had opposed the advance to second grade in government because it meant a diminution of his authority, but by 1804 he had changed his position, moving with the tide of public opinion and convinced that his own strength in the territory was secure. In any case, he was wrong, for opposition to his views became steadily more vocal in the next seven years.

Harrison's principal opponents were members of the antislavery party who sharply resented his approval of a resolution favoring suspension of Article Six in the Ordinance of 1787, which had forbidden the bringing of slaves into the territory. At the same time, the proslavery group, who came mainly from the western region of the territory, Illinois and the Wabash Valley, expressed animosity toward the governor because he opposed the movement to establish a separate territory of Illinois. When that division finally came in 1809, Harrison's ablest adversary, Jonathan Jennings, an antislavery man from Charlestown, was elected as Indiana's delegate to Congress. During the last three years that Harrison was in office, Jennings vigorously proposed a variety of bills in Congress designed to harass him and reduce his authority. There was even a petition subscribed to by the citizens of Harrison County demanding his removal from the governorship. It got nowhere.

In the sense that George Washington was "the father of his country," William Henry Harrison was hardly "the father of the Northwest," as he has sometimes been called. He was an administrator rather than a leader, a politician and not a man who had the interests of his people always at heart. That he was a good administrator is attested to by his reappointment to office three times by the Federal government during shifts of party power; and he was an able politician because he trimmed his sails skillfully to those shifts, entering office by the endorsement of Federalists and remaining in it under Republican administrations. Paradoxically Harrison's later role in national politics, especially his campaign for the presidency in 1840, built credit to his account in the popular mind for acts in Indiana Territory that were not altogether creditable—the victory at Tippecanoe, for example—and at the same time brought accusations down upon his head, such as the charge of land-grabbing, that cannot be supported without reservations. It is nevertheless true that he guided the new ship of state north of the Ohio through very troubled waters for twelve years without serious mishap although also without any bold distinction as a navigator. When he quit his office to fight in the War of 1812, leaving behind first John Gibson as acting governor and then Thomas Posey as his appointed successor, Indiana Territory had emerged from a chaotic wilderness to a reasonably stable community, on the verge of statehood and ready for the great influx of settlers that began about 1815.

Chapter Four

☆

Utopia on the Wabash

UTOPIA came to the banks of the Wabash two years before Indiana became a state. At New Harmony, in the heart of the wilderness and within a span of a dozen years, groups of men and women put into practice not one, but two, of the major social concepts that flourished among visionaries in the nineteenth century. The town became world-famous and is still so. And yet what happened to New Harmony as the years passed is typical of what has happened to other small towns with less auspicious beginnings in Indiana and elsewhere, so that the story of this Posey County community is both a distinguished exception and an illustration of the commonplace in Indiana's history.

Soon after the first Utopian society was founded at New Harmony, Lord Byron was writing about it from Italy in his *Don Juan,* satirically, it is true, but also with a grudging admission of its success:

> Why called he "Harmony" a state sans wedlock?
> Now there I've got the preacher at a deadlock.
> Because he either meant to sneer at Harmony
> Or marriage, by divorcing them thus oddly.
> But whether Reverend Rapp learned this in Germany
> Or no, 'tis said his sect is rich and godly.

Many other Europeans were not content, like Byron, with a distant view of the town; they made the hard journey across the ocean and through the forests to see for themselves the pious members of the first community at work, and after Robert Owen moved in with his Community of Equality, their numbers increased. Owen's experiment was debated in Congress and studied with varying degrees of approval and disapproval by governments abroad. What is more, New Harmony remained a cultural center in America long after its Utopianism became a matter of history, with notable scientists and philosophers and at least one President of the United States among its guests. Today, people from all over the world still converge upon the town as tourists to see the streets and buildings where, twice, men and women tried to make the world a better place.

Called the Harmony Society, the first community venture was based, like the communities of the Shakers, on a belief in the imminent Second Coming of Christ, though no violent physical manifestations of spiritual ecstasy shook the stolid German peasants who poled their boats up the Wabash from the Ohio in the spring of 1814 and camped their first night at what is now the corner of Church and Main Streets. These founders of New Harmony, some five or six hundred strong, came from Pennsylvania to the southwest corner of Indiana to await the millennium. The nearest town of any size was Vincennes, forty miles upstream, with a population of 3,000; Evansville was three years old, a cabin or two on a muddy riverbank; Princeton, hardly more than a clearing with a few homes huddled together, was a year or two older; the rest was forest. Before the Harmonists came to Indiana Territory, they had awaited the millennium for eleven years on the banks of Connoquenessing Creek, near Pittsburgh, after emigrating from Württemberg in 1803. But the Pennsylvania land was "too brocken & too cold for to raise Vine," and vine-growing was the special skill they had brought from Germany. Their hearts had been set on an estate in the fertile Wabash Valley for a long time before they were able to buy 24,734 acres there from the government for $61,050. In New Harmony, which they called Harmonie, they waited eleven years more; then they returned to Pennsylvania to wait again. They continued to wait until 1905, when there were only two of them left and one of these pronounced the long vigil over and became the executor of the large fortune they had accumulated in their century of existence.

The Harmonists' spiritual leader, George Rapp, was fifty-six years old when he came to Indiana, six feet tall, robust, somewhat heavy-featured, blue-eyed, white-bearded, and strong of will. In Germany, he had been a Separatist, formally breaking away from the established church in his thirtieth year and beginning to preach in his own house. He preached the basic doctrines of Lutheranism, but he believed that the Lutheran Church in Germany had lost sight of these doctrines in the luxury and confusion of its ceremonies. Ultimately he became convinced that the First Resurrection, promised in the Book of Revelation, would come in his own lifetime. He remained so firmly convinced of this that, on the day of his death in his ninetieth year, he said, "If I did not believe the Lord intended me to present my people to Him on the last day, I would think I was dying."

Father Rapp thought that "the last day," when Satan would be shut up in the bottomless pit and Christ would begin his reign of a thousand years on earth, was an event not simply to wait for but also to prepare for. He believed the Lord helps those who help themselves but expects them to help each other as well. On the basis of a verse in The Acts—*And the multitude of them that believed were of one heart and of one soul: neither said any of them that ought of the things which he possessed was his own; but they had all things common*—he persuaded his followers to surrender to him and his "associates" all their worldly goods and the products of their labors and to ask in return only meat, clothing, lodging, "and all such instruction in church and school as may be reasonably required."

George Rapp married young and had two children of his own, a son and a daughter, but in his middle age he adopted a young man, who was known afterward as Frederick Rapp, and Frederick became the chief of his "associates," his business manager. Frederick managed shrewdly and wisely and, while the Harmonists were in Indiana, was elected as a delegate to the state's first constitutional convention and appointed as a member of the commission that later chose the site of its second capital. By the time the Harmonists brought their religious communism to Indiana, Frederick Rapp's management had made them rich. After they had paid for the Indiana land and before they sold their Pennsylvania holdings, they still had $12,000 left on deposit in a Pittsburgh bank.

Shortly before they came to the Wabash country, the Harmonists began to practice celibacy, for which Father Rapp had also found authorization in the Bible, not only from Saint Paul, who urged Christians to "abide," but from Genesis, too. He interpreted the story of the Creation and of Adam's Fall as meaning that Adam was originally bisexual, capable of reproduction without assistance from a woman. "So God created man in his own image," says the Bible; "in the image of God created he him; male and female created he them." Rapp argued that the "them" referred to Adam alone and that the end of the statement, which appears in Genesis before the female element was taken from Adam to create Eve, proves that Adam was originally a male-and-female creature. The ultimate creation of Eve took place, Rapp argued, to satisfy Adam's restlessness and loneliness after he had named all the animals in Eden and noticed that, unlike himself, their male and female elements were in separate bodies. Curiously, Rapp believed that if man abjured the sexual relationship, he would someday return to the pristine, bisexual, self-reproductive state in which God had first designed Adam.

Marriages in the Harmony Society were not dissolved when the rule of celibacy was adopted. Husbands and wives continued to live together but were expected to "abide," as Saint Paul put it. A few children were born in the years that followed, but only a very few. The parents were not banished or even punished, except by patriarchal and communal disapproval, which must have been hard to bear in such a small society. No new marriages were performed, of course, and among the first buildings the Harmonists began to construct in New Harmony, after they had finished their steepled frame church, were dormitories for men and dormitories for women.

Everything the Württembergers built at New Harmony was substantial and strong: four dormitories of brick, each large enough to house about sixty people, each with a kitchen and a community room; a fine house for Father Rapp and his family;

two granaries of brick and stone; a water mill and dam; a textile mill; a dye house; two sawmills; a hemp and oil mill; two large distilleries; a brewery, in which the pump was operated by a large dog walking on a treadmill; forty two-story brick and frame dwellings and eighty-six log dwellings, all with fences, stables, and gardens.

The buildings were a triumph of construction. The larger of the two brick-and-stone granaries, the dam, the dye house, part of Father Rapp's house, a score of the other houses, and two of the dormitories are still standing after a century and a half. The houses and dormitories were insulated against heat and cold with soft bricks and with slabs of wood wrapped in clay and straw, known as "Dutch biscuits." The same stove heated the first and second floors by means of a flue on the second floor, and the buildings were rudimentarily air-conditioned by tunnels into the cellars. They were so firmly mortised and tenoned by square pegs driven into round holes that they could not sag or lean. The timbers that went into the houses were cut in standard sizes at a central sawmill and numbered with an adz, so that they were interchangeable, and by this convenient uniformity of materials the Harmonists pointed the way toward modern prefabrication.

By 1822, the Harmonists had all but created a Paradise on the banks of the Wabash in advance of the millennium. A hundred and thirty new members had come from Württemberg in 1817 and joined the original group, signing away not only their property but also the right to claim any wages or compensation should they choose to quit the society. Delegates had gone back to Germany and returned with 20,000 gulden in inheritances due the emigrants. Flatboats were leaving regularly for New Orleans loaded to capacity with agricultural products and whiskey, which the Harmonists never drank, limiting themselves to the small rations of beer and wine that Father Rapp doled out to them; and the factories of the town were turning out about $100,000 worth of goods a year—woolens, silks, wagons, hats, rope, and leatherwork. The homes the workers lived in were a striking contrast to the Hoosier backwoodsmen's pitiful, dark "log-holes," as one early traveler called the pioneers' cabins; their streets were broad and clean, shaded by Lombardy poplars and mulberries; the hillsides surrounding their village were covered with vineyards and orchards; and great flocks of Merino sheep grazed in their pastures. By the ingenious invention of a movable greenhouse set on grooved tracks, which made it possible to cover large plants in inclement weather but also to expose them fully to the summer sun when desirable, they even raised such exotic fruits as figs, lemons, and oranges in the variable Indiana climate.

They led a quiet, well-ordered life. Each morning they were wakened to the day's labor by the mellow tones of French horns. After the community milk wagon had made its rounds and the chickens, the only domestic creatures that refused to adapt to community ownership, had been fed, the workers marched singing to their allotted tasks in the fields and shops. At nine o'clock they paused for lunch, at noon for dinner, at four for *vesperbrot,* and at sunset they came home for supper. Sometimes the band played while they worked in the fields, and in the shops fresh flowers decorated their workbenches. At night, the shepherds slept under the stars in a house on wheels known as "Noah's Ark," while in the village the slumbering Harmonists were secure in the knowledge that the watchman was crying the hours: "Again a day is past, and a step made nearer to our end. Our time runs away and the joys of heaven are our reward."

Yet over this bucolic paradise there lay a solemn air. Travelers who passed through New Harmony between the years 1814 and 1825 repeated over and over the same observations. The Harmonists, they said, seldom conversed in the streets, and they never laughed. They loved music, but music seemed to be the only sound that ever broke the silence of the town. They refused to discuss their religion and were not cordial to strangers. In fact, most of them could not speak English. But by 1822, their town built and finished, their labors had become so light that the only occasion when they were all called out at once was "in the event of sudden bad weather, when the hay or corn is cut, but not carried."

Perhaps it was the increase of the Harmonists' leisure that brought an angel to Father Rapp in a dream in 1822. This angel gave him the specifications for a new church that would require great labor in the building. Rapp told his people about the dream, and the construction of the church began under his supervision. Made of brick and in the shape of a cross, the transept and nave were each one hundred and twenty feet long. At the center, the ceiling was twenty-eight feet above the floor, and twenty-eight columns of cherry, walnut, and sassafras supported the roof, each column hand-turned and polished from a single tree butt about twenty feet in circumference. Atop the church was a dome encircled by a railed balcony where the community band could play on summer evenings. Frederick Rapp, who was something of an artist as well as a shrewd businessman, carved and gilded a rose on the stone lintel of the main door. Today, this door and lintel, which are all that remain of the church, form the west entrance of New Harmony's schoolhouse, built on the church site in 1913. The church, after being partially dismantled, was completely torn down about a hundred years ago and the bricks were used to build a wall around the Harmonists' cemetery. An English traveler, seeing the imposing church before it was finished, wrote in his journal: "I could scarcely imagine myself to be in the woods of Indiana . . . while pacing the resounding aisle and surveying the stately colonnades."

But the church was finished sooner than the angel and Father Rapp had planned, and Harmonist hands were once more idle. They continued to build dormitories and acquire land, but even so there was not enough work to keep them busy all the time. George Rapp and his associates decided to sell their little Zion on the Wabash, at a sacrifice if necessary, and begin another community elsewhere. They had other reasons for moving that clinched the decision: New Harmony was a profitable agricultural community, but they had cherished visions of an industrial enterprise and now they realized such a venture would be more profitable in the East; furthermore, Frederick Rapp was beginning to dream of high finance, of trafficking in money as well as goods. The West was not altogether what they had expected.

When finally the Harmonists left New Harmony, the long-awaited angels of Judgment Day had not yet appeared, but by that time gossip about Father Rapp and another angel besides the one in his dream was troubling the leaders of the Harmonists much more than the Lord's delay. The gossip concerned a slab of limestone that Frederick Rapp had bought as a curiosity in St. Louis in 1819. The stone was intagliated with the delicate tracing of naked human footprints, which, said the Harmonists' Hoosier neighbors, Father Rapp used to deceive his people. According to the gossips, Rapp told the Harmonists that Gabriel had come down out of heaven to advise him to lead them out of New Harmony against their will and Gabriel had left his footprints on the stone where he alighted.

The story was apocryphal. Frederick Rapp was showing the stone to visitors soon after he brought it to New Harmony and was explaining to them its origin and his reason for buying it, which was simply to possess an ornamental curiosity. But the slander haunted the Harmonists the rest of their days; as late as 1914, their executor, John S. Duss, was referring to it in his letters as "this damphoolishness," and today's tourist in the town is still occasionally shown the old footprints and told the libelous tale.

The man who bought New Harmony, lock, stock, barrel, and alleged angel tracks, was Robert Owen, the British industrialist and reformer who had made a fortune in the textile business. He too was a chiliast of sorts, like Rapp, but whereas Rapp waited for the millennium, Owen announced that he was bringing a millennium to Indiana himself. At New Lanark, in Scotland, he had established a school to reform the character of the working class and had long preached his doctrine that man is not responsible for his acts and can be saved from ignorance and poverty only by the improvement of his surroundings. Owen regarded all religions as "superstitions," and by 1825 his public attacks on organized faiths of all kinds had lost for him much of his influence and popularity in the British Isles, and he was ready to seek fresh fields for his Utopian projects. When he was approached by George Rapp's agent in Scotland as a prospective buyer of the town on the Wabash, the agent was so astonished by Owen's immediate interest that he said to one of Owen's sons: "Does your father *really* think of giving up a position like this, with every comfort and luxury, and taking his family to the wild life of the far west?" Owen came to America and in New Harmony closed the deal with Frederick Rapp on Sunday, January 2, 1825. Accounts of the price vary from $50,000 to $190,000; whatever the figure, he got a bargain.

Although he was a man of high humanitarian purposes, many years ahead of his times, Robert Owen suffered all his life from an inability to stay on any job long enough to see it well done; he was inclined to mistake the word—his own word—for the deed. He had no more than signed the papers for the purchase of New Harmony when he was off to Washington to tell America about his plans as if they were already a *fait accompli*. In two speeches before joint sessions of Congress, with the President of the United States and members of the Supreme Court in attendance, he exhibited a model of the town he planned to build at New Harmony and, with only a hazy explanation of its governmental structure, predicted the spread of communities like his all over the United States and a consequent release from ignorance and oppression such as mankind had never before witnessed. Immediately afterward, having set up no kind of organization in New Harmony whatsoever and with only his son William, just turned twenty-three, left there as his representative, he published a manifesto inviting any and all who dreamed of a socialist millennium to move to the town on the Wabash at once. The result was that by the time he returned to New Harmony three months later, about a thousand men and women had moved into the town before the last of the German Harmonists had moved out and people were living there two and three families to the house.

Undismayed, Owen rechristened the town New Harmony, dedicated the Harmonists' brick church to free thought and free speech, renaming it The Hall of New Harmony, and promptly made therein the first of the many speeches that were to be his substitute for action. "I am come to this country," he announced, "to introduce an entire new state of society, to change it from an ignorant, selfish system to an enlightened social system which shall gradually unite all interests into one, and remove all causes for contests between individuals." He then outlined, in general terms, a constitution for a Preliminary Society, pointing out that for a while he would keep the property in his own hands and the people must temporarily accept "a certain degree of pecuniary inequality," although thenceforth there would be no social inequality. Three days later the community adopted his constitution.

This constitution was mostly preamble, establishing very little beyond the fact that "persons of color" were not to be included in the social equality, that the society was not answerable for its members' debts, that those who did not want to work could buy credit at the community store by paying cash quarterly in advance, and that everyone must try to be "temperate, regular, and orderly" and set a good example for everybody else in order to achieve the goal of "universal happiness." The actual government of the society was to be by a committee which Robert Owen would appoint, but neither its size nor its function was defined, unless the statement that it "would conduct the affairs of the society" can be regarded as a definition. As soon as the constitution was adopted, Owen appointed four members of the governing committee and allowed the society to elect three more "by ballot among themselves"; and then he was off again, to the East, to spread the news of New Harmony further, and to Scotland, to settle his financial affairs. This time he was gone seven months.

During the first month of his absence, the Preliminary Society ran well enough on the momentum of its first enthusiasm. In accordance with the program Owen left behind for them, the members danced on Tuesday nights in The Hall of New Harmony, the committee held a business meeting on Wednesday nights, there was a concert on Thursday nights, and on Sundays there were lectures in the Harmonists' old frame church, which the newcomers called "The Steeple House." "Here there are no brawling braggarts and intemperate idlers," one Owenite wrote back home to his son. He described how well the postmaster lived with his wife and several sons on the $1.54 a week that he earned in credit at the community store by being not only postmaster but also a committeeman, superintendent of the farms, and a selling agent for the store. But by midsummer, discontent and dissension had set in. "The idle and industrious are neither of them satisfied," one member wrote to a friend, "the one contending that they do enough for their allowance, the other thinking themselves entitled to more." At the same time, this letter-writer's wife was telling her aunt in Pittsburgh, "The hogs have been our Lords and Masters this year in field and garden. We are now . . . without vegetables, except what we buy; and I believe we shall go without potatoes, turnips, or cabbages this winter, unless they are purchased."

Her prediction came true, and by the time Owen returned, in January, 1826, the society was in chaos and splinter groups were in the process of forming both within and on the periphery of the town. Owen, however, was so delighted by what he thought he saw that he announced the time had come, a year in advance of his original plan, for the formation of a permanent "Community of Equality." Another constitution was drawn up, not greatly different from the first, and in a short time the threatened splinter groups were a reality. One of them called itself Feiba Peveli, employing a scheme of nomenclature devised by an English architect in which letters were substituted for the numerals in latitudes and longitudes. This architect, one Stedman Whitwell, proposed the renaming of Pittsburgh as Otfu Veitoup, New York as Otke Notive, and New Harmony itself as Ipba Venul.

It was at this point that William Maclure came on the scene at New Harmony as Owen's partner and a financial backer. Like Owen, Maclure was a wealthy man, a Scot who had accumulated a fortune in an English-American export business. Some twenty years before, he had made a geological survey of the United States, traveling alone, crossing and recrossing North America many times between the Atlantic Coast and the Rockies and the St. Lawrence River and the Gulf of Mexico. Unlike Owen, he was a practical, levelheaded man, less of a visionary although more of a philanthropist. His primary interest in the New Harmony community was its educational experiment, and he soon began to look upon his partner's social theories with a jaundiced eye. Before the year was out, Maclure and Owen quarreled, dissolving the partnership, and thereafter Maclure's sole participation was in the conduct of the schools.

Maclure came to New Harmony in January, 1826, aboard a keelboat of his own purchasing at Pittsburgh. It was named *The*

Philanthropist but rechristened for posterity by Owen as "The Boatload of Knowledge." It carried an astonishing intellectual cargo on one of the most hopeful and halting voyages in the history of the Ohio River. Among the boat's passengers were Thomas Say, the American naturalist; Charles-Alexandre Lesueur, the French naturalist; Madame Marie Duclos Fretageot, a Pestalozzian schoolmistress from Paris via Philadelphia; Robert Dale Owen, Robert Owen's oldest son, future founder of the Smithsonian Institution and crusader for women's rights; and a score or more of teachers and pupils for the school system that was to make New Harmony famous in the history of American education.

In New Harmony, these people and others of equal renown who followed them wrangled deplorably over the nature of universal happiness and the proper pursuit of it. They were required by Owen to wear a ludicrous costume—white pantaloons buttoned over a boy's jacket without a collar, compared by one observer to "a feather-bed tied in the middle." But in spite of their dress and their inability to manage their everyday lives, there was a persistent charm in their initial naïve enthusiasm for the New Moral World that Owen dreamed of. Most of them were not designed by nature or experience to do the work they needed to do to keep the community going, but they tried at first to do their share of the harsher chores. Thomas Say developed such blisters that he could hardly shake hands with the Duke of Saxe-Weimar Eisenach when the Duke visited the town. Robert Dale Owen spent a day sowing wheat and got a sore arm and, after that, lent a hand in the community bakery and spoiled the bread. Charles-Alexandre Lesueur preferred zoological expeditions to teaching in the school. Plaiting his beard and tucking it into his waistcoat, he fled to the woods as often as possible with his three dogs—Penny, Snap, and Butcher—to collect specimens. One of these was a skunk, which his French biographer, a hundred years later, described as the first "pool-cat" ever to be sent alive to Europe. There is no record of what happened to it, or its recipient. Joseph Neef, a pupil of the Swiss educational reformer, Pestalozzi, struggled to control his old-soldier's profanity in the schoolroom but had a hard time of it, perhaps because he carried a spent bullet in his head from the Battle of

Arcola and because not all the children of New Harmony were so phenomenally shy as Sir Charles Lyell, the Scottish geologist, observed them to be when he visited the town. Old man Greenwood, discouraged by the pursuit of happiness with the handicap of advanced age, marched about town carrying a twelve-foot iron rod every time there was a thunderstorm; he wanted to die but thought it was God's privilege, not his, to do the job.

Meanwhile, everybody read and thought and wrote and wrote and talked and talked and talked, when they were not attending lectures in The Steeple House or dancing the night away in The Hall of New Harmony. Lovers wandered in the mystic labyrinth that the Harmonists had designed with tailored hedgerows and a small temple at the center and which the Owenites allowed to grow into a jungle. Picnickers gathered in the neglected vineyards and boating parties drifted on the river. One day the picnickers took axes with them and chopped down several trees as preparation for the new town that Owen planned to build; but they were soon leaning on their ax-helves listening to another speech by Mr. Owen and singing a song, which began:

> Ah, soon will come the glorious day,
> Inscribed on Mercy's brow,
> When truth shall rend the veil away
> That blinds the nations now.

A duel was fought in the Harmonist cemetery, but with no casualties, and two women engaged in fisticuffs in front of Community House No. 4 without serious damage to each other. Single gentlemen complained that their socks were stolen from the community-house washlines, and Madame Fretageot told the Duke of Saxe-Weimar Eisenach, in German, that Mr. Owen's democracy was harmful to the manners of the young. The schoolchildren played tricks on their mathematics instructor, Monsieur Guillaume Sylvan Casimir Phiquepal d'Arusmont, and Monsieur Guillaume Sylvan Casimir Phiquepal d'Arusmont eventually gave up in despair and married Frances Wright, the feminist. A group of dissenters built a coffin and would have buried "Owenism" if the coffin had not been smashed by unidentified persons the night before the funeral. It is little wonder that the Harmonist factories stood idle, the Harmonist millwheels no longer turned, the Harmonist fences broke down, the hogs had the run of fields and gardens, and there weren't even cabbages to store when the second winter came.

Owen's experiment at New Harmony lasted altogether about two years and ended in failure, but with Owen and Maclure still owning most of the property. Owen tried to save his dream by frequent reorganizations and, toward the last, by offering land for lease or sale to anyone who would attempt to establish a community according to his design. On July 4, 1826, once more mistaking the word for the deed, he sought to free the community of all its troubles by making a "Declaration of Mental Independence." On this date, the fiftieth anniversary of American political independence, he announced, "I have calmly and deliberately determined upon this eventful and auspicious occasion, to break asunder the remaining mental bonds which for so many ages have grievously afflicted our nature and, by so doing, to give forever FULL FREEDOM TO THE HUMAN MIND." (The capitals are Owen's.) Less than a year later, he delivered two successive farewell addresses in New Harmony, on May 26 and 27, 1827. Thereafter, deeding his property over to his sons, he left the community to its own devices and took off in pursuit of a new dream: He would ask the government of Mexico to give him Coahuila and Texas for his next experiment, in the expectation that the United States and Great Britain would support his sovereignty in that vast borderland. Owen died in 1858, at the age of eighty-seven, a spiritualist, on familiar terms with Napoleon, Shakespeare, and Benjamin Franklin.

Where George Rapp, believing that the "last day" was at hand, built New Harmony as if it were going to endure forever, Robert Owen, convinced that a new world was just beginning, erected nothing permanent on the banks of the Wabash. What one sees of old New Harmony today is the work of the Germans; there is not a single visible structure left that was created in Owenite days. And yet, with all the monuments to the Germans' industry, it is difficult to determine what went on in their minds and spirits as they worked in the Indiana wilderness, while the stamp of the Owenites' intellectual independence and cultural aspirations shaped the history of the town throughout the nineteenth century and is still apparent. Owen was not a practical reformer, but he was a prophet and a catalytic agent among other dreamers. He created in New Harmony a lasting spirit like his own by his sincere good will and his personal magnetism, "gentle bore" though he was, according to Macaulay.

Specifically, Owen shaped New Harmony's future by the remarkable group of people he brought to Indiana, many of whom remained, and by leaving behind four remarkable sons and one remarkable daughter, who composed the town's "first family." The people of New Harmony like to speak of the period immediately following Owen's community days as "the Golden Age." Certainly the town remained for a long time as lively and exciting as it was when Robert Owen was proclaiming his miracles of Mental Independence and the New Moral World. Indeed, throughout most of the nineteenth century, the town was a cultural if not a celestial Zion unlike anything else in the vast, raw, and often ugly newness of the Middle West. Although the population has never much exceeded one thousand, it has supported a library, a museum, an art gallery, several lecture series, the Thespian Society, a theatre, and two newspapers of national reputation and a half dozen of regional fame. As if such adornments were not enough, the first woman's club in America was organized in New Harmony in 1859 (or 1825). In fact, about the only civic virtue the town has failed to acquire in its sevenscore and twelve years to the date of this writing, either by its own initiative or by the generosity of its numerous benefactors, is a public sewage system. But with a millennium of one sort or another always just around the corner, such a preparation for permanence on this earth has perhaps seemed superfluous.

After Owen's departure, Maclure became the first citizen and major patron of New Harmony. Like Owen, Maclure never spent more than a month or two at a time in the town; the climate was too much for him. But unlike Owen, he knew the value of able lieutenants in his absence: Madame Fretageot, who served the New Harmony school system until 1831; Thomas Say, who remained in the town until his death in 1834; and Maclure's brother, Alexander, who died in New Harmony in 1850 and is buried with Say in a vault on the lawn of the Maclure home that had formerly been George Rapp's. William Maclure did more for the community in outright gifts and, through his agents, gave it more guidance than it received from the man whose name is more often associated with its history. Under Maclure's direction, New Harmony had the first free-public-school system in America for boys and girls alike and the first trade school, supported by his generosity, until finally the state of Indiana adopted a school system supported by taxation. Through Maclure's generosity also, the Workingmen's Institute was founded, a society of mutual self-improvement for the common man; and largely because of his spirit New Harmony's public library remains today remarkable for its size—a large, two-story brick building, housing 18,000 volumes available to a population of about a thousand. When Maclure died in Mexico in 1840, he left a sum of about $80,000 that helped establish 144 libraries in the state of Indiana and 16 in Illinois.

Shortly before the German Harmonists left Indiana, they bought a printing press for the publication of George Rapp's *Thoughts on the Destiny of Man,* in German and in English. When Robert Owen came, he purchased a new Stansbury press in Cincinnati and had it shipped to the town on the Wabash. On this press, *The New Harmony Gazette* was published regularly every week for three years, from 1825 until 1828, edited first by William Owen and Robert Jennings and later by Robert Dale Owen and Frances Wright, who finally took the journal to New York City and renamed it the *Free Enquirer.* The motto of the *Gazette* was, "If we cannot reconcile all opinions, let us endeavor to unite all hearts"; but it was, of course, primarily the organ of Owenism, and it published many of the treatises and speeches of the British reformer written before the New Harmony venture, as well as essays and editorials from the pens of two of his sons, Miss Wright, and William Maclure.

William Maclure sent up a press from New Orleans in 1827 for the use of students in his School of Industry, and on it was printed the first issue of his *Disseminator of Useful Knowledge,* a bimonthly that, for the better part of a decade, was the official organ of the town. It had two mottoes: "Ignorance is the fruitful cause of human misery," and, later, "He who does his best, however little, is always to be distinguished from him who does nothing." In time, the *Disseminator's* press produced a number of books in New Harmony, among them Maclure's *Opinions on Various Subjects,* in three volumes; schoolbooks for use in Mexico; Michaux's *North American Sylva;* and Thomas Say's *American Conchology.* Mrs. Say and Charles-Alexandre Lesueur drew the sixty-eight illustrations for this beautiful book. Pupils in the New Harmony schools did the coloring. Later, Josiah Warren, inventor of "the time store" and founder of The Village of Modern Times on Long Island, came to town and invented his speed press, the first to print a newspaper on a continuous sheet.

The inspiration of William Maclure and Gerard Troost, the Dutch geologist, and the presence in New Harmony of Maclure's large geological collection are indirectly responsible for the town's being a headquarters of the U.S. Geological Survey from 1839 until 1856. When young David Dale Owen joined his father in the community, he had already abandoned the career of an artist after studying for a while with Benjamin West and was contemplating the practice of medicine, but the sight of physical suffering was so painful to him that he abandoned that career too and turned to a study of Maclure's collections. Ultimately he was appointed U.S. Geologist. The "laboratory" he built on Church Street in 1858 remains today one of the most distinguished and interesting houses in New Harmony. David Dale in turn inspired his younger brother, Richard, to become a geologist, and Richard was for a while David's assistant. After distinguishing himself in the Civil War, Richard became a professor of Natural History at Indiana University and later was chosen as the first president of Purdue, but he always maintained a residence in New Harmony and spent the last eleven years of his life there in retirement, dying in 1890. These two brothers were, in large part, responsible for the visits of many famous scientists to New Harmony, including John James Audubon, Sir Charles Lyell, and Prince Maximilian of Wied-

Neuwied, who brought with him the young Swiss painter, Karl Bodmer.

The oldest Owen brother, Robert Dale Owen, was in and out of New Harmony all his life, sometimes maintaining a home there, sometimes paying his sister and brothers long visits. In the 1840's, he served two terms in Congress as a Representative from southern Indiana and, while in Washington, wrote and introduced the bill that created the Smithsonian Institution, which David Dale Owen helped to design. In 1850, New Harmony sent Robert Dale Owen to Indiana's second constitutional convention, where he served in the vanguard of those fighting for the rights of women. From New Harmony, the oldest Owen son wrote the letter to President Lincoln that is said to have persuaded him to issue the Emancipation Proclamation. Owen spent his last years at Lake George, New York, where he died in 1877, but sixty years later his remains were brought back to New Harmony and buried beside those of his first wife.

Robert Owen's granddaughter, Constance Fauntleroy, who had lived abroad with the Robert Dale Owens when her uncle was American chargé d'affaires in Naples and who had been educated in Europe, organized the Minerva Society, a woman's literary club, in New Harmony, and Uncle Robert Dale wrote its constitution. Before that, in 1825, Frances Wright had gathered a Female Social Society about herself in New Harmony: so whichever is "the first woman's club in America," New Harmony can claim it. Today "the Fauntleroy home," built by the German Harmonists, is a museum.

The tradition of the theatre was perhaps the longest-lasting in New Harmony's story. It began with William Owen. After Robert Owen returned to England, all five of his children and their mates and offspring lived for a while, according to his wish, in an enormous house known as "the Mansion." One of them was William, who was married to Mary Bolton in 1837 in a triple ceremony with two of his brothers, whose brides were daughters of Joseph Neef. William did not live long enough to become as famous as Robert Dale, David Dale, and Richard, but locally he made a name for himself by founding the Thespian Society in 1828. His spirit inspired New Harmony's theatre for almost a century thereafter. The old "Opera House," originally a Harmonist dormitory, is still standing.

The inherited wealth that preserved the gracious living and culture of New Harmony well into the present century and that is still in evidence there was shored up against depletion by the fertility of Posey County farms, and during the town's long history some new fortunes were derived therefrom. But by 1900 most of the famous citizens of New Harmony had either died or departed, and by 1920 the town began to suffer the fate of many other small rural communities in Indiana. The prosperity and magnetism of cities were attracting its most enterprising citizens. Many of the town's children went off to college and did not return, and the automobile, the metropolitan movie palace, city banks, city supermarkets, radio and, soon thereafter, television destroyed the old self-sufficient community life for those who were left behind. After the 1920's came the Depression, and then World War II. By the 1950's the town, like most remote small towns in the state, had become a derelict, too far from any city to become a residential suburb, too near to have a life of its own. The children who passed in and out of the schoolhouse door that Frederick Rapp had made for Father Rapp's church in 1822 were still told about their remarkable past, but they no longer felt they were a part of it.

Now the state has taken over some of the Harmonist buildings; and in the 1960's a trust, originated in Texas by the wife of a descendant of Robert Owen, erected in New Harmony a large edifice designed by Philip Johnson and called "the Roofless Church" and adorned it with a "Descent of the Holy Spirit" by Jacques Lipchitz. Across the street, at the edge of the Wabash River bottoms, where tall corn still grows, a small park was created and named for Paul Tillich, and in June, 1963, Dr. Tillich came to New Harmony to dedicate the site of a "Cave of the New Being." After his death, his ashes were brought to New Harmony in 1966 and buried there. The trust owns a number of old Harmonist houses, has painted them various colors, furnished them, and opened them to invited guests. These attractions have increased the number of sightseers in New Harmony in recent years. In 1964 civic leaders organized the New Harmony Associates to preserve the town's historic treasures and spread more widely a public appreciation of them; and in 1965 the state of Indiana initiated plans for a large recreation park for tourists in the vicinity of the village.

So New Harmony seems once more on the verge of prosperity and, with it, whatever kind of universal happiness prosperity creates.

Chapter Five

☆

Horse-Trading and Logrolling

IN ITS beginnings, Indiana was a young man's country. Exploring and settling an unfamiliar territory, enduring the hardships of travel on uncharted rivers by canoe or flatboat and overland on foot and horseback, fighting and negotiating with Indians, surveying the land, clearing forests, building homes, breaking new soil, mauling rails, laying up fences, eking out crops from stump-studded miasmal earth, and taking the chances of ague, fever, and chills—these were not for the aged or aging. Old people seldom migrated to the West in its first development. Consequently, the young, carrying full responsibility for creation of a new society, matured fast, and if a niche awaited them in history they had to find it early.

When Jonathan Jennings came on the scene in Indiana in 1806, he fitted into the pattern already set. La Salle was twenty-three when he left France for Canada, twenty-six when he discovered the Ohio; George Rogers Clark came to Kentucky at nineteen, was twenty-five when he led an army into the Northwest and twenty-six when he marched it across the drowned lands of the Wabash to capture Vincennes; William Henry Harrison arrived at the outpost of Cincinnati at eighteen, was twenty-three when the Northwest Territory sent him to Congress, and had just turned twenty-seven when he became governor of the newly created Indiana Territory. So it was with Jonathan Jennings. He disembarked from a Pittsburgh flatboat at Jeffersonville when he was only twenty-two; he was elected territorial delegate to Congress at twenty-five; he was thirty-two when he became the first governor of the state of Indiana.

Jennings was born in New Jersey, but his parents took him at the age of two to Fayette County, Pennsylvania, and there he spent his childhood and early youth. His father was a Presbyterian preacher, and both his parents had degrees in medicine. The boy attended the Presbyterian school at Canonsburg, where he learned some Greek and Latin; afterwards he studied law. When he came to Indiana, he was a young man of medium height, with blue eyes, fair complexion, and sandy hair, pleasing in manner though somewhat slovenly in dress with a carelessness that would increase as he became corpulent in his last years. From Jeffersonville he soon moved to Charlestown and then to Vincennes, where in 1807 he was admitted to the bar. His legal fees were meager, however, and he had to supplement them by working at the land office and later becoming an editorial associate of Elihu Stout on the *Western Sun*, which Stout had founded in 1804 as the *Indiana Gazette*, Indiana's first newspaper. Stout was a proslavery man, and Jonathan Jennings, brought up in a Northern clergyman's family in abhorrence of slavery, soon abandoned the relationship with Stout and decided to return to Clark County. There he expected the political atmosphere to be more congenial, and there too lived a young woman, Anna Hay, whom he admired. In letters back home to his sister in Pennsylvania he had already announced his intention to marry as soon as he found a young woman to his liking.

The story is told that as the young lawyer was preparing for the journey over the Vincennes Trace to Charlestown, his former employer at the land office, Nathaniel Ewing, suggested that he look around in the eastern counties for a good candidate for Congress, and Jennings promptly proposed himself. Ewing agreed that he would be acceptable if he could gather round him the support of the antislavery faction in the region to which he was going; he would need that support to offset the votes of "the Virginia aristocrats," sometimes called "the Vincennes Junta," whose stronghold was the western part of the territory. At that time there were no political parties in Indiana, but already voters were dividing into two factions: "the people" and "the aristocrats," or those who wanted more democracy and those who wished to retain political power in the hands of a few. The former group was largely anti-slavery as well as anti-Harrison, the latter proslavery and pro-Harrison. As soon as Jennings arrived at Charlestown, he began a canvass of the political situation.

In 1809, there were only four counties in Indiana Territory. Dearborn was a sharp wedge thrust upward along what was known as "the Gore," from the Ohio River between the mouth of the Kentucky and the First Principal Meridian, which was then, as it is now, the Indiana–Ohio line, to a point on that meridian several miles southwest of Fort Recovery. Clark lay just west of Dearborn, another north-pointed wedge, but much broader at its base. It encompassed the land between the Ohio and the East Fork of the White River from a point on the First Principal Meridian a few miles north of the apex of Dearborn and down the fork of the White to Delaney's Creek. Harrison was a rectangle below the East Fork of the White stretching southward to the Ohio, bordered on the east by Clark and on the west by the Second Principal Meridian. Knox, the original county, was everything else in the territory, with the white population concentrated along the lower Wabash, especially at Vincennes.

Jennings soon learned that the most intransigent of his political foes in the eastern counties would be General James Dill, an officeholder in Dearborn appointed by William Henry Harrison, and Captain Samuel Vance, Harrison's brother-in-law, who also lived in Dearborn. But when the election came, the candidates who opposed Jennings were not these men but Thomas Randolph, a "Virginia aristocrat," and John Johnson, a native of Kentucky, both of Knox County. The campaign was bitter. Stout, of the *Western Sun,* opposed his former associate editor vigorously. At a party in Vincennes on July 4, Governor Harrison offered as a toast: "Jonathan Jennings—the semblance of a delegate—his want of abilities, the only safety of the people—three groans!" Jennings was not an orator. He solicited votes by traveling about through the woods and meeting people, often taking off his coat and pitching in with them at their work. He was also a busy letter writer and became in time what is sometimes called a "home congressman" because of his direct personal contact with his constituents. Throughout his political career, the windowpanes of many cabins and schoolhouses in Indiana were Jennings' letters that had been greased with lard to make them translucent and serve as glass. At the end of the campaign, having concentrated his efforts in Clark and Dearborn, he carried those counties by enough margin to outweigh the pro-Harrison sentiment of Knox and Harrison counties. The vote was Jennings 428, Randolph 402, and Johnson 81.

Randolph contested the election, and the House of Representatives came close to declaring it null and void, but Jennings was finally seated. Two years later, he defeated Randolph again, and this time he and his bride rode on horseback all the way from Charlestown to what was then called "Washington City." In succeeding elections Jennings won against two more "Virginia aristocrats": Waller Taylor and Elijah Sparks. By the time the first constitutional convention was held, in 1816, William Henry Harrison had left Indiana, Thomas Randolph lay buried at Tippecanoe, and Jennings was the undisputed political leader of the territory.

The year Jennings was first elected to Congress, 1809, was also the year of the separation of Illinois Territory from Indiana Territory. Michigan Territory had been removed four years earlier. The separation of Illinois left Indiana with its present boundaries, excepting the Indiana–Michigan line, which would later be moved ten miles north to where it is now, and a small strip of land west of a line north of Vincennes and east of the Wabash, which had gone with Illinois but would be returned to Indiana when it became a state. By that time, 1816, the territory would have fifteen counties: Switzerland, carved out of Dearborn; Franklin and Wayne, formed from parts of Dearborn and Clark; Dearborn, widened; Jefferson, Jackson and Washington, formed from the northern portions of Clark and Harrison; and Orange, Perry, Gibson, Posey, and Warrick, taken mainly from Knox below the East Fork of the White River. Knox, incidentally, the mother of Indiana counties, was finally reduced to its present shape the following year.

The second division of Indiana Territory—that is, the separation of Illinois—not only gave the state approximately its present boundaries, it also added impetus to the sentiment for removal of the capital from Vincennes to a town more centrally located in the territory that remained. Although during much of this time Jennings was away in the new Federal capital on the Potomac, he still had a voice in debates at home and ardently supported the movement for a new territorial capital. When Governor Harrison vetoed a bill from the territorial legislature authorizing removal of the government to Madison, Jennings, on January 20, 1812, presented to Congress a "representation of sundry inhabitants of Indiana Territory complaining of the arbitrary conduct of the Governor of that Territory." The argument of the "sundry inhabitants" was that Harrison's extensive landholdings in and around Vincennes had motivated his opposition to the change and had inspired his tyrannical use of the veto power. But there was no way to override this veto, and the transfer of government had to await Harrison's departure for the war. When the move was finally made, in 1813, the village of Corydon, seat of Harrison County, won the coveted honor.

The War of 1812 postponed the advance from territory to statehood in Indiana. In the fervor of patriotism, territorial politicians put away their differences and closed ranks against the common enemy. At the same time, beneath the surface, the war broadened the sentiment for statehood to the degree that when the fighting ceased there was no longer much opposition to the advance. Harrison had done well for the territory, especially by his extinction of Indian claims; when he left for the war, one third of Indiana land was already in the white man's possession. But with the coming of the war many of the Indians allied themselves with the English and were soon striking southward into the territory they had relinquished, and the pioneers along the Lower Wabash and the Ohio, especially after the Pigeon Roost Massacre, became convinced that a state government would give them more security than Washington could give them, preoccupied as it was with many other affairs. As soon as Harrison carried the war into Canada and the Indian menace subsided, political maneuvering revived in Indiana and the issue of statehood came alive again.

Indiana's House of Representatives had sent a memorial to Congress late in 1811 asking for statehood and, at the same time, requesting the right to elect its county sheriffs, whom the governor appointed at that time, and Jonathan Jennings had presented this memorial to Congress several weeks before he made his "representation" about the governor's "arbitrary conduct" in regard to the location of the territorial capital. In the spring of 1812, Congress approved the resolution and proposed that an enabling act for Indiana's admission to the Union should be submitted when its population reached 35,000. Thus Congress was willing to waive the requirement of 60,000, just as it had waived the population requirement when Indiana became a territory. But it was 1814 before the territorial legislature got around to authorizing a census, and the returns from the census would not be completed for another year after that.

In 1812, the population of Indiana was estimated at 30,000; it would be more than double that figure before Indiana became a state. In the four intervening years, especially the last two, new settlers arrived in the region in increasing numbers, coming mainly from the South, although the New England Yankee, with his strange speech and his sharp eye for a bargain, was already beginning to put in an appearance on the Hoosier scene. As early as 1808, Frederick Mauck had begun to operate a ferry across the Ohio between Mauckport and Brandenburg, Kentucky, and at this point settlers poured into Indiana from Kentucky and the Carolinas for the next fifteen years, setting the stamp of their customs and speech so firmly upon southern Indiana that it is still in evidence there. Downriver, other immigrants from the South were crossing into Warrick County at or near Rockport, which is now in Spencer County, or dropping still farther downstream to Mc-Fadden's Landing (now Mount Vernon), which was established in 1805. These settlers laid out many new towns along the streams and rivers and among the hills south of the East Fork of the White—Evansville in 1812, Salem in 1814, Vernon in 1815, Paoli in 1816; and settlements already established, like Jeffersonville, Charlestown, Brookville, Lawrenceburg, Madison, and Corydon, grew rapidly round the tree stumps, mudholes, hogs, and garbage that obstructed their "streets." An exception was New Albany, founded by the Scribner brothers from the state of New York in 1813. Many of the new settlers squatted for a while, perhaps even bought land from the government, and then restlessly moved on. The adventurous probed as far northward into the forest as the Ten O'Clock Line and clustered in remote places like Spencer and Bloomington, which were founded in 1815 and 1818.

When finally the census was made, it reported 63,897 white inhabitants within the boundaries of the territory. There were several hundred Negro slaves and free Negroes—there would be a few slaves in the state as late as 1840—but they, like Indians, did not count. At once the legislature prepared another appeal for statehood and sent it off to Congress. Jonathan Jennings was chairman of the committee in Congress to which the new memorial was referred, and he wasted no time. On January 5, 1816, eight days after Congress received the memorial, he introduced a bill for an enabling act.

In their memorial the territorial legislators left no doubt as to where they stood on the subject of slavery, stating clearly that they were opposed to "involuntary servitude"; and consequently the argument, long popular among some Hoosier chroniclers, that Indiana's early history was the story of a redemption from slavery is without grounds. The memorial also asked for seven per cent of the receipts from Federal land sales, confirmation of the grant of a township for an academy and of one section of land in each township for the maintenance of public schools, a township for a capital site and another for a college, and the salt licks and coal mines that until then had been reserved for the United States.

Congress wrote the enabling act in six sections. In the first five, after authorizing the inhabitants of the territory to form for themselves a constitution and assume for their state "such name as they shall deem proper," the act defined the boundaries, gave suffrage to all male citizens of the United States who had resided within the territory at least one year and had paid a county or territorial tax, set the election day for representatives to the constitutional convention on the second Monday of May, allotted five representatives each to Franklin, Clark, Harrison, Washington, and Knox counties, four each to Wayne and Gibson, three each to Dearborn and Jefferson, and one each to Switzerland, Perry, Posey, and Warrick, authorized the representatives to meet in the territorial capital on the second Monday of June and organize a government that would be "republican, and not repugnant to the articles of the Ordinance of 1787," and promised the new state one representative in the House of Representatives of the United States until the next general census was taken.

The sixth section of the act offered five propositions for the "free acceptance or rejection" of the convention. These propositions varied only slightly from the requests in the territory's memorial. They suggested that the section numbered sixteen in each township should be granted to the township for the use of schools; that all salt springs be granted to the state, although the land involved was not to exceed thirty-six sections in all; that five per cent, not seven, of the profits from Federal land sales should be granted, not outright to the state, but for use by Congress toward the building of public roads and canals, three fifths of the money to be spent within the state and two fifths for roads leading to the state; that one entire township should be reserved for the use of a seminary of learning and vested in the legislature of the state for the sole use of such a seminary; and that four sections of land be granted to the state "for fixing their seat of government thereon."

It was a foregone conclusion that "such name as they shall deem proper" would be *Indiana,* for already the inhabitants of the region thought of it only by the name of the people they had taken it from. Many modern Hoosiers who still have difficulty with place names and are likely to call Indianapolis *Indanapolis,* Terre Haute *Terry Hut,* and Brazil *Brayzil* should be grateful that a plan for the Northwest Territory conceived by Thomas Jefferson thirty years before was not in effect when the enabling of the territory toward statehood became possible. If Jefferson had had his way in Congress in 1784, Indiana today would be not one state but parts of six states, and Evansville would be in Polypotamia, Fort Wayne in Metropotamia, Terre Haute in Illinoia, Gary in Assenisipia, Madison in Pelisipia, and Brookville in Saratoga. However, there would have been no Indianapolis at all to twist the tongue over.

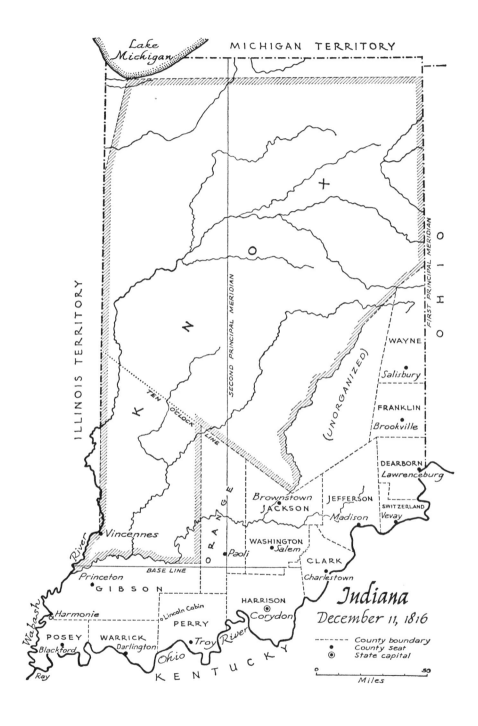

Lake Michigan

MICHIGAN TERRITORY

ILLINOIS TERRITORY

O H I O

SECOND PRINCIPAL MERIDIAN

FIRST PRINCIPAL MERIDIAN

(UNORGANIZED)

TEN O'CLOCK LINE

K N O

O R A N G E

WAYNE
Salisbury

FRANKLIN
Brookville

DEARBORN
Lawrenceburg

SWITZERLAND
Vevay

JEFFERSON
Madison

Brownstown
JACKSON

Vincennes

WASHINGTON
Salem

Paoli

CLARK
Charlestown

River

BASE LINE

Princeton
GIBSON

HARRISON
Corydon

Wabash

Harmonie

Lincoln Cabin

PERRY

POSEY

WARRICK
Darlington

Troy

River

Ohio River

Blackford

Ray

K E N T U C K Y

Indiana
December 11, 1816

- - - - - County boundary
⦿ County seat
◉ State capital

0   50
Miles

News of the enabling act did not reach Vincennes until May 2, and Elihu Stout complained in the *Western Sun* the next day that only eleven days were thus left in which to choose the candidates to be voted for on May 13. In making this protest, however, Stout ignored the lively debate to which he had been opening the pages of his newspaper ever since the passage of the territorial memorial four months before. The assumption in this debate was that passage of the enabling act was a certainty, as indeed it was, the vote in Congress standing 108 to 3. Stout himself had already proposed five nominees to represent Knox County, protesting as he did so that he had not consulted any of them about their willingness to run. Travelers in Indiana during the brief election campaign and immediately following it reported that the chief arguments of the people seemed to concern the slavery question, but the election of delegates had little to do with that issue, for Indiana had no choice but to come in free. In the end, the election was mainly a repudiation of Harrisonism and a victory for Jennings and the "people's party."

Considering the speed with which the delegates were chosen, the forty-three men who assembled at Corydon on June 10, 1816, were not only remarkably representative of the people of Indiana but were also an able and responsible group, though hardly distinguished. Most of them were farmers, some were already officeholders, about a dozen were preachers, a smaller number were lawyers. None of them was ever to become famous outside the boundaries of the state, but twenty-three of them later served in the Indiana Senate and seventeen in the House, one became governor, two became members of the national House of Representatives, two United States senators, and three served as highly respected judges in the state. Among the more notable Hoosier names were those of James Noble from Brookville, one of the two first Hoosier senators; John DePauw, son of an officer with Lafayette and father of the man whose name supplanted Asbury's at Indiana Asbury College; John Badollet, a friend of Albert Gallatin; David Maxwell, later a trustee of Indiana University; and Frederick Rapp, business manager of the Harmonist Society. William Hendricks, the first representative of the state and afterwards governor and

United States senator, served as secretary of the convention although he was not an elected delegate.

The convention was in session eighteen weekdays between June 10 and its adjournment with task accomplished on June 29. The official meeting place of the delegates in Corydon was the county courthouse that had been constructed four years earlier. Designed by Dennis Pennington, who was a delegate at the convention, this first state capitol still stands, forty feet square, its walls of blue limestone, its hipped roof surmounted by a bell tower. Because the June weather in southern Indiana was hot, the delegates often assembled for committee sessions under a "Constitutional Elm" on Big Indian Creek nearby. The village was too small to accommodate all its guests, and most of them slept at an inn a mile east of their meeting place, on the road to New Albany.

After electing Jonathan Jennings president, William Hendricks secretary, and Henry Batman doorkeeper, the convention considered contests over the seating of two of the delegates. Dan Lynn's opponent had challenged his election in Posey County, and some of the delegates suspected that Frederick Rapp of Gibson had been illegally elected. In those days the Gibson–Posey line ran through the heart of New Harmony, and Rapp's challengers charged that many of the German Harmonists of Posey had crossed Church Street into Gibson to vote for Father Rapp's adopted son and make certain his election. But the testimony in each case was vague, and both Lynn and Rapp were seated.

From these items of business the convention moved on to draw up its rules and regulations and to award the contract for such printing as would be required during the assembly. Mann Butler, editor of the *Louisville Correspondent,* got the contract, and immediately Elihu Stout of the *Western Sun* was heard from again. What right, he demanded, had the convention to award the contract outside the territory? The answer was that the convention had no choice in the matter, there being no other press near enough at hand for their purposes. Anyhow, Mann Butler was already proclaiming to the readers of his journal that the gathering at Corydon was most admirable for its decorum, manliness, and acumen. Would Elihu Stout have done the same?

At the afternoon session of June 11, when it was moved that it was "expedient, at this time, to proceed to form a Constitution and a State Government," as the enabling act directed, eight delegates voted that it was not expedient. The ones who dragged their heels—John Boone, a relation of Daniel, of Harrison; Hunt, Maxwell, and Smocke of Jefferson; Johnson and Polke of Knox; and Rapp and Robb of Gibson—were probably influenced by Stout's arguments in the *Western Sun* that statehood would mean increased taxes. More than three times their number voted in the affirmative, and the convention proceeded to its business as scheduled.

A faint shadow of proslavery sentiment cast itself over the convention on June 20 when John Johnson of Knox, who a year before had handed down a judgment from the bench of the Supreme Court of the territory upholding ownership of a slave in Vincennes, proposed an amendment to the antislavery article. Johnson moved that the convention change the preliminary draft of the statement about slavery, reading, "no alteration of this constitution shall ever take place," so that it read, in this regard, "it is the opinion of this convention that no alteration of this constitution ought ever to take place." Johnson's amendment would have weakened the antislavery article and left the subject open for future consideration. Although most of the delegates from the western counties supported him in this maneuver, they were outnumbered and his motion lost.

With one exception, there was little that was original in the constitution that the delegates finally signed at Corydon. They copied large parts of Articles I and III word for word from the Ohio Constitution. Others of the twelve articles closely resembled the Kentucky and Pennsylvania constitutions as well as that of Ohio. But such copying was natural; these three states were the birthplaces of many of the delegates. Moreover, the plagiarism was justifiable; these were practical men, and with no Gouverneur Morris among them to polish up their style they could hardly have improved upon the precedents in constitution-making that had already been set. Yet, during those long hot days in Corydon, they did produce one section in the charter that was entirely their own and shone as a credit to their foresight and intelligence, if not their literary skill. This was Article IX, written by John Badollet.

Article IX gave Indiana the distinction of being the first state in the Union to acknowledge and assume responsibility for educating its citizens. It provided not only for public schools but also for public libraries and urged the passage of laws by the General Assembly for "the promotion and improvement of arts, sciences, commerce, manufactures, and natural history." Although the intentions of the article were not to be realized for many years, largely because of legislative neglect and mismanagement and because, for a time, opening the state to development and physical improvement seemed more important to its citizens than the opening of minds, those original intentions were nonetheless genuine and laudable, a signal honor to the new state. Because there was nothing like this article in any of the eighteen previous state constitutions that had been written up to that time, the article deserves a full reading here as one of the monuments of American history:

ARTICLE IX

Sec.1. Knowledge and learning generally diffused through a community, being essential to the preservation of a free Government, and spreading the opportunities and advantages of education through the various parts of the country being highly conducive to this end, it shall be the duty of the general assembly to provide by law, for the improvement of such lands as are or hereafter may be granted by the United States to this state, for the use of schools, and to apply any funds which may be raised from such lands, or from any other quarter, to the accomplishment of the grand object for which they are or may be intended. But no lands granted for the use of schools or seminaries of learning shall be sold by authority of this state, prior to the year 1820, and the monies which may be raised out of the sale of any such lands, or otherwise obtained, for the purposes aforesaid, shall be and remain a fund for the exclusive purpose of promoting the interest of literature and the sciences, and for the support of seminaries and public schools. The general assembly shall, from time to time, pass such laws as shall be calculated to encourage intellectual, scientifical, and agricultural improvement, by allowing rewards and immunities for the promotion and improvement of the arts, sciences, commerce, manufactures, and natural history; and to countenance and encourage the principles of humanity, honesty, industry, and morality.

Sec.2. It shall be the duty of the general assembly, as soon as circumstances will permit, to provide by law for a general system of education, ascending in regular gradation, from township schools to a state university, wherein tuition shall be gratis, and equally open to all.

Sec.3. And for the promotion of such salutary end, the money which shall be paid as an equivalent by persons exempt from militia duty, except in times of war, shall be exclusively, and in equal proportion, applied to the support of county seminaries; also, all fines assessed for any breach of the penal laws, shall be applied to the said seminaries, in the counties wherein they shall be assessed.

Sec.4. It shall be the duty of the general assembly, as soon as circumstances will permit, to form a penal code, founded on the principle of reformation, and not of vindictive justice; and also to provide one or more farms, to be an asylum for those persons who by reason of age, infirmity, or other misfortunes, may have a claim on the aid and beneficence of society, on such principles, that such persons may therein find employment, and every reasonable comfort, and lose by their usefulness, the degrading sense of dependence.

Sec.5. The general assembly shall cause at least ten per cent to be reserved out of the proceeds of the sale of town lots, in the seat of justice of each county, for the use of a public library, for such county; and at the same session, they shall incorporate a library company, under such rules and regulations as will best secure its permanence, and extend its benefits.

The Constitution of 1816 was the matrix of government in Indiana for the next thirty-five years. It was not submitted to popular vote in its original form and there were no provisions for amending it, but the delegates agreed that it should be reviewed by popular referendum at least every twelve years. Under this provision, proposals for calling a new constitutional convention were offered to the voters of the state in the general elections of 1823, 1828, and 1840, but all failed to win a majority. In 1846, such a proposal did receive a vote of 32,468 to 27,123, but the General Assembly refused to provide for an election of delegates to a constitutional convention on the grounds, that the total vote cast in favor of a new convention was less than a majority of the total number of voters in the state. It was not until a fifth voting took place, in 1849, that the General Assembly called for a convention to rewrite the constitution.

The Constitution of 1816 was indisputably a victory of the Jennings party over the Harrison party in all its effects, and the most obvious effect was the election of state officials that followed in August of that year. Jennings won the governorship over Thomas Posey by a vote of 5,211 to 3,934, and Hendricks defeated two opponents in the race for Congress by a sizable majority. In November, the General Assembly met and chose James Noble and Waller Taylor to represent the state in the United States Senate. Jacob Piatt Dunn, in his *Indiana and Indianans,* points to Taylor's election by the House as an example of "the liberality of the controlling party to the minority." Taylor, who had tried to provoke Jennings to a duel in 1809 and who ran against him in his second race for Congress in territorial days, was indeed one of William Henry Harrison's most ardent partisans; but the only other example of "liberality" that Dunn can muster is John Johnson, one of the ablest lawyers in the state, whom Jennings appointed to the Supreme Court. The rest of the evidence points to the determination of the controlling party simply to control.

After Jennings was elected to a second term as governor, he ran for Congress while still holding the gubernatorial office. Winning a seat in Congress, he resigned as governor and left his lieutenant governor, Ratliff Boon, to hold the position until Hendricks could resign from Congress and get himself elected to the governorship in 1822. When Hendricks finished a term as governor, the Indiana General Assembly made him a United States senator in place of Waller Taylor. Meantime, Jennings certainly had his eye on James Noble's seat in the Senate, but in 1830 Jennings's friends as well as his enemies decided to remove him from his congressional post in "Washington City," where the temptations of drink had become too much for him. Retired from politics to his farm near Charlestown, he died there in 1834.

Thus, in the first dozen years of state government, horse-trading and logrolling became the tradition of Indiana politics, a tradition that has given Indiana the reputation of being the most politically minded state in the Union. In those first days of statehood, the practices of "the controlling party," plus the great power of the General Assembly under the first constitution, reduced executive authority to a minimum and, compounded by the second constitution, has made strong leadership difficult in the state except by the czarist methods adopted by its two most memorable governors, Morton and McNutt. Doubling the size of the white man's share of Indiana by acquisition of "The New Purchase," an acquisition instrumented with dubious legality by Governor Jennings in a dual officeholding capacity in 1818, and removal of the state government in 1824 to Indianapolis, a city created for that purpose, did not ameliorate the situation. As the "people's party," the men in control had begun their crusade against the Harrison forces with laudable intentions and at Corydon framed, on the whole, an excellent constitution, but their idealistic beginnings quickly deteriorated into a selfish trade in public offices that revealed them as clever politicians but hardly statesmen.

With the growth of Jacksonian Democracy in the West and a consequent shifting of loyalties, the founding fathers lost their power as a party by 1830. The Democrats and, later, the Whigs developed the party caucus and party organization, but these improvements in political machinery failed to improve the quality of office seekers and officeholders. Although there were able men among them, Governors James Ray, Noah Noble, David Wallace, Samuel Bigger, James Whitcomb, and Paris Dunning are hardly names to conjure with in a state's history; nor do the names of the United States senators from Indiana during that period (1830–50) trip readily from even a Hoosier schoolboy's lips. In those early days of the Republic, who were Hanna, Tipton, Smith, White, Hannegan, and Bright in a Senate that shone with such illustrious men as Clay, Calhoun, and Webster?

Edward A. Hannegan's oratory is said to have rivaled Webster's in the 1840's; ladies flocked to the Senate gallery to hear him speak; but what Hannegan said on those occasions was largely bullyragging bombast to the popular tune of "Fifty-Four Forty or Fight," which, if listened to, would have got the United States into war with Britain and Mexico simultaneously and might have lost for this country more Western territory than that which Hannegan would have had Americans do battle for. Perhaps Hannegan's chief claim to fame is local, rather than national or even statewide; by the drunken murder of his brother-in-law in Covington in 1852 he drove from that town two young prosecuting attorneys who were reluctant to bring him to trial, and thus he gave Terre Haute claim to Daniel W. Voorhees, "the Tall Sycamore of the Wabash," and Crawfordsville the Byzantine study and bronze statue of Lew Wallace, author of *Ben-Hur*. The United States Senate heard no Hoosier eloquence like Hannegan's again until Voorhees himself was sent there in 1877 and, later, Albert J. Beveridge preached the doctrine of manifest destiny; often their speeches too were no more than flashes of liquid fire, like Hannegan's, giving off more heat than illumination.

Indiana voted for Andrew Jackson in 1824 as well as in 1828 and 1832, and after Jackson's unsuccessful first try for the presidency, when John Quincy Adams was installed in the White House by vote of the House of Representatives, Jacksonian Democrats were united in Indiana by resentment of what they called "the theft of the presidency." When the hero of New Orleans won the office in 1828, he strengthened his followers' machinery in Indiana by introduction of the "spoils system." By 1832, Jackson men filled all the appointive offices in the state and most of the county and township elective offices, even though by that time Jackson had cooled Hoosier enthusiasm for his brand of democracy by pocket veto of a bill to improve the Wabash River. This veto along with vetoes of bills to aid the National Road and the harbor at Michigan City probably cost Jackson's successor, Van Buren, Indiana's vote in the Electoral College in 1836.

At the same time that Indiana Democrats were supporting Old Hickory they were casting their votes for National Republicans or Whigs for state offices. For one thing, the opposition produced abler and more persuasive candidates on this level than they themselves could offer; for another, Republicans and Whigs were identified in the state with a program of internal improvements that no Hoosier had it in his heart to oppose. During the supremacy of the Jackson Democrats, the governor's chair in Indianapolis was occupied by Ray, Noble, and Wallace, all Republicans or Whigs. On the other hand, when the Whigs finally grew into national stature, they introduced the practice of voting the straight ticket from the national down to the township level, and soon all parties learned the lesson. Samuel Bigger was the last Whig governor (1840–43).

Starting as a nonpartisan movement in 1836, the Harrison campaign of the Whigs took Indiana by storm in 1840. Animosities of territorial days were forgotten. In fact, the only survivors of those days seemed to be veterans who had fought at the general's side at Tippecanoe. Whigs ferreted them out for public display in such droves that somebody in the state should have wondered how it was possible that Harrison's original army numbered only a thousand men. But apparently in the excitement of the day nobody paused long enough to clear his head of hard cider and contemplate statistics. William Henry Harrison had at last given Hoosiers a hero of national eminence. No longer "a Virginia aristocrat," he became "a man of the people," a Hoosier himself, opposed to Little Van, "the used up man," who according to the political smear of that period lived in decadent luxury in the White House. What honest Hoosier would want to vote for a man who drank champagne, and, worse, perfumed his whiskers? When an Eastern newspaper retorted to the Whig sneer with a sneer of its own, that a log cabin and hard cider would be good enough for Harrison if he were president, the log cabin and hard cider became the proud symbols of the man who had once lived affluently at "Grouseland" in Vincennes.

The Whigs held their state convention in May that year at Tippecanoe, and although it was a rainy May, the multitude assembled at Indianapolis and marched through the mud to the battleground in a procession that was said to be twenty-five miles long. On the way, farmers regaled the faithful with Hoosier hospitality strongly fortified by hard cider. Thereafter, torchlight parades, banquets, barbecues, logrollings, and speechifying filled the Hoosiers' days and nights until election day. Enormous floats representing canoes and log cabins were dragged through the streets of cities and villages; cider flowed like Wabash water in floodtime; and Old Tippecanoe himself came "home" and spoke at Madison and New Albany and Vincennes.

One of the principal organs of the Democrats was the *Wabash Enquirer,* published at Terre Haute by George Chapman, but Mr. Chapman seemed to lack confidence in Little Van's chances of success until one of the party leaders got after him and gave him a lesson in the writing of political editorials. "You must never express any doubts, Chapman," the politician admonished. "You must always appear sure and confident. You must crow, Chapman, crow!" Thereafter, Chapman dutifully crowed; but unfortunately for the Democrats, his instructions leaked out, and soon every Whig newspaper in the state was taunting its opponents in big black letters: "CROW, CHAPMAN, CROW!" From this episode, it is said, on the banks of the Wabash was born the Democratic Rooster.

It was also at this time that "O.K." found a place in American speech, deriving from the Democratic O.K. Clubs secretly named for Old Kinderhook, Van Buren's home in New York. Unable to solve the riddle of the letters, the Whigs finally surmised that "O.K." was Andrew Jackson's abbreviation of "oll korrect." Van Buren's political daddy, they pointed out, had never excelled at spelling.

When the high jinks were finally over, Harrison carried the state by a vote of 65,276 to 51,695, and two years later Hoosiers were delighted when dapper little Martin Van Buren, making a tour of the West with a hope of running again, was dumped out of a stagecoach at Plainfield into a mudhole on the National Road— and not, according to the local gossip, entirely by accident. Nevertheless, the Democrats were back in power in the state the very next year, with James Whitcomb in the governor's office and about to move on to the United States Senate, at which time Reuben and Elizabeth Riley of Greenfield would name a son for him. The Democrats remained in Indianapolis until the Civil War, and it was a Democratic General Assembly that authorized the second constitutional convention, which gathered in the capital in the fall of 1850.

Much of the sentiment for revision of the constitution grew out of the spirit of Jacksonian Democracy. Citizens of Indiana had begun to feel that their government was too far removed from their control. They wanted more frequent elections and more elective offices. The General Assembly had too much power. It passed local as well as state laws; it chose too many state officials; it granted divorces; and because there was no requirement that the laws it passed should be confined to one subject, it often enacted hidden legislation by attaching riders to popular bills in the House and Senate. At the same time, for reasons of economy and in contradiction of their desire for increased democracy, the people regarded annual sessions of the General Assembly as unnecessary. Hoosiers were also worried about the public debt, for ventures into banking and internal improvements in the 1840's had got the state into financial difficulties.

In contrast to the small number of delegates that had met in Corydon in 1816, one hundred and fifty elected representatives convened at Indianapolis in 1850 to frame the new document; and instead of doing the job in less than three weeks, they deliberated more than four months. The larger number of hands at work on the new constitution and the longer time employed in the accomplishment of their task produced both advantages and disadvantages: More opinions were heard and these opinions were explored more thoroughly, but the resulting document was bulkier and less malleable. Schuyler Colfax had begged the constitution-makers to confine themselves to principles and to write a brief and simple charter. "If it could be written on two sheets of paper," he argued, "so much the better." But when the work was finished, Robert Dale Owen, one of the principal authors of the second constitution, had to apologize for its length and admit that even the men who made it "would be somewhat puzzled to sit down and enumerate" its departures from the original charter. The second constitution was twice the length of the first, and it read more like a code than a constitution.

But the new constitution accomplished what the people wanted and reflected the temper of antebellum Indiana. Its bill of rights reworded the bill of rights of the first constitution, except that a more vigorous insistence upon separation of church and state hedged against the increase of foreigners, then mainly Germans and Irish. At the same time, the voting franchise of white male citizens was expanded to include "foreigners who had been in the United States one year, and in the state six months, immediately before any election, and who shall have declared under oath their intention to become citizens." This hospitality did not extend to free Negroes, however. Their further immigration into the state was forbidden, and those already residents were urged to go elsewhere.

As expected, the delegates to the convention adopted biennial sessions of the General Assembly, limiting regular sessions to sixty-one days and special sessions to forty, prohibited state legislation on many local and special subjects, and required that each law passed by the General Assembly should concern itself with only one subject. The new constitution abolished county seminaries and urged development of common schools, but it ignored the requirements of higher education, reflecting the popular suspicion of a "godless" state university, an anxiety which in that period resulted in denominational colleges being better attended and more generously supported than the state institution at Bloomington. It denied the General Assembly the right to incur "'any debt, except to meet casual deficits in the revenue, to pay the interest on the present state debt, or to repel invasion, or suppress insurrection," and it prohibited the state's being a stockholder in any bank, corporation, or association.

The convention adjourned February 10, 1851, and in August of that year the citizens of Indiana approved its work by a vote of 113,230 to 27,638. Strongest sentiment in favor of the new constitution appeared in the northern third of the state. Ohio County alone recorded a majority vote against ratification, although Switzerland and Vanderburgh came very close to doing so.

Since the adoption of this constitution more than a century ago, amending it has proved difficult for the same reason that the calling of the second constitutional convention was itself long delayed in spite of the people's obvious desire for a new charter. Not until 1880—fifteen years after the Civil War—was the constitution amended to admit Negroes into the state. On several occasions—in 1897 and 1899, for example, when James A. Mount was governor —the electorate cast majority votes in favor of amendments, but on each occasion the Indiana Supreme Court ruled that there was no ratification because the majority of the votes cast was not a majority of the citizens eligible to vote. The same situation occurred in 1906 and 1919, during the administrations of Governors J. Frank Hanly and Thomas R. Marshall. Marshall, governor from 1909 to 1913, tried an original approach to the problem; he persuaded the General Assembly to draw up a new constitution and present it to the people, hoping thus to detour around the majority requirement for passage of amendments and at the same time obviate the necessity of a constitutional convention. But again the Supreme Court stepped in, declaring that the legislature had exceeded its authority. During the administration of Marshall's successor, Samuel M. Ralston, the General Assembly made another attempt at amendment; on this occasion the voters rejected the change.

The struggle for constitutional amendment was frustrated until the 1930's and then changes became possible only when the Supreme Court reversed the previous judicial interpretations of the majority requirement. The two amendments that were finally adopted, during the administration of Governor Paul V. McNutt (1933–37), authorized a state income tax and gave the General Assembly the right to prescribe qualifications for the practice of law. The income tax won by a ratio of seven to two; the so-called "lawyers' amendment," a reform long sought, carried by a two-to-one vote.

The second constitution extended the term of the governor from three to four years and made him ineligible for reelection in any eight-year period. This change might have strengthened the governorship if it had not at the same time, set gubernatorial elections in Indiana in the same years as presidential elections. The consequence was that governors were seldom chosen for their merits alone; in every instance but two, their success at the polls reflected the political sentiment of the state in the national election. Thomas A. Hendricks and Thomas R. Marshall are the two exceptions. In 1872, Hendricks, a Democrat, won the governorship although the state cast its presidential vote in the Electoral College for the Republican candidate, Grant. Indiana might have gone Democratic that year in the national election too, if the Democratic candidate had been anyone but Horace Greeley. Most Democrats in the state were themselves indifferent to him, especially Daniel W. Voorhees, who at first refused to support him. Hendricks won by only a thousand votes, and his General Assembly was Republican. Again, in 1908, Marshall, a Democrat, won in spite of a Republican victory for Taft in the Electoral College vote. Marshall's margin over his opponent, James E. Watson, was narrow, but so was the margin of Taft and Sherman over Bryan and John Worth Kern, who was an Indianan. The Democrats, with Kern on the national ticket, and the Socialists, led by Debs, also a Hoosier, together polled more votes in Indiana than the Republicans in the national election. On the two occasions in this period when Indiana did not follow the national trend, giving majorities to Tilden in 1876 and Hughes in 1916, governors of the same party as the state's presidential choice were elected: James D. Williams, a Democrat, and James P. Goodrich, a Republican.

Governors of Indiana of the period from the Civil War to World War I compose, like the pre-Civil War governors, a creditable but not very distinguished list of names. In chronological order, they were: Conrad Baker of Evansville, Thomas A. Hendricks of Shelbyville, James D. Williams of Knox County, Isaac P. Gray of Union City, Albert G. Porter of Indianapolis, Alvin P. Hovey of Mount Vernon, Ira J. Chase of Danville, Claude Matthews of Vermillion County, James A. Mount of Montgomery County, Winfield T. Durbin of Anderson, J. Frank Hanly of Warren County, Thomas R. Marshall of Columbia City, Samuel M. Ralston of Lebanon, and James P. Goodrich of Winchester. Eight of these fourteen executives were Republicans; six were Democrats.

It was during the period from the Civil War to World War I that Indiana became known as "the mother of vice presidents." Schuyler Colfax served under Grant during the General's first term, but Grant rejected him the second time around because he found Colfax "too ambitious." Perhaps he also had doubts about

Colfax's honesty. Thomas A. Hendricks served under Cleveland for one year of Cleveland's first term and died in office. Charles W. Fairbanks was vice president under Theodore Roosevelt, who said of his running mate's candidacy, "Who in the name of heaven else is there?" Thomas R. Marshall, who described the vice presidency as "a disease, not an office," endured the ailment for two full terms under Wilson.

In seven elections two of these men, plus four more who can be called "Hoosiers," met defeat in races for the vice presidency. George W. Julian was the Free-Soil candidate in 1852. Joseph Lane, although he was identified with Oregon when the Southern Democrats nominated him with Breckinridge in 1860, had spent thirty-three of his fifty-nine years in Indiana and served in the state's legislature. In 1872, the year he was elected governor, Hendricks, opposed to Greeley's nomination, also ran for vice president as a "straight Democrat" or "reform" candidate with Charles O'Conor, and then as a regular Democrat with Tilden in 1876, before he was finally elected with Cleveland in 1884. William H. English, Democrat, ran with Winfield S. Hancock against Garfield and Arthur in 1880. John Worth Kern, Democrat, ran with Bryan in 1908. Fairbanks, vice president under Theodore Roosevelt, ran with Hughes against Wilson and Marshall in 1916 and lost.

The two presidents that Indianans claim as Hoosiers were not natives of the state. William Henry Harrison was born in Virginia; Benjamin Harrison, his grandson, was born in Ohio, although he was an Indianapolis lawyer when elected in 1888. By the elastic definition of the term that includes the two Harrisons, Lincoln is sometimes called a "Hoosier," but only the most ardent Indianaphiles suggest that he was a "Hoosier president." Lincoln spent fourteen years of his youth in Indiana but was born in Kentucky and elected to the presidency from Illinois.

Definitions must be similarly stretched to include most of the "Hoosier" aspirants to the White House who ran for the presidency but never got there. One John P. St. John was the first among them. In 1884 he was the Prohibitionist candidate for the office. He came from Franklin County, Indiana, but by the time he entered the national battle against John Barleycorn he had long been a Kansan. In 1916, the Prohibition Party chose J. Frank Hanly to lead its ticket. Hanly had previously been a Republican governor of Indiana (1905–1909), but he was born in St. Joseph, Illinois, and received his common school education in Champaign County of that state. Presidential candidates Eugene V. Debs, Socialist, and Wendell L. Willkie, Republican, were both authentic, native-born, Hoosier-educated Indianans; but Willkie was a Wall Street lawyer when he was nominated in 1940, although he promptly loosened his tie and hurried out to Elwood, Indiana, to make his official acceptance speech, and Debs, though he maintained residence in Terre Haute, conducted the most effective of his numerous races for the presidency from a Federal prison in Georgia.

Chapter Six

☆

Into the Twentieth Century

A PERENNIAL figure in Indiana's public life for more than fifty years of the nineteenth century and a man of principle and integrity, who deserves a larger place in the history of both the state and the nation than is usually accorded him, was George Washington Julian. Whig, Free-Soiler, Radical Republican, Liberal Republican, Democrat, and finally Gold Democrat, George W. Julian was born May 5, 1817, in a log cabin a mile and a half southeast of Centerville. At the northern boundary of white civilization, the cabin had been used five years before as a block house against Indian raids. Julian's parents, who were Hicksite Friends, had come to Indiana from North Carolina, and like many other early immigrants to the state, they left the South because they disapproved of slavery. Julian's ancestry was German and French, the name being originally St. Julien.

Six feet two and powerfully built, Julian was noted in his youth for his feats of strength, and his reputation in this regard probably aided him as much as his love of books in his early career as a pioneer schoolteacher. When he was eighteen, he worked for five days on the new National Road, receiving $4.20 for his labors with a shovel. The next summer he was a rodman on the Whitewater Canal. While he was teaching, he began to read law and was licensed to practice in 1840. That was the year of the Harrison "hard-cider campaign," and he participated in the march from Indianapolis to the meeting at Tippecanoe Battleground in the rainy weather of May. In September, he went to Dayton, Ohio, to

107

hear Old Tippecanoe speak and had his pocket picked while he was standing in the crowd listening to the oratory. Later he described his youthful enthusiasm for Harrison as "lunacy," for he soon conceived a fixed disapproval of military men as presidents.

Another lawyer in Centerville in those days was Oliver P. Morton, later the Civil War governor of the state and always, even when they were members of the same political party, a rival of Julian's. The two men were married in Centerville the same year, in 1845. Morton was then a Democrat, Julian still a Whig. As a Whig, Julian was elected to the state legislature in that year but alienated himself from the rank and file of his party in Indianapolis by opposing capital punishment and legislative divorces. In the legislature with him were Dennis Pennington, who had designed the capitol at Corydon; Conrad Baker, a future governor, successor to Morton; Joseph Lane, then a resident of Vanderburgh County; and Reuben Riley, who would sire the Hoosier poet a few years later. Among the other unpopular stands that Julian took during this period was his opposition to the calling of a second constitutional convention. "The people of Indiana are attached to their constitution," he said in 1847. "It is the work of their forefathers. Under it for thirty years they have enjoyed a degree of prosperity unsurpassed by any state in the Union."

Even more unpopular was his growing opposition to slavery. He wrote two letters on the subject to the Centerville *News-Letter* that were published in other journals throughout the state and got him labeled an Abolitionist. He was then still a Whig; but being unable to support a military man for president who would take no stand on the issue of slavery, he could find no place for himself in the party's ranks behind Zachary Taylor. In 1848, he attended the national Free-Soil convention in Buffalo, where he finally accepted Van Buren as a candidate when Van Buren consented to an anti-slavery platform. When he returned to Indiana, people whispered that he carried a lock of Frederick Douglass's hair in his pocket, and "Abolitionist" was the mildest of the epithets they flung at him. His brother Jacob was so embarrassed by the family "disgrace" that the two young men dissolved their law partnership.

Julian held firm to his convictions and in 1850 got the Free-Soil nomination to run for Congress in his district. Whig opposition was strong and the campaign bitter, but Julian won and went to Washington. There he and his wife stayed first at the United States Hotel but, finding Senator Jefferson Davis of Mississippi their table-mate in the dining room, they soon moved to more congenial surroundings. The young congressman's maiden speech in the House drew a letter of commendation from Charles Sumner of Massachusetts, who remarked:

> The old parties seem now, more than ever, in a state of dissolution. The cry will soon be
> "Mingle, mingle,
> Ye that mingle may."

In Congress, Julian was also interested in the land question and spoke in favor of providing free homesteads to landless settlers in the West. The Homestead Bill appealed to him as an antislavery measure.

Defeated for renomination to Congress in 1852, largely because of the antagonism of Oliver P. Morton, who was opposed to abolition, Julian went to the national Free-Soil convention at Pittsburgh and won the nomination for vice president, to run with John P. Hale of New Hampshire. The party was badly defeated, and he returned to the practice of law in Centerville, where, the next year, in a courtroom, an opposing lawyer cut his throat in an altercation. Julian recovered, and his assailant was fined $25 for "contempt of court." Throughout this period, Julian was active in antislavery and woman's rights campaigns, fought the Know-Nothing Party, which had a strong following in Indiana, and was active in the formation of the new Republican Party.

In Indiana this new party was called the People's Party. Oliver Morton left the Democrats and became its unsuccessful candidate for governor in 1856. That year, Julian went to Philadelphia to attend the first national Republican convention, which nominated John C. Frémont. Democrats supporting Buchanan, bigoted Know-Nothings joined by Whigs in support of Fillmore, and the new and "radical" Republicans headed by Frémont created a bitter and ugly three-way campaign on the eve of the Civil War, as a contemporary Currier and Ives print vividly illustrates. It portrays Frémont receiving representatives of the various groups composing the new party: a Negro insisting that the "Poppylation ob Color" should come first; a Catholic priest demanding that the "power of the Pope" be put on a firm footing in America; an old woman who would abolish marriage; a drunken laborer proposing the equal division of property; a female advocate of woman's rights smoking a cigar; and a Puritan who would make "the use of Tobacco, Animal food, and Lagerbeer a Capital crime." In the cartoon, Frémont is promising everything to everybody.

In 1860, Julian was elected to Congress again, this time as a Republican, and he was reelected in 1862, 1864, 1868, and 1870. During these years he was always a Radical Republican, often in disagreement with Morton and many other members of his party, including Lincoln. After Lincoln's death, he was at odds with President Johnson and Morton over Reconstruction. He favored immediate Negro suffrage, would have delayed the restoration of Southern states to the Union, and advocated hanging all leaders of the Confederacy for treason. Indiana's newspapers bitterly denounced him, and on one occasion he was attacked and beaten in the Richmond, Indiana, railroad station. Gradually he came to believe that his party's only motive in politics was to keep the nation permanently divided and itself permanently in power. It was during this period in Congress that he presented, in 1868, the first resolution for a woman's suffrage amendment.

In 1872, Julian declined another nomination for Congress and, disillusioned by his party's preference for military heroes as candidates for president, moved with the Liberal Republicans toward support of the Democrats. He favored Greeley against Grant in 1872 and in 1876 actively supported Tilden against Hayes. He was by that time a Democrat, and when finally the Democrats came back into power in 1885, Cleveland appointed him surveyor general of New Mexico. But he was a Democrat in the same way that he had been a Republican, a man of independent mind. Three years before his death, he came out of retirement at the age of seventy-nine to speak against the candidacy of William Jennings Bryan. He was convinced that Democrats were wrong in endorsing the free coinage of silver in the ratio of sixteen-to-one. Julian died in Indianapolis in 1899.

Right or wrong, farseeing or fanatic, quixotic and obstructive as he may have seemed at times even to his friends and family, George W. Julian moved often in advance of the thinking of his times and stood consistently by the principles he conceived and believed in, frequently to the disadvantage of his political career. A man who, in perspective, rises above the ruck of mediocrity that characterized the latter half of the nineteenth century in the politics of both the state and the nation, he is a striking contrast to his contemporary and political opposite, Daniel W. Voorhees, who was far better known in his own time and far more successful even though he too, throughout most of his career, represented a minority in the nation's political thinking.

Voorhees, a Democrat, an exponent of popular sovereignty, opposed to the war, opposed to emancipation, and in the Gilded Age of the 1870's and 1880's an enemy of the Eastern moneyed interests, served thirty-one years in Congress as representative and senator as against Julian's twelve. Voorhees was only an advocate of borrowed ideas and never a philosopher who produced his own; consequently, he knew when and how to compromise, even to reverse himself. But Julian and Voorhees had one quality in common, personal honesty. It is perhaps more for that virtue, in a period of shabby public morals, than for his brilliance as an orator and his long and steadfast service to his party in Indiana, that the Tall Sycamore of the Wabash should be remembered in the company of distinguished Hoosier politicians.

Tall Sycamore of the Wabash Voorhees was called not only because he was tall—over six feet, massive of head, and broad of shoulder—but because, in the excitement of forensics, his hair stood out like the quills of a sycamore's buttonball. Born in Ohio in 1827, Voorhees was brought to Fountain County, Indiana, when he was two months old and lived for a time, like Julian, in a log house. But his father was more prosperous than Julian's and soon built a two-story brick house, the first of its kind in the region. The Voorhees family were Methodists, Daniel's father of Dutch ancestry, his mother Irish, and they sent their son to Indiana Asbury College (later DePauw) with the expectation that he would become a minister. But young Voorhees discovered early that he had a talent for oratory and after graduation he began to read law in the office of Henry S. Lane, later a Republican governor of Indiana, and in 1850 began practice in Covington, where he soon became Edward A. Hannegan's partner.

Governor Wright appointed Voorhees prosecuting attorney for the criminal court, and his courtroom performances immediately created a following for him as he rode the circuit in western Indiana. In those days the defense was allowed the final plea before a jury, and it was said that it was Voorhees' eloquence, on the occasions when he stood for the defense, that brought about the repeal of the Indiana code that established that order of speaking. Whether this legend is true or not, within ten years Voorhees had a national reputation, having appeared in the courts of sixteen states.

Not of national renown at the time but significant now in the light of history were the debates between Voorhees and James Wilson over the issue of slavery in 1856, two years before the Lincoln–Douglas debates in Illinois. Wilson, a young graduate of Wabash College, was a Republican, Voorhees' opponent in his first race for Congress. They began their series of debates in Delphi, then moved on to Lafayette and other towns. The position of Voorhees was similar to that of Stephen A. Douglas: "I do not favor the institution of slavery, I don't want it here; but they have a right to it elsewhere; property in slaves is not to be distinguished from other kinds of property which are protected by the same constitution." When Voorhees lost the election by 230 votes, he moved from the district to Terre Haute, keeping a pledge that he said he had made regarding the Congressional race. There were many in Covington, however, who believed he made the move because he was reluctant to prosecute his old law partner, Hannegan, for murder.

In 1859, Governor Ashbel P. Willard's wife's brother, one John E. Cook, was rounded up among the followers of John Brown at Harper's Ferry and charged with treason and murder, and Voorhees, then United States District Attorney for Indiana, went to

Charlestown, Virginia, to plead in Cook's behalf. A few of the words he spoke in the Virginia courtroom will illustrate the character of Voorhees' oratory: "I come from the sunset-side of your western mountains, from beyond the rivers that now skirt the borders of your great state; but I come not as an alien to a foreign land, but rather as one who returns to the home of his ancestors, and to the household from which he sprang." Voorhees' ancestors came from New Jersey and Maryland, via Kentucky, but apparently he was thinking of political ancestors, not those of blood; for he continued, "Nor do I forget that the very soil on which I live in my western state was once owned by this venerable commonwealth as much as the soil on which I stand." In the end, Cook was acquitted of the charge of treason but was found guilty of murder and hanged. For Voorhees, however, appearance at the trial was a personal and political success. His speech received praise from all parts of the nation.

Elected to the House of Representatives in 1860, Voorhees found himself immediately confronted by the problem of Sumter's fall and South Carolina's secession. He had opposed the use of force against the South, but now, he said, it was a matter of preserving the Union and he favored its defense. However, he continued in opposition to the freeing of slaves, and when Lincoln issued the Emancipation Proclamation in 1862, he protested: "Ten days before he issued it he said he had not the power to promulgate such a document and that it would do no good if he did. In that he was right for once. But I suppose he gave way to pressure. Yes, pressure. He was pressed. By whom? By Horace Greeley, that political harlot."

By that time the young congressman's name had been linked with that of Clement Vallandigham of Ohio in the activities of the Sons of Liberty, and in 1864 his political enemies raided his Terre Haute law office and professed to have found copies of the ritual of the Copperheads and several incriminating letters. Voorhees first protested that the wrong office had been burglarized, then said that the materials had been "planted." He denied that he was a member of the conspiratorial group of Southern sympathizers, whose goal was withdrawal of the Middle Western states from the Union, but the evidence is reasonably strong that he was a member.

In 1872, before the national Democratic convention met, Voorhees strenuously opposed the candidacy of Horace Greeley, whom he had called "that political harlot" ten years before; but when Greeley got the Liberal Republican nomination and the Democrats endorsed him, the Tall Sycamore bent with the political wind and remained in the ranks of his party. Four years later, he was campaigning for "Blue Jeans" Williams, the Democratic candidate for governor; and that shrewd countryman from Knox County had hardly more than ambled across the threshold of the executive mansion and kicked off his boots when he was able to reward Voorhees for his services. Oliver P. Morton died and Williams appointed Voorhees to Morton's United States Senate seat. Voorhees remained in the Senate the rest of his life, except for the last month of it. He was defeated in the Indiana legislature in January 1897, served out his term until March, and died in April. In his twenty Senate years, Voorhees was the tireless champion of agriculture in the West against the bankers of the East.

Voorhees was a convivial and kindly man, a beguiling storyteller, folksy in his manner and speech. He loved birds, the poems of James Whitcomb Riley, the Bible, and horses. Senator Hoar of Massachusetts once said of him, "Sometimes when Voorhees speaks, I can hear the whirr of the threshing machine, the whinny of a colt, or the tinkle of a cow-bell as lowing cattle stand waiting before the bar." Although sometimes excessive and vituperative in his oratory, the Hoosier Senator retained loyal friends among Republicans and Democrats alike throughout his life. He was a generous man, not only with his own money but with the government's as well, especially in the distribution of pensions. Senator Vest of Missouri remarked that Voorhees "could have put Aladdin's lamp in the hands of a receiver in thirty days." His personal honesty, however, was never questioned, and he survived without a blemish on his character during the corruption of the 1870's that led to an attempt to impeach his fellow Hoosier, Vice President Colfax, at the time of the Crédit Mobilier scandal. Republican Hugh McCulloch of Fort Wayne, Secretary of the Treasury under

Lincoln and Johnson, wrote about Democrat Voorhees in his *Men and Measures:* "He could speak eloquently before he could speak correctly. . . . As a lawyer he may not have ranked among the highest, but as an advocate . . . it would be difficult to find his peer."

The Republican opponent whom Voorhees defeated in the senatorial election in the Indiana legislature in 1879 was Presbyterian Benjamin Harrison, an Indianapolis lawyer who had moved to the state from his native Ohio after receiving his education at Miami University in Oxford, Ohio, and a year or two of reading law in Cincinnati. Harrison's first political office was that of reporter of the Supreme Court, to which he was reelected while in the field with the Union army. In 1862, Governor Morton asked him to raise a regiment in Indianapolis and, when the task was completed, put him in command of it as a colonel. He emerged from the war a brevetted brigadier general. In 1876 he opposed "Blue Jeans" Williams in the race for the governorship that Voorhees won for Williams. Retaliating against the Republicans' ridicule of Williams's bucolic clothes and manners, the Democrats labeled Harrison "the kid-glove candidate." Years later, in a campaign biography written in 1888, Lew Wallace tried to remove the epithet which was then still clinging to Harrison.

> He was not then, is not now, and had really never been extreme in his ideas or dress. On the contrary he was habitually somewhat negligent in that respect. It is true he affected clean shirts when he could get them, not so much for the sake of appearance as for comfort. . . . His clothes were of good material but plainly cut and made. He wore no jewelry on finger or shirt front. He combed his hair at least once a day, and thought he violated no canon of propriety by brushing his teeth in the morning.

This is probably a more comprehensive portrait of Benjamin Harrison than Lew Wallace intended.

Three years after the unsuccessful race against Williams for the governorship, Harrison lost to Voorhees in a contest for the United States Senate. He was finally sent to the Senate in 1881, however, and in 1888, as James G. Blaine's choice, won the Republican nomination for president of the United States over a dozen other candidates, among whom was another Hoosier, Walter Q. Gresham. The Electoral College gave the election to Harrison, although Cleveland led him at the polls by 100,000 votes.

Whatever Benjamin Harrison wore on his hands, his mind and his conscience seem to have been permanently sealed off from reality by some kind of hermetic material. His election was achieved by bribery and fraud in the two pivotal states of New York and Indiana; and yet when he was notified that he had won—by a margin of only 2,348 votes in his home state—he observed piously, "Providence has given us the victory." To this observation Matt Quay, chairman of the Republican National Committee, retorted: "Think of the man! He ought to know that Providence hadn't a damn thing to do with it!"

In Indiana it was money alone that gave Harrison the victory, money spent more generously by Republicans than the Democrats that year could afford to spend it—and more recklessly. William W. Dudley of Richmond, treasurer of the Republican National Committee, who had lost a leg at Gettysburg, lost his head in the course of the campaign and wrote to the Republican county chairmen of his state a circular letter which a Democratic postal clerk purloined from the mails and gave to the Indianapolis *Sentinel* on the eve of the election. The letter instructed the county chairmen to "divide the floaters into blocks of fives and put a trusted man with necessary funds in charge of these five, and make him responsible that none get away and that all vote our ticket." From Bloomington that year, an Indiana University professor reported in *The Nation* that he saw a Republican worker drive up in a buggy with two Negroes "and deliberately place Republican ballots in their hands in full view of the assembled crowd, the negroes handing in the ballots through the window without even alighting from the buggy." When the Indianapolis *Sentinel* published the Dudley letter in late October, Dudley could only say, "Somebody has been robbing the mails!" Against the Indiana University professor's allegation, the defense of the Bloomington *Telephone*, a Republican newspaper, was that the Democrats did the same thing. Both were right. No politician in Indiana needed tutoring

Fluorspar figurine from Angel Site

La Salle

The Little Turtle

Tecumseh

The Prophet

Anthony Wayne at the Greenville Council, 1795

Drawings by George Winter: Frances Slocum, The Deaf Man's
Village, and Bishop Bruté with the emigrating Potawatomi

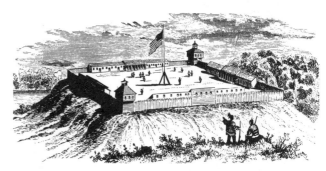

Fort Sackville, Vincennes, 1778

George Rogers Clark

Fort Wayne, 1812

Fort Harrison, 1813

William Henry Harrison

Jonathan Jennings

The territorial capitol, Vincennes

The first state capitol, Corydon

Harrison home, "Grouseland," Vincennes

Lesueur drawings: The Boatload of Knowledge on the Ohio River,
a flatboat, a keelboat, and the Steeple House at New Harmony

Muséum d'Histoire Naturelle du Havre

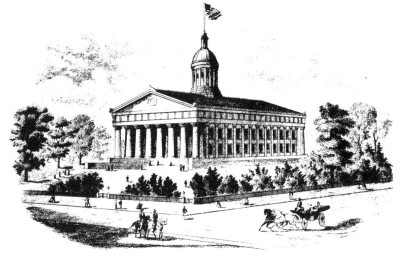

The first capitol in Indianapolis

Christian Schrader drawings of Indianapolis: governor's house and market scene

Indiana State Library

Richmond street scene, drawn by Lefevre Cranstone

Christian Schrader drawings: old Union Depot and the Tumbles, Indianapolis

OR THE BATTLE GROUND

"Every man to his tent!"

TO THE BOYS OF INDIANA.

you know that the greatest and most universal gathering of the People; of Farmers, Mechanics, Laborers, and all classes of community, who are in favor of

HARRISON and **TYLER**

Are to meet upon the BATTLE FIELD OF TIPPECANOE on the

29TH OF MAY,

welcome the Old Soldiers once more to that scene of glory, where everlasting benefits were wrought in blood for Indiana?

Announcement of Whig Rally, 1840

The Spirit of '76

The *Governor Morton* and the Washington Street bridge, Indianapolis

George W. Julian

Daniel W. Voorhees

Edward A. Hannegan

Indiana State Library

Benjamin Harrison

Albert J. Beveridge

Indiana State Library

Eugene V. Debs

Paul V. McNutt

Wendell L. Willkie

Indiana State Library

Indiana Historical Society Library

The present state capitol

Ninth Indiana Volunteers at Danville, Ky., October 1862

Oliver P. Morton

Eleventh Indiana Volunteers swearing to avenge Buena Vista, Indianapolis, May 1861

Harper's Weekly

Camp Morton near Indianapolis, September 1862

Soldiers' Reunion, Indianapolis, September 20-21, 1876

Morgan's Raiders at Salem, July 10, 1

State homecoming, Indianapolis, May 7, 1919

Evansville shipyards during World War II

Lincoln cabin, Spencer County

Camp meeting, Indiana, 1829

The Road to the West, drawn by George Tattersall

The first steamboat in the West, 1811

Passengers on a canalboat

Ferry owner's broadside,
Vincennes, 1825

Steamboat at wharf, drawn by Lefevre Cranstone

Basil Hall drawings: Steamboat passengers and captain

J. F. D. Lanier home, Madison

Andrew Wylie home, Bloomington

Levi Coffin home, Fountain City

New Albany, largest city in Indiana, 1850

Monon Railroad broadside, 1860

The Oliver chilled-steel plow

The Studebakers' blacksmith shop, South Bend

Burns Harbor plant, Bethlehem Steel

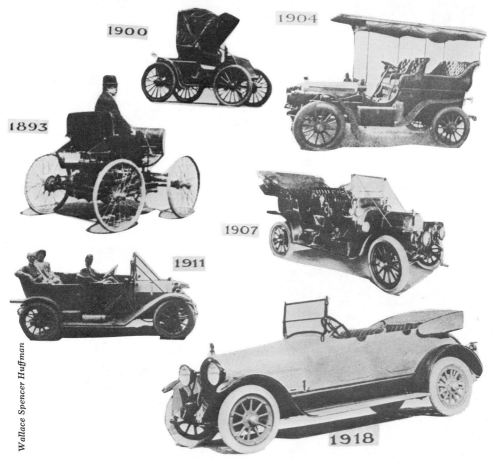

1900
1904
1893
1907
1911
1918

Wallace Spencer Huffman

A quarter century of Haynes cars, Kokomo

The start of the 500-mile race, 1965

Indianapolis Motor Speedway

Edward Eggleston birthplace, Vevay

Lew Wallace

Booth Tarkington

Indiana State Library

Theodore Dreiser

Lilly Library, Indiana University

Showboat *Majestic* on Ohio River

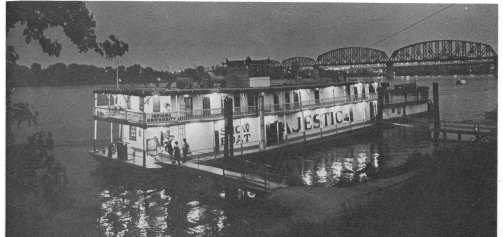

from W. W. Dudley. Both parties had been "sugaring" voters for years. It just happened that in 1888 the Republicans had more money. When Harrison arrived at the White House, still attributing his victory to Providence, he did not reward the one-legged war veteran, who by that time was in disgrace even in his own party; instead, the new President gave the judgeship of the Circuit Court of Appeals in Indianapolis to William A. Woods, who, by reversing previous rulings in the Dudley case, had made Dudley's conviction impossible.

Harrison wore kid gloves on his mind and possibly his conscience through four years in the presidential office while the fat national treasury he had inherited from his predecessor shrank to such a point that he failed of reelection in 1892. His presidency did, however, make one creditable contribution to Indiana's history; in 1889, an indignant state legislature adopted the Australian ballot in order to prevent another election quite so disgraceful as his of the preceding year. The Harrison administration also left behind in Indiana two physical reminders of its existence. The Harrison home at 1230 North Delaware Street in Indianapolis, which Harrison built in 1872 and where he lived until he died in 1901, was a national center of social activity in the 1880's and 1890's and is now a museum; and the Columbia Club on Monument Circle in Indianapolis, social hub of Hoosier Republicanism, is an outgrowth of the Harrison Marching Club of 1888.

At the dedication of the Columbia Club's new building on New Year's Eve, 1900, under the light of his own electrically illuminated portrait and just three months short of dying, Benjamin Harrison made a speech that had in it some of the quality of prophecy. It lifts him out of the light of his own aristocratic but undistinguished image into the light of the twentieth century that lay ahead. That night he shared honors at the Columbia Club banquet with the brilliant, newly elected, junior Republican senator from Indiana, Albert Jeremiah Beveridge, aged thirty-seven and just back from a trip to the Philippines. Speaking last on the program, following Beveridge, Harrison took up the young man's challenge and defended a policy of respect for the autonomy of other nations against Beveridge's proposal of a blatant American imperialism. "Hail to Columbia," the old man concluded, "the home of the free, from which only freedom can go out."

Maybe William Henry Harrison's grandson had always been on the side of the angels, after all. Just maybe it was only his kid gloves that were at fault. Once before, at the time of his grandfather's candidacy, Hoosiers had lost their heads over an "aristocrat." Maybe it was all because those kid gloves attracted to Benjamin Harrison's side too many men who were themselves considerably less than angels. Maybe. But it is hard to forget "Providence" and William W. Dudley and Judge Woods.

Harrison had snubbed Albert J. Beveridge when Beveridge first came to Indianapolis in 1886. At least, so Beveridge remembered the incident years afterward. A young man who believed in starting at the top if he could, Beveridge went first to Harrison's office to ask if he could read law there. He had met Harrison on several occasions and was sure that the most prominent lawyer in the town could not fail to remember him. But Harrison failed; he received the young man coldly and dismissed him with the curt aloofness that would later affront many of his own party's leaders when he became President. A few years later, Beveridge found himself opposing Harrison in a courtroom and attacked the older lawyer's arguments with vigor. Offended by the impertinence of a novice, Harrison suggested that his opponent had "better linger in Jericho until his beard has grown."

Beveridge was born in Ohio in 1862, grew up in Illinois, and attended DePauw University, where David Graham Phillips was his roommate and James E. Watson was his rival in forensics. Even as a boy, ambitious, energetic, relentless in his pursuit of success, he could not wait for his beard to grow. Before he went to college, he wrote to a dozen college presidents informing them that he had no money and asking them how a boy who wanted to go to college could do so without money. The president of DePauw was the only recipient of the letter who replied to it, but he had no answer to the question. When, later, an Illinois lumberman staked Beveridge to a start at college, Beveridge chose DePauw and, on his arrival at Greencastle, went directly to the president's home and asked directions to the cheapest rooming house in town. Having thus attracted attention to himself at the top, Beveridge set about cultivating his gift for oratory, practicing long hours before a mirror, and won all the prizes in forensics that the university had to offer.

Once started in Indianapolis, with the firm of McDonald and Butler, Beveridge joined the Meridian Street Methodist Church, which at that time was the Sunday gathering-place of the pious and powerful of the Republican Party, and became locally famous for the grace with which he ushered the "best" people of the city to their pews. He also joined the Indianapolis Literary Club and accepted every speaking engagement that came his way. By 1889, he was ready to ask the Indiana General Assembly for a seat in the United States Senate, although several of his close friends advised him to let his beard grow in Jericho a little longer. The General Assembly put him in the Senate seat, but only after the eleventh ballot, and he won the office for a second term in 1905. Thereafter, his races—in 1910 as a Republican, in 1914 as a Progressive, and in 1922 as a Republican again—were unsuccessful. He spent his last years in literary pursuit and died in Indianapolis in 1927.

In his early days in politics, Beveridge's heroes were Beveridge, Napoleon, and Richelieu, in that order. The victory of the United States over Spain confirmed him in his belief that the Anglo-Saxon race was destined by God to rule and improve the world and that his mission in life was to act as the prophet of imperialism. He preached his doctrine brilliantly in the Senate and on the lecture platform the breadth and length of the country until late in his first term in the Senate when he was struck by the lightning of political liberalism. He became then, with Theodore Roosevelt, a trust buster and cast in his brilliant talents with the lot of the new Progressive Party.

Perhaps Beveridge discovered the common man too late in his career; by the time he was ready to do battle in the common man's cause, the common man had chosen other leaders. There are many, however, who argue that the fault lay with Beveridge's constant, humorless obsession with his own image, no matter what cause he was espousing. If so, it is unfortunate that the "cheapest rooming house" in Greencastle in the early 1880's was still prosperous enough to afford a mirror, for Albert J. Beveridge had one of the best minds that ever became concerned with politics in Indiana.

A contemporary of Beveridge and a striking contrast in many ways was Eugene V. Debs (1855–1926), a native of Terre Haute. Debs's parents owned a small grocery store and they could have used their son's services in it, but his compassion for others who lived in poverty was so strong that they feared he might give food away instead of selling it; so, at fifteen, he went to work at the Vandalia carshops. Within a year, he was firing a locomotive. Soon after that, he went into politics, beginning as a Democrat and getting elected as city clerk. Later, he was a member of the General Assembly, where his nominating speech for Daniel W. Voorhees to the United States Senate won him a local fame in Indiana that he could have capitalized upon. But his experience on the railroad had already brought him to wondering whether anything could ever be done for labor within the ranks of the two major political parties. When the first all-inclusive union of railway men was organized and he was offered its presidency, he gave up his political prospects and accepted the office. In 1894, while serving a term in jail for his part in the strike against the Pullman Company in Illinois, he was converted to Socialism.

For the next thirty years, Debs was the leader of the Socialist Party and five times its candidate for the presidency. Like many other Americans, he opposed America's entrance into World War I and said so. But even after war was declared he continued to speak in behalf of peace until he was finally arrested for violation of the Espionage Act and sentenced to ten years in prison. Debs never acknowledged the justice of his punishment and refused to ask for pardon, even after the war was over. "It is the government that should ask me for pardon," he said. Apparently many Americans agreed with him, for when he ran for the presidency in 1920 as Convict Number 2273, he polled 901,062 votes. He was released from prison in 1921 but was never officially pardoned.

In 1922, Indiana's Governor Warren T. McCray, addressing a gathering of the American Legion in Indianapolis, expressed regret that an archtraitor had his home in Indiana; and when a motion was made to have members of the state Legion convention march past the Debs home at 451 North Eighth Street in Terre Haute shouting "Traitor!" McCray approved. "For this extremely patriotic speech," Debs retorted, "Governor McCray was lauded as a great American patriot. . . . It so happened that . . . he was at the same time fleecing, plucking, and skinning suckers in a dozen states." For these activities, using the mails to defraud, Governor McCray was, two years later, sentenced to a ten-year term in the same prison from which Debs had been released.

Eugene Debs possessed rare combinations of qualities, both as a man and as a politician. He combined gentleness with courage and, perhaps more remarkably, an uncompromising devotion to principles with an excellent talent for organization. He was one of those unusual men in political history who have known the secret of holding theoretical and practical idealists together. Nevertheless, he spoke the truth as he believed it as bluntly to his friends as to his enemies. A year before his death, at the age of seventy, when most men are sentimental about the friends who still rally round them, Debs stood on a platform in Steeg Park in Terre Haute, tall, lean, bald, bent forward from the waist, his long arms giving powerful emphasis to his speech as he flung these unadorned words at the group of laboring men who had gathered to hear him: "The politician tells you how intelligent you are to keep you ignorant. I am going to tell you how ignorant you are to make you intelligent. Do you suppose that if you acted intelligently you would be the ones who build palaces and live in hovels?"

In 1922, a man named D. C. Stephenson came to Indiana from Texas and that spring, at Evansville, entered the Democratic primary as a candidate for Congress. He lost the nomination by an overwhelming majority to William E. Wilson, who was elected in November. By that time, Stephenson had shifted his political allegiance to the Republicans and was emerging as the state's principal organizer of the Ku Klux Klan. Before long, he was Grand Dragon of the Klan in Indiana and had moved to Indianapolis, where he established a luxurious suite of offices and was able to announce unchallenged, "I am the law in Indiana."

In the mid-twenties the times were ripe for an organization

like the Klan not only in Indiana but throughout the nation. Woodrow Wilson's internationalism had been repudiated and insularity was the order of the day, best represented in Indiana perhaps by the Hoosier hominess of Senator James E. Watson, last of the brass-voiced orators of the string-tie and campaign-hat era. Corruption too had been the order of the day during Harding's administration, and his successor in the White House was an apostle of mediocrity and laissez-faire. In Indiana, Governor McCray was sentenced to the penitentiary, his elected successor, Ed Jackson, would later be indicted for offering bribes, and the Klan candidate who defeated Congressman Wilson in Evansville in 1924 would be sent to Federal prison for selling post-office appointments. America, in those years, was in the doldrums of a vulgar prosperity from which any kind of "crusade" would be a relief and to which the bigoted preachments of the Ku Klux Klan had a special appeal.

White Protestant Americanism was the "ideal" the Klan set up for the smug and self-righteous who shared in the nation's prosperity and for the malcontents who had no share in it. If a man was rich he could attribute his riches to his God-given right as a one-hundred-per-cent American to be rich and to be suspicious of anyone not of his kind, like Eugene Debs, who wanted others to share the wealth with him; if a man was not rich, he could at least be proud that he was not a Catholic who worshiped in Latin, a Jew who had a foreign-sounding name, or a Negro whose skin was black. Complacency and boredom, combined with an unacknowledged sense of guilt, can demoralize a nation and a state as much as division or dissension.

They demoralized Indiana more than most states in those years, largely because of the diabolical skill of D.C. Stephenson in organizing prevalent forces of evil and suborning religious as well as political leaders. Processions of robed Klansmen marched into churches on Sunday mornings and laid sums of money on offertory rails, and all too often the money thereafter talked from the pulpits. The Klan's *Kourier* solicited the membership of native-born, white, Protestant Hoosiers and offered Klectokons, the Klan's regalia, for sale, putting over two million dollars in Stephenson's pockets in eighteen months. The Horse Thief Law, which in 1852 had authorized associations of citizens to arrest individuals and punish them without bringing them to trial, was revived, and the Klan's Horse Thief Detective Association entered homes without warrants, flogged citizens it wished to intimidate, raided stills, burned barns, and collected protection money. Parades of hooded men and women marched through the streets of towns and cities. Crosses burned in the fields and on people's lawns. Because of the secrecy of the organization, no man could be sure whether his neighbor or even his best friend was a Klansman or not. A quiet terror pervaded the state.

As Secretary of State under Governor McCray, Ed Jackson issued the Klan its charter in Indiana, and in 1924 the Klan rewarded Jackson by electing him governor. But power eventually corrupted the efficiency of the Klan. The leaders began to quarrel among themselves. Stephenson broke with the national organization, and then local Klaverns began to "banish" him throughout the state over various disputes. But he remained "the law" in Indiana until April, 1925, when he was arrested for sadistic sexual assault on a young Indianapolis woman. When the young woman died, the charge was changed to murder, and eventually Stephenson was sentenced to life imprisonment at Michigan City's state prison.

With Stephenson's passing from the Hoosier scene, the Klan too passed away, and since those evil days Indiana has proved herself time and again, at the polls, by her laws, and by the practices of her people, emancipated from those old hates and fears. Although Jackson's successor, Harry G. Leslie, was criticized for laxness in keeping some of the old Klan appointees in office, the Klan died while he was in office, and it has shown no signs of successful revival in the nine administrations of his eight successors—Paul V. McNutt, M. Clifford Townsend, Henry F. Schricker, Ralph F. Gates, George Craig, Harold W. Handley, Matthew E. Welsh, and Roger D. Branigin.

Typical of the latter-day up-and-coming Hoosier in politics and yet unique was Paul Vories McNutt, who would have been the Democratic nominee for the presidency in 1940 if he had had his way and if Franklin D. Roosevelt had not outmaneuvered him. McNutt was born in the next-best-thing to a log cabin—a plain, frame, one-story, five-room house—in a small town, Franklin, an ideal starting point for anyone with political aspirations in Indiana. Like many another Hoosier boy of his era, he conceived presidential ambitions early in life. At the age of ten, in Martinsville, where the family moved after a brief sojourn in Indianapolis, he got himself elected secretary of the Epworth League by canvassing its members as they entered the Methodist Church and afterwards unblushingly nominating himself. Not surprisingly he was soon thereafter superintendent of the Sunday school. He was also editor of the high school paper, president of his senior class, and principal thespian in the dramatic society.

As a student at Indiana University, just down the road from Martinsville, McNutt joined the right fraternity for his purposes and quickly became a "Big Man on Campus," would indeed have been the "Biggest" if it had not been for one rival, a classmate, Wendell Willkie. Even so, his picture appeared eleven times in the university's annual, *Arbutus,* and his campus biography was the longest in the book. For his law degree, McNutt went to Harvard, but he overcame that political handicap in Hoosierdom by joining the Bloomington chapter of the American Legion when he returned to Indiana as a law professor. By 1925, aged thirty-four, he was Dean McNutt, the youngest dean of an accredited law school in the nation. By 1928, although he had no overseas service to his credit in World War I, he was the American Legion's national commander, having been progressively, before that, local and state commander. In 1933, he was inaugurated governor of Indiana. In the election he had outstripped the Roosevelt landslide in the number of Hoosier votes he received.

This spectacular success at the polls may have been McNutt's first and worst political blunder; at least, he should not have allowed it to go to his head. By his own admission he was off and running for the White House and might indeed have got there if Franklin Roosevelt had not, first, astutely exiled him to the U.S. High Commissionership of the Philippines and, then, slyly appointed him Federal Security Administrator in Washington where he could keep an eye on him. In the end, McNutt saw his old college rival, Willkie, run on the Republican ticket in 1940 for the office that he had coveted as a Democrat. Like many Hoosiers who get ahead in the world, he left the state, making his home in New York, where he died in 1955.

Norman Thomas once called Paul McNutt "a Hoosier Hitler." A journalist writing in a national magazine described him as "a platinum bust of Sitting Bull," implying that the bust was hollow. With prematurely white hair, gleaming teeth, the build of an athlete, a deeply tanned skin suggesting the strain of Indian blood that he was proud of (Virginia Indian, not Hoosier!), Paul McNutt was a handsome man, and vain. When his Republican predecessor in the statehouse, learned that McNutt intended to wear a morning coat and striped trousers at his inauguration, he remarked, "That fellow struts like a stud horse at a county fair."

But even McNutt's bitterest enemies in the state had to admit that, whether by good means or bad, he saved Indiana from bankruptcy, taking over a large deficit in 1933 and leaving a surplus of more than $10,000,000 in the state treasury four years later. Although he was both hated and admired in his own time, and probably very little loved even by those who rode on his coattails, he ranks with Oliver P. Morton, the Civil War governor, as an executive who regarded election to his office as a mandate from the people to exercise authority and who exercised it, if indeed for his own good as well as the public's. Certainly by the Reorganization Act of 1933 McNutt's rubber-stamp legislature wrought a more radical change in the state's government than any that had been effected since the adoption of the second constitution eighty years before. It was McNutt who, not without dust and heat, finally brought Indiana alongside its contemporaries in the Union.

The Reorganization Act, although later repealed, reduced the state's clumsy 169 agencies to eight departments (executive, state, audit and control, treasury, law, education, public works, commerce and industries) and placed the governor beside the elected administrative officer as the head of each. It also gave the governor the right to transfer agencies from one department to another, thus increasing his authority even more, but at the same time, if the authority was not abused, making possible greater flexibility and efficiency in governmental processes. One consequence of the change was the accusation, not unjustified, that the governor was creating a political machine for himself; but equally valid was McNutt's counterclaim that he had modernized Indiana's government so that it could operate like the big corporation that it was, instead of ambling along at the pace of the 1850's, an amateur ill-informed assemblage of men and women who had little more than their own local and selfish interests at heart.

Since the 1930's—with Democrats Townsend, Schricker, Welsh, and Branigin and Republicans Gates, Craig, and Handley in the governor's mansion—the government of Indiana has continued to evolve and keep apace of the times. Once tolerant of slaves within their territory, inhospitable toward Negroes until well after the Civil War, seduced by the bigotry of the Ku Klux Klan in the 1920's, and capable of a lynching, in Marion, as late as 1930, Hoosiers nevertheless moved earlier than most Americans in de-segregation of schools and businesses, so that now, with progressive but sound and workable legislation on their books, they have made their state a model among all states of the Union in such matters. They have also passed from a provincial suspicion of the Federal government to the point where they not only accept its assistance but ask for it and are even willing to exchange favors with Washington, as in the offer of state land in 1965 for the use of a Federal atomic plant. What is more, the state now does what it once protested the Federal government should not do; within its boundaries it gives its component communities assistance in self-development.

There is still opposition in Indiana to many of the changes that have taken place, and a swing of the pendulum in the opposite direction is possible, although it is not likely to be extreme. It is in the nature of democracy to advance cautiously; that is, in the end, one of its advantages over more extreme forms of government. But whatever happens in Indiana, its government is tempered no longer by the kind of thinking that in 1816 made some men favor statehood chiefly because it would open to themselves more avenues to officeholding and made other men oppose statehood simply because it would cost too much, nor by the condition of mind that in 1850 made people fear their elected representatives for their cleverness more than their stupidity and seventy-five years later still made them mistrust some of their neighbors because of strange religions or dark skins. Dying at least, if not yet dead, is the spirit that held Indiana for years just outside the Union for which it fought more generously and gallantly than most Northern states in the conflict of 1861–65 and that kept it for several decades, reluctant, at the threshold of the twentieth century, long after many of its own sons, in industry, commerce, education, science, the arts, and occasionally in politics, had marched boldly through the door.

Chapter Seven

☆

Five Wars

... the Second Indiana, which had fallen back as stated, could
not be rallied and took no further part in the action, except a
handful of men, who under the gallant colonel, Bowles, joined
the Mississippi regiment and did good service, and those fugitives who, at a later period in the day, assisted in defending the
train and depot. . . .

The author of these opprobrious words was General Zachary
Taylor, "Old Rough and Ready," writing his official report of the
Battle of Buena Vista in which some 5,000 American troops, about
one third of them Indiana volunteers, defeated some 20,000 Mexican regulars under General Santa Anna on a sunny, deep-gorged
plain near Saltillo, Mexico, on the 22nd and 23rd of February,
1847. They were words that would be in part responsible for
Zachary Taylor's failure to carry Indiana in the presidential election of 1848 and that would rankle in the hearts of Indianans for
another dozen years thereafter.

At the time of the official report, everyone knew who was in
command of "the Mississippi regiment," whose valor, if only by
the inference to be drawn from the juxtaposition of phrases in the
General's report, made the retreat of the Second Indiana seem by
contrast all the more craven. The colonel of that Mississippi regiment was General Taylor's son-in-law, Jefferson Davis, and although Jeff Davis most certainly distinguished himself by his conduct at Buena Vista, obviously the General was prejudiced.
Furthermore, by the time the voters were casting their ballots in

1848, a military court of inquiry had definitely established that "the gallant colonel, Bowles," cited in the General's report, was ignorant of company, battalion, and brigade drill and was solely responsible for the Second Indiana's retreat. The men of the Second Indiana had not turned and fled in fear, as the report implied; their commanding officer, Bowles, acting without any authority from his superiors, had ordered them to cease firing and withdraw. True, Bowles joined the Mississippi regiment thereafter and conducted himself creditably, but the majority of the Indianans also rejoined the battle. It was not true that "they could not be rallied." Nevertheless, the damage had been done to the reputations of the men of the Second Indiana, and it was not easily undone. The truth about them was not fully published until almost a century later. Meantime, Hoosiers had no opportunity to redeem their honor on the field of battle until the Civil War.

The state of Indiana was not prepared for the Mexican War when it was declared on May 13, 1846. In territorial days, the militia had maintained high standards and a full complement of men, but after the War of 1812 was won and Indian hostilities had diminished, there was little glory in militia duty and hardly any need for an armed force. By 1846, there were only about a thousand inventoried firearms for militiamen in the state, and the men who continued to drill were often derisively called "the cornstalk militia," because they used cornstalks as rifles and wore corntassels in their hats to resemble military plumes. The adjutant general of Indiana in 1846 was an able man, David Reynolds, who proved himself equal to the emergency, but he was severely handicapped by inadequate records, insufficient pay, and a complete absence of funds. The governor of Indiana, James Whitcomb, was an able man too, but he was a bookish man, hardly qualified to organize a military expedition.

Among the people of the state there was no lack of enthusiasm for the war. It was sometimes called "the Democrats' war," but Hoosier Whigs and Democrats alike supported it. Already some Hoosiers had traveled to Texas and back, as early as the 1820's when Texas was still a part of Mexico and later when it was an independent republic. Almost everyone in Indiana had heard tales of the Alamo and firsthand accounts of life on the southwestern plains. Young Indianans were eager for adventure in romantic Mexico and boasted that they would raise the Stars and Stripes over "the Halls of Montezuma." Nineteen days after Governor Whitcomb issued a call for volunteers, on May 22, 1846, Indiana's quota of thirty companies, or about three thousand men, was filled. In that year the state's population was about three quarters of a million.

The recruiting was undertaken by individuals, young men like nineteen-year-old Lew Wallace, for example, who opened an office on Washington Street in Indianapolis, hung out a flag and a four-sided transparency that read, "For Mexico, Fall In," and with a drummer and fifer paraded the streets until enough men had fallen in to form a company. Such companies, from all over the state, converged as rapidly as they could upon Camp Clark, near New Albany, where they were organized into regiments. At that time there was only one railroad in Indiana. It ran between Madison and Edinburg. To Edinburg the new recruits from the central and northern parts of the state came afoot or in farm wagons and took "the cars" south. From points along the Ohio River they came by boat, the "Indiana Riflemen" of Vanderburgh County, for example, traveling upriver under the command of Captain William Walker aboard the steamboat *Thomas Metcalfe*. Volunteers from the vicinity of Fort Wayne used the Whitewater Canal and the upper Ohio.

Women as well as men were active in the war effort. They made uniforms on short notice and created beautiful silken flags for their favorite companies and regiments. The state banks contributed their share by loaning money for the maintenance of the new soldiers until government funds became available. The Indianapolis and Madison branches each placed $10,000 at the disposal of the state, and the Lawrenceburg branch agreed to honor the governor's draft for a similar amount. Those that were unable to supply cash, like the Vincennes, Terre Haute, and South Bend branches, submitted their regrets along with their good wishes to the men who had volunteered.

At Camp Clark the initial blush of the recruits' enthusiasm began to fade when they discovered that politics would play a role in their fates. Governor Whitcomb was on hand, along with Lieutenant Governor Paris C. Dunning. The Lieutenant Governor took charge of dispensing political favors and soon earned for himself the epithet of "Big Dog" at the camp. The men were authorized to elect their officers, but most of them had never heard of that political device known as "the slate," and they were puzzled by the maneuvering that offered them little or no choice in the final voting. As a consequence, all three of the originally elected regimental colonels were Democrats, members of Governor Whitcomb's own political party: James P. Drake, First Regiment; Joseph Lane, Second Regiment; and James H. Lane, Third Regiment. When Joseph Lane was advanced to the rank of brigadier general, it looked for a time as if a Whig might have a chance at the colonelcy of the Second, but the votes of one company were conveniently "lost" and ultimately, after the troops reached the mouth of the Rio Grande, the command of the regiment went to William A. Bowles, another Democrat.

At the beginning, not one of these regimental officers knew the manual of arms, much less the principles of military tactics on the battlefield, and most of the lower-ranking company officers were similarly ignorant of military procedures. Colonel Drake was a jovial innkeeper from Indianapolis; Colonel James Lane was a lawyer and politician; Colonel William Bowles was a doctor who, in 1840, had built the first resort hotel at French Lick Springs. Drake loathed horses and would have been much happier walking at the head of his regiment; James Lane hated authority and, by the eve of Buena Vista, hated Joseph Lane as well, for the two Lanes were at that time preparing for a duel; Bowles preferred to hunt botanical specimens in the fields and woods when he should have been drilling his men. Joseph Lane, the brigade's general, was a farmer, a storekeeper, a politician, and a man of many other enterprises. Because he had grown up as a frontiersman on the Ohio River, he had learned how to use a rifle expertly, but as a general he carried a sword and pistols.

Lane received his appointment to the generalship of the Indiana brigade almost by accident. Everyone in Washington was lobbying for such posts, and one day, according to the Indianapolis *Sentinel,* one of the Indiana senators, either Hannegan or Bright, asked Representative Robert Dale Owen whom he intended to recommend from his district. "Why, I had no thought of offering a name," Owen is reported to have said. "There are no applications from my district, but if you think I should offer a name, I shall hand in that of Joe Lane." When the appointment of Lane was confirmed, President Polk said to Owen that he hoped the Congressman had considered his recommendation well before making it. Owen replied that he knew nothing about Lane's military talents but there were "about him those elements of character which in all times of difficulty prompt each one to rally round him instinctively as a leader." Such "elements of character" were admirable, but they were hardly enough to qualify a man for a generalship.

And yet Joe Lane, unacquainted with the simplest rudiments of military drill when he took command and further handicapped by unseasoned troops and unprofessional officers, became one of the most distinguished commanders of the Mexican War, the equal of Scott and Taylor in courage and tactical skill if not in historybook fame. Affectionately called "Old Rough and Ready No. 2" by his men, he won the praise of the military court of inquiry that finally exonerated the men of the Second Indiana, if not their colonel, after Buena Vista; and later, commanding the Fourth and Fifth Indiana Regiments, which were mustered in 1847 and included a young second lieutenant from Liberty, Indiana, named Ambrose E. Burnside, he directed the advance from Vera Cruz via Puebla to Mexico City with a brilliance that won him the title of "the Marion of the Mexican War." Thus, more often than not, men like Lane and the volunteers who fought at his command have won America's wars.

In the two years of the conflict, Indiana sent about 5,000 men to Mexico, of whom 542 were killed. When the survivors returned, via the Mississippi and Ohio rivers or the old Natchez Trace, all the towns of Indiana feted them at banquets and barbecues. At New Orleans, landsharks had cheated most of them out of their bounties of 160 acres of land in the West and they were destined to remain in Indiana and try to recoup the financial losses they had suffered by going off to war. For a while, members of the First and Third Indiana regiments tormented those of the Second by reminding them of the disgrace of General Taylor's report. But the First could boast no real superiority because they had seen no action in the war, and in their hearts the Third knew well enough that the Second were not cowards, for they had seen them in action and fought at their sides at Buena Vista. As for the Fourth and Fifth, they could boast unchallenged about what they did at Vera Cruz and Puebla and Mexico City, because they were the only Indiana regiments that were there. Meantime, Colonel Bowles returned to Indiana too, to everyone's great surprise. He said he would write a full acount of his part in the Battle of Buena Vista, but he never got round to it. As for Joe Lane, "Old Rough and Ready No. 2," he could have had anything he wanted from Indiana's Democratic Party in that postwar period, but he chose instead to go to Oregon as the appointed governor of that territory. A dozen years later, when he was a candidate for the vice presidency with John C. Breckenridge, Indiana gave him only 12,000 of the 270,000 votes that were cast in the state. But by that time other matters were on Hoosiers' minds, and another war was in the offing.

On the September day in 1847 when Lieutenant U. S. Grant ingeniously planted a howitzer in the belfry of a suburban church and Mexico City sent out a white flag of surrender, Oliver Hazard Perry Throck Morton, in Centerville, Indiana, was less than a month past his twenty-fourth birthday. Although young Morton was still a Democrat at that time in his life, he had taken no part in "the Democrats' war." Born in Salisbury, Wayne County, he had attended a private school in Springfield, Ohio, was apprenticed for a while to a hatter, studied at the Wayne County Seminary, and had gone to Miami University in Oxford, Ohio, where Benjamin Harrison, ten years his junior, would be a student later. In 1847, when the Mexican War was coming to a close, Oliver Hazard Perry Throck Morton—better known as Oliver P. Morton—was admitted to the bar in Indiana, and that year he began the practice of law in Centerville, becoming a rival of George W. Julian in the courtroom and in politics. Thirteen years later, in the summer of 1860, Morton was deep in his second campaign for a major public office in Indiana and on the threshold of fame. He was then just thirty-seven years old.

In 1856, Morton had failed in a race for the governorship as a "People's Party" (or Republican) candidate against Ashbel P. Willard of New Albany. Now, in 1860, he was the Republican candidate for lieutenant governor, although the goverorship itself was still his goal. There had been five successive Democrats in the governor's mansion in Indianapolis in the previous seventeen years, and Morton and his running mate, another Lane, this one from Crawfordsville and named Henry S., had devised a scheme which, if successful, would give the state of Indiana two Republican governors in quick succession. According to their plan, immediately after they took office, a Republican General Assembly would put Governor Henry S. Lane in Democrat Graham Fitch's seat in the United States Senate and Morton would succeed Lane as governor.

In the summer of 1860, it would have been almost impossible for the plans of Morton and Lane to go agley. Morton had once been a Democrat; Lane was originally a Whig; there was at least one other former Whig on their ticket; there were also a Fillmore elector of 1856, a former Liberty Party man, and one young Republican with no previous affiliations outside that brand-new party. It was a ticket that could be made to appeal to almost everybody except radical abolitionists like George W. Julian at one extreme of the political spectrum and the Peace Democrats at the other. With Albert Lange running for the office of state auditor, the ticket should also attract the new and rapidly growing German vote. Furthermore, in Abraham Lincoln the party had a candidate for president who should hold the abolitionist and antiabolitionist Republicans together without offending the sympathetic Union Democrats, for Lincoln seemed not yet to have committed himself to anything beyond the preservation of the Union. On the other hand, the Democrats were divided in their presidential choice between Douglas and Breckenridge, and some Hoosier Democrats might go so far as to join the old Whigs and vote for Bell rather than accept the label of disloyalty that Oliver P. Morton was determined to brand them with before the campaign was over. Indiana had thirteen electoral votes in 1860; only three Northern states—New York, Pennsylvania, and Ohio—had more than that; the national Republican Party would have to concentrate on such an important state with both money and speakers. It was a very good year for Hoosiers of the new party.

In the October voting, Lane and Morton defeated Hendricks and Turpie by 10,000 votes; in November, Lincoln carried the state by a majority of 6,000 over all three of his opponents, and seven of the eleven men elected to the U. S. House of Representatives were Republicans. Among them was Schuyler Colfax of South Bend, who would be speaker of the House from 1863 to 1869 before going on to the vice presidency under Grant. As for the four Democrats, who all came from southern counties as was expected—Vanderburgh, Vigo, Washington, and Dearborn—two of them were War Democrats who could be counted on to support Lincoln, at least short of emancipation. The most noteworthy of the minority group of congressmen was Daniel W. Voorhees of Terre Haute, elected for his first term in Washington. Maybe Voorhees was a Peace Democrat, maybe a Constitutional Union Democrat; no one was quite sure then, perhaps not even Voorhees himself; and historians cannot agree about him now.

Among the rewards Indiana Republicans received for their victory at the polls was the appointment of Caleb B. Smith of Indianapolis as Lincoln's Secretary of the Interior. Smith had seconded Lincoln's nomination at Chicago. He was a man in whom Lincoln never had much confidence, but it was something to have a Hoosier in the Cabinet. Later, Hugh McCulloch of Fort Wayne would become Secretary of the Treasury. Lincoln stopped over in Indiana on his way to his inauguration, at Lafayette on February 11, 1861, and the next day, his fifty-second birthday, at Indianapolis. By that time, according to plan, thirty-seven-year-old Oliver P. Morton was the governor of Indiana. He would remain governor for the next six years, until he too, like his predecessor, was sent to the United States Senate by the legislators. Morton remained in the Senate until his death, in 1877.

South Carolina seceded from the Union on December 20, 1860. By February 1, 1861, six more states had joined her, and a week later the Confederate States of America organized at Montgomery, Alabama. On April 12 Fort Sumter was fired upon, and on April 14 it fell. On the 13th of April the Indianapolis *Sentinel* presented the news of Sumter to Hoosiers with gloomy headlines:

THE IRREPRESSIBLE CONFLICT INAUGURATED
CIVIL STRIFE COMMENCED IN CHARLESTON HARBOR
THE ABOLITION WAR OF SEWARD, LINCOLN AND COMPANY
The Abolition and disunion administration have attempted the coercion of the Confederate States. Such are the first fruits of Republicanism—the end no one can foresee.

The Indianapolis *Sentinel,* it goes without saying, was a Democratic newspaper.

The rapid sequence of events between Lincoln's election and his inauguration stunned Hoosiers as it stunned everyone else in the North, but in Indiana the blows seemed to fall more directly and more ominously than in most of the other loyal states. The majority of Hoosiers were of Southern ancestry. Many had relatives in the South. The political sympathies of Indiana were also closer to the South than to the East. Since Andrew Jackson's time, Democracy had usually prevailed in the state, and in 1860 only the fear of disunion had brought enough varied political elements together to elect Republicans Lane and Morton. Finally, what was happening was happening just next door. An alien nation controlling the Mississippi could cut off and destroy a large part of Indiana's commerce. Worse still, if Kentucky followed the other slave states, the border between the two belligerent nations would be the Ohio River and Indiana soil could well become a battleground.

But when Sumter fell, Democrats as well as Republicans in Indiana rallied to the cause of the Union, just as Whigs had joined Democrats in the Mexican War. Governor Morton appointed Lew Wallace, a former Democrat, adjutant general of the state, designated the Indianapolis fairgrounds as "Camp Morton," the rallying point for organizing regiments, and called for volunteers. Within five days Indiana filled its military quota.

The Hoosier volunteers organized in six regiments that were numbered from the Sixth to the Eleventh in recognition of the previous five regiments of the Mexican War. The Eleventh, a colorful outfit called the "Indiana Zouaves," was the first to leave for duty at the front. On the day that Adjutant General Wallace gave them their regimental banners he made the men kneel and swear that they would never desert their colors and would avenge the disgrace that General Taylor's report had brought upon Indiana fighting men after Buena Vista. On June 3, Indiana troops saw their first action, at Philippi, Virginia, where they prevented the Confederates from seizing the Baltimore and Ohio Railway. By that time, back home in Indiana six more regiments had enlisted and organized, and a militia, called the "Indiana Legion," was in readiness to defend the state against invasion.

Like the Indiana of 1846, the state was not prepared for war when war came in 1861. In disregard of the earlier experience, the state government had neglected the militia. Once more there were no trained soldiers and no trained officers on duty. There were, however, a few residents who had graduated from West Point and resigned and gone into business, among them Thomas A. Morris, Joseph Reynolds, and Milo Hascall; and a dozen or so veterans of command from the Mexican War were still on hand, although they had left military service when that war was over and had been for many years civilians. In this latter group were Robert Milroy, Ebenezer Dumont, Lew Wallace, Mahlon D. Manson, Nathan Kimball, James M. McMillan, Alvin P. Hovey, and Jefferson C. Davis. By the end of the first year of the war, all these officers were back in uniform and 61,341 Indiana men had enlisted, almost twice the state's quota of 38,832.

No matter what the sentiments of Indianans might be about states' rights and slavery, it was obvious that Indiana was going to play an important role in the war. Indiana was the fifth largest of the states that remained in the Union. It bordered the South; at least, it bordered the controversial commonwealth of Kentucky. Most of its railways ran north and south, and it stood on the north bank of a four- or five-hundred-mile stretch of a river that was an important artery between East and West as well as North and

South. Finally, its production of wheat (16,848,000 bushels in 1860), corn (71,588,000 bushels), and hogs (3,099,000) made it a principal source of food for the Federal army. The population of Indiana in 1860 was 1,350,428.

In spite of the gloomy headlines in the Indianapolis *Sentinel,* everyone believed in the beginning that the war would be over in a few months, and the new soldiers marched off to the battlefront singing and frolicking as if they were going to a picnic. But as the winter wore into the spring of 1862 and the hot Hoosier summer followed, the temper of the people of Indiana changed. Although Kentucky was apparently saved for the Union, the Hoosier border counties along the Ohio were vulnerable to raids. On July 18, for example, Colonel Adam Johnson, with thirty Confederate cavalrymen, crossed the river at Newburgh, captured the town, and demanded a ransom of $20,000 from its bank. Although Grant had begun to win victories in the West—at Forts Henry and Donelson and at Shiloh—they were bloody victories; and although McClellan in the East would later receive praise from Robert E. Lee as the ablest of his opponents in the war, he seemed always reluctant to move forward and was forever quarreling with his commander in chief in the White House. By midsummer of 1862, it was obvious that the war would last a long time, and it was beginning to look like a war not only to save the Union but also to end slavery. To many Middle Westerners, even to some Republicans, this new prospect was not pleasing. Oliver P. Morton himself had run on a platform that refused to endorse the exclusion of slavery from the territories.

Indianans not only shared the national discontent of 1862, their own discontent was exacerbated by their local view of the war. Indiana regiments, involved in almost all the fighting East and West, had suffered heavy losses in killed and wounded and deaths from disease. Four Indiana regiments under Burnside had been disastrously crushed at Fredericksburg. At Shiloh, Indiana's own General Lew Wallace had taken the wrong road on his way to the battle and prolonged the carnage by his delay, and he would never have a battle command again. Steamboats from Evansville and other Ohio River ports were bringing back the wounded from

Tennessee in frightening numbers. Perryville, strategically a Federal victory, was from the Hoosier civilian's point of view a senseless slaughter of green Indiana troops. As for Indiana's governor, he was endeavoring to be "the soldier's friend" with motives that could be variously interpreted and in ways that seemed unrelated to his duties as governor; he meddled in the military campaigns, had quarreled with General Buell, whom he would finally connive to remove from his command, and seemed to think he was the governor of Kentucky as well as Indiana. Morton quarreled also with General William "Bull" Nelson over the best way to defend Louisville and was present in the parlor of Louisville's Galt House when General Jefferson C. Davis murdered Nelson. Back home, where Morton's administration tried to brand every critic of the government as a traitor, many civilians were worried about the suspension of habeas corpus for persons charged with disloyalty. Finally, although the state had produced far more than the number of volunteers the Federal government had asked for, the Federal government had at first discontinued enlistments, fearing it could not equip all the men who were ready to fight, and then, finding the army inadequately manned, had reversed itself and ordered the state to institute a draft by counties. Men who had offered their services and had been turned away were not happy over the prospect of being coerced into fighting. When the census for the draft was taken, in some counties the eligible men all went visiting in neighboring counties and left at home only the women, the aged, and the sick.

On September 22, 1862, on the eve of the state election, Lincoln issued the Emancipation Proclamation. Paradoxically, Democrat Robert Dale Owen had been urging him to make this move while Republican Governor Morton was begging him to delay, at least till after the election. All summer long, the Republicans had been trying to shore up against their obvious gradual loss of strength by spreading "atrocity" stories about the Confederate army, by accusing Democrats of disloyalty, by probing into the activities of the Sons of Liberty, and by arranging election-time furloughs for soldiers at the front whose loyalty to the party could be counted upon. But after the Emancipation Proclamation was signed, these efforts were of no avail. In October, the Democrats sent a majority to the General Assembly, and in November the proportion of Indiana Republicans and Democrats in the U. S. House of Representatives was reversed, only four Republicans retaining their seats. The legislature promptly elected two Democrats, Thomas A. Hendricks and David Turpie, to the United States Senate. One of these men replaced Unionist Joseph A. Wright, who had in his turn replaced Democrat Jesse D. Bright when Bright was expelled from the Senate on February 5, 1862, for addressing a letter to "His Excellency, Jefferson Davis, President of the Confederate States."

What happened after the election of Senators Hendricks and Turpie is of no credit to either political party on the home front in Indiana. The Democrats proposed to take time out from the war's problems to gerrymander the state so that they could not be dislodged at the next election; and the Republican assemblymen, to prevent a quorum and paralyze the state government, removed themselves to Madison where they could cross the river and escape arrest if there should be an attempt to coerce them. Morton himself could have called them back and then vetoed the reapportionment bill when and if it was passed; but Morton had other plans; he waited until the legislature adjourned without passing an appropriations bill and then, instead of calling a special session for that purpose, as the state constitution provided, he proceeded to operate the government single-handed, without a legislature, for the next two years.

For money Morton sought out James F. D. Lanier, formerly a Madison banker, who had earlier furnished $400,000 through Winslow, Lanier and Company of New York to equip Indiana's first volunteers. Lanier loaned Morton an additional $600,000 now to pay interest on the state debts, and from the Federal War Department and the contributions of individuals in nineteen Indiana counties Morton got a half million dollars more. These funds Morton kept in the safe in his office in Indianapolis and distributed them on his own responsibility, without taxation and without legislative sanction. His excuse for not depositing the money in the state treasury was that the treasurer was a Democrat and probably would not pay it out as he directed.

In April, 1863, General Burnside, commander of the Department of the Ohio, strengthened Governor Morton's hand against his critics by declaring that sympathy for the enemy "would not be tolerated and any newspaper that attempted to bring the war policy of the government into disrepute" would be prosecuted. Burnside ordered such prosecutions by military courts in disregard of the continued existence of functioning civil courts in the Department of the Ohio. In Indiana, fanatics soon took the "prosecution" into their own hands. Mobs that included soldiers home on furlough destroyed the Richmond *Jeffersonian,* the LaPorte *Democrat,* and the Vincennes *Sun* and attacked the offices of the Princeton *Union Democrat,* the Terre Haute *Journal,* the Rockport *Democrat,* and the Franklin *Herald.* The editor of the Plymouth *Democrat* was arrested and the newspaper was placed under a $5,000 bond not to violate the order from Cincinnati.

In May, when the Democrats held a convention in Indianapolis, General Hascall mobilized infantry, cavalry, and artillery to prevent a "revolution." Many Democrats were arrested in the city and searched for concealed weapons, and apparently many of them were armed. Voorhees spoke at the convention without interruption, but soldiers with fixed bayonets moved in when Senator Thomas A. Hendricks took the platform and at that point the convention was adjourned. That night, soldiers boarded departing trains and searched the homeward-bound convention members for weapons. As one of the trains was crossing Pogue's Run, the occupants of one coach threw a shower of pistols out the windows into the water. This little opera bouffe later came to be known in local history as "The Battle of Pogue's Run."

Since the election of 1862, Morton had kept the Copperheads of Indiana under close surveillance; in 1864, running for reelection, he made his campaign against Democrats synonymous with a campaign against "treason." Meantime, the Knights of the Golden Circle, organized in the 1850's as a society advocating annexation of all of Mexico and with its first chapter believed to have been established in Indiana at Paoli by Dr. William A. Bowles, "the gallant colonel" of Buena Vista, had evolved into the Sons of Liberty, presumably dedicated to the ultimate secession of the Northwest and the formation of a separate confederacy. Very few of the society's members ever "saw the elephant," as the saying went in those days; that is, they had no knowledge of what was afoot in the inner circle of hard-core extremists. But Morton accused the Democrats of arming and drilling under the cloak of the Sons of Liberty, and he encouraged Union Clubs and Union Leagues to arm and drill in retaliation. His opponent in 1864 was Joseph E. McDonald, who had been nominated by an overwhelming vote over the extremist Lambdin P. Milligan and whose loyalty could not be impugned; consequently, others in McDonald's party bore the brunt of Morton's attack.

The secret activities of the Sons of Liberty could not have been very secret, for Governor Morton installed spies in the order, among them one Felix Stidger. Stidger reported to the governor that plans were in progress for an uprising in Indianapolis on August 16, 1864, at which time the Sons of Liberty planned to seize the fairgrounds and release Confederate prisoners held there. There was indeed a hare-brained plot of some sort in progress among the hotheads of the society, including the aging Dr. Bowles, but responsible Democrats got wind of it in time and forestalled it. It is significant that the governor, however, waited till well after the alleged date of the uprising before he made a move. Then General Hovey arrested Harrison Dodd, an Indianapolis printer, and on September 22 brought Dodd to trial before a military court. A few days before election Dodd escaped and fled to Canada. Morton said Dodd's escape was proof of his guilt. Democrats said Morton helped Dodd to make his getaway. Whatever the truth of the matter, Dodd was found guilty *in absentia* and sentenced to be hanged. Soon after Dodd's arrest, General Hovey arrested William A. Bowles, Stephen Horsey, Lambdin P. Milligan, Horace Heffren, Andrew Humphreys, and Joseph J. Bingham. Bingham was the editor of the Indianapolis *Sentinel.* The first three of these men were sentenced to be hanged; Humphreys was to be confined for the duration of the war; and the other two, turning state's evidence, were released. Afterwards, in *ex parte Milligan*, the Supreme Court of the United States ruled that the military court had no jurisdiction in the case since the civil courts were functioning in the region at the time, and all three of the condemned men escaped the rope.

Throughout the war there was in Indiana strong and bitter feeling against both Morton and Lincoln, but recent scholarly investigations of the Copperhead movement in the state have established that the widespread disloyalty attributed to Indianans was largely a contemporary Republican canard. There can be no doubt that Oliver P. Morton, working by his own choice almost single-handed, preserved the state's resources for the Union cause; but it is equally certain that he could have done the job just as well, and possibly better, by inspiring the confidence and cooperation of his fellow Hoosiers instead of claiming for himself and his party a monopoly of patriotism. Such a course of action would at least have invalidated the charge, in large degree justified, that he used the war for the advancement of his party and his own career. If Democrats were indeed plotting to withdraw Indiana from the Union and abet the Confederate cause, they were strangely indifferent to their one great opportunity to achieve that end when John Hunt Morgan invaded Indiana in the summer of 1863. On that occasion their failure to aid Morgan should have been proof to the governor that his suspicions, if they were honest suspicions, were unfounded.

That summer, after capturing Columbia, Lebanon, and Bardstown in Kentucky and destroying large quantities of Federal stores, Confederate General John Hunt Morgan disobeyed General Bragg's orders and, with 2,400 seasoned cavalrymen, crossed the Ohio River from Brandenburg, Kentucky, to Mauckport, Indiana, on the morning of July 8. Morgan's reasons for entering Indiana that July morning were cogent. Bragg and Rosecrans were facing each other in Tennessee, neither ready to strike. They had already engaged in one major battle at Stone's River, and each could claim a sort of victory, Bragg's statistical, Rosecrans' strategic, but neither's decisive. Bragg's force was smaller than Rosencrans', but it was in top condition, had the advantage of shorter supply lines, and was maneuvering on familiar terrain. If Burnside could be detained in the North by Morgan's raid, the chances were good that the Confederates in Tennessee would at least hold their own.

Elsewhere, conditions seemed to favor a bold Confederate action of the sort Morgan was about to undertake. Down the Mississippi, Grant was still hammering at Vicksburg and had not yet overpowered it when Morgan left Tennessee. In the East, the Confederate army had won two major victories at Fredericksburg and Chancellorsville, and so far as Morgan knew when he stood on the banks of the Ohio, Lee was still marching into Pennsylvania. Finally, in the North, there were draft riots and a growing weariness of the war.

How much these last two considerations weighed in Morgan's decision is a matter for conjecture. He spoke on several occasions of joining Lee in Pennsylvania but at the same time he was making definite plans to recross the Ohio at Buffington Island above Cincinnati. The project of union with Lee was probably only an alternative to be resorted to if the crossing at Buffington Island failed. As for the dissidence in the North, Morgan would naturally have welcomed a large-scale revolt, but there is no good evidence that he counted on Copperhead support in Indiana, in spite of attempts to prove that he was deeply involved in "the Northwest Conspiracy." For one thing, Morgan's first raid into Kentucky the year before had taught him not to expect recruits from Southern sympathizers. If his own fellow Kentuckians would not rally round him, he could hardly expect disaffected Hoosiers to do so. Moreover, his treatment of the few Copperheads who approached him in Indiana demonstrates his lack of confidence in them.

"Good," he is reported to have said to one protesting Hoosier sympathizer as he took the Hoosier's horse. "Then you ought to be glad to contribute to the South."

The crossing of the Ohio got off to a bad start. Although Morgan easily captured two steamboats for the ferriage, a party of home guards has established themselves on the Indiana side behind houses and haystacks. The raiders' Parrott guns had to be put into action to silence the single Hoosier fieldpiece before the crossing could commence. Then, after the Second Kentucky and the Ninth Tennessee were over the river and the home guards were retiring, a Federal gunboat steamed round the bend and began tossing shells alternately at the raiders on the Indiana shore and those who had not yet left Brandenburg on the Kentucky side.

The appearance of the gunboat brought the ferrying to an abrupt halt and put the entire Confederate force in a hazardous position. Delay was dangerous, because pursuing Federal cavalry would soon be coming up through Kentucky. Yet if the crossing was abandoned, half the troops would be left stranded on the Indiana shore. Morgan opened up on the gunboat with every piece of artillery at his disposal, but for two hours he could not drive her off. When the situation had come to seem almost desperate, however, the gunboat suddenly turned and fled, her ammunition exhausted.

That night, after putting the torch to the two steamboats they had used and setting them adrift, Morgan's men camped at Frakes Mill, six miles north of the river. Behind them, one of the boats, the *Alice Dean*, did not burn completely, and for many years a part of its carcass was still visible in the water where it sank. As late as the summer of 1965 parts of it were still being salvaged from the bottom of the river.

The next day, Morgan's raid was in full swing. Morgan possessed what the English call "a good eye for a country," but he amplified his vision and prehension by using his troops as an insect uses its antennae. They rode usually in fours, and at every crossroad those at the head of the column fanned out, foraged and scouted for several miles on both sides of the main force, and then rejoined it in the rear. Thus was Morgan not only kept informed of any threat on his flanks, he kept the countryside in a wide area through which he passed in constant alarm and confusion as to his whereabouts and the direction he was taking.

A Canadian telegrapher named George Ellsworth, but called "Lightning" by the raiders, further extended Morgan's vision and his knowledge of the purposes of his adversaries. Ellsworth had the rare skill of mimicry at the telegraph key. By watching a captured operator work or by listening to an operator on a tapped wire, he could soon imitate the man's style so well that he was able to deceive other operators and get information from them. He could also send out false information and even false military orders. His expert faking made it possible for Morgan virtually to assume command of the enemy forces surrounding him and to put them almost anywhere he wanted them.

At Corydon, Indiana, the raiders met their first serious resistance. Outside the town, four hundred home guards barred their way. Before the defense could be broken—by shelling the town behind the home guards—sixteen Confederates were killed. Three of the defenders were killed, two were wounded, and one dropped dead of a heart attack. The battle of Corydon was the only pitched battle north of the Mason and Dixon's Line, besides Gettysburg, officially recorded by the War Department. In spite of the setback, Morgan was in town that day in time for noonday dinner at the Kintner Hotel. It was while he was dining there, on July 9, that the innkeeper's daughter told him of Lee's defeat at Gettysburg almost a week before. There is no evidence that he considered turning back when he received this information. From Corydon, Morgan advanced to Salem, Vienna, and Lexington; but nine miles below Seymour he began to swing eastward toward the Ohio line.

When the news of the invasion reached Indianapolis, there was a brief time of panic and confusion, and if Morgan had pushed straight on from Salem on July 10, he might have captured the city and released and armed, from the arsenal, the several thousand Confederate prisoners held there. In twenty-four hours, however, it was too late for a such a dream. Governor Morton had the situation in hand; General Lew Wallace, home on leave and on a fishing trip on the Wabash, was in the saddle and on his way downstate to help General Edward H. Hobson, who was hot on Morgan's trail. From Cincinnati, Burnside had dispatched General Henry M. Judah to head the raiders off if he could. But far more damaging to Morgan than the combined efforts of these three generals was the disaster that had befallen his own men by this time; demoralized, they had begun to loot and to straggle.

From the beginning, horses had been taken as needed. This was the custom of cavalrymen, both Union and Confederate. It not only gave the raiders fresh mounts, it denied them to pursuers. Apparently Morgan himself at first tried to see that exchanges were as just as possible under the circumstances, but in his swift, zigzag movements he lost contact with and control of many of his men. By the time they reached Salem, the plenitude of Hoosier shops and stores after impoverished Dixie was too much for them. To use the euphemistic words of Morgan's lieutenant, General Basil Duke, they developed "the propensity to appropriate beyond limit or restraint."

General Duke could be—and was—more specific. Describing the raid for the *Century Magazine* thirty years later, he wrote:

> The weather was intensely warm,—the hot July sun burned the earth to powder, and we were breathing superheated dust, —yet one man rode for three days with seven pairs of skates slung about his neck; another loaded himself with sleighbells. A large chafing-dish, a medium-sized Dutch clock, a green glass decanter with goblets to match, a bag of horn buttons, a chandelier, and a birdcage containing three canaries, were some of the articles I saw borne off and jealously fondled.

At Harrison, Indiana, twenty-five miles from Cincinnati, all detachments that could be reached were drawn in and a strong provost guard kept the stragglers under some control as the raiders crossed into Ohio. From there on their holiday was ended. Morgan was no longer a wolf on the prowl; he was now a fox in flight, and the hounds were baying all around him. Yet they would not capture Morgan himself and the 364 men who stayed with him to the end until he was almost at the Pennsylvania line in eastern Ohio.

The failure of Morgan's raid to inspire an uprising in Indiana is good evidence that Hoosiers were not disloyal in any large number. That they were, on the contrary, more generously devoted to the Union than the inhabitants of most states in the North is proved by their military record. To the Union cause Indiana contributed 129 infantry regiments, 13 regiments and three companies of cavalry, one heavy artillery regiment, and 26 batteries of light artillery—a total of 196,363 men. Many Indiana women also volunteered, as nurses, and some were at the front. Of the men, 7,243 were killed and 17,785 died of disease in the war. The Nineteenth Indiana (a part of the "Iron Brigade") lost 15.9 per cent of its men killed in action, the Twenty-Seventh Indiana 15.3 per cent. Indiana troops were involved in 308 military engagements beginning with Philippi on June 3, 1861, and ending with Palmetto Ranch, Texas, May 13, 1865, the last battle of the war. Fourteen Indiana regiments were engaged at Shiloh alone, and of the 13,000 casualties in that fight 1,300 were Indiana men. Indiana ranked second after Delaware in the percentage of men of military age who served in the Union army; Delaware's percentage was 74.8 and Indiana's 74.3.

Thirty years is about the limit of man's endurance of peace. Between the Civil War and the Spanish-American War thirty-three years elapsed; but during the last three of those years the newspapers of the United States were fighting gallantly on their front pages and persuading President William McKinley against his will that it was our duty, indeed our religious duty, to lick the Spaniards. Then the *Maine* blew up in Havana harbor, and the President was persuaded, though still against his conscience. If the Mexican War can be called "the Democrats' war" and the Civil War was, in a sense, "the Republicans' war," the Spanish-American War was "everybody's war." By the time we got into it, just about everybody was for it except President McKinley, who might himself have settled our differences with Spain and prevented it if he had acted promptly and firmly enough. For a brief time, all Americans, regardless of party, were inspired by a high idealism; we were going to free the enslaved people of Cuba. Then, of a sudden, the war was over. We had freed Cuba and got Puerto Rico and Guam into the bargain. But we found ourselves then with another war on our hands, with some wild Moros in the Philippines who were not interested in the blessings of American civilization. Many Americans had never heard of the Philippines before, and in spite of the eloquent jingoism of Albert J. Beveridge, even more Americans thought we ought to bring our soldiers home. But nations can be like small boys at times; once they have got themselves into a fight they cannot get out of it, no matter how much they might want to. Indeed the Spanish-American War might be called "a small boys' war." Did not the British ambassador in Washington a few years later indiscreetly say that it was easy to get along with tempestuous Teddy Roosevelt if one always reminded oneself that the President was a six-year-old boy? Teddy and the small boys of America probably enjoyed the Spanish-American War more than anyone else, unless it was Albert J. Beveridge, who got elected to the United States Senate as soon as the war was over.

Mr. Dooley, reviewing Theodore Roosevelt's *The Rough Riders,* wrote: "I haven't time f'r to tell ye the wurruk Tiddy did in armin' an' equippin' himself, how he fed himself, how he steadied himself in battles an' encouraged himself with a few well-chosen worruds whin the sky was darkest . . . But if I was him I'd call th' book 'Alone in Cuba.' "

Mr. Dooley was unfair, of course. There were others in Cuba besides Teddy Roosevelt and his horseless "Rough Riders," and there were a great many ardent young Americans who wanted to go to Cuba but never got there. In Indiana, when Governor James A. Mount called for members of the National Guard to volunteer at the Indianapolis fairgrounds, more men turned up than could be accepted under the state's quota. One Indiana battery and one company reached Cuba as the war ended. Two Indiana regiments were later sent to the island for police and sanitation duty. One of the Hoosiers in Cuba was William E. English, aged forty-eight when he was wounded at Santiago while serving without pay as an aide-de-camp to dashing sixty-two-year-old ex-Confederate General Joe Wheeler. English, a former Hoosier congressman, was the son of William H. English, once a candidate for vice president. When he returned from the war, he became president of the board of park commissioners of Indianapolis and national commander of the United Spanish War Veterans.

Were these men, too old for war, playing a backyard game of good guys and bad guys? Perhaps. But they played with live ammunition and real typhoid fever, which proved deadlier than Spanish bullets. Although only 289 Americans were killed in the whole conflict (about half the number that Indiana alone lost in the Mexican War, only one twenty-fifth of the Hoosiers killed in the Civil War, fewer than the traffic fatalities of a single modern holiday weekend in the United States), thirteen times the number killed died of disease, a far greater proportion than that of the costly Civil War. Not a war at all, then? A self-inflicted pestilence? But any soldier, sailor, or civilian killed in Cuba or the Philippines, whether by fever or by enemy fire, was just as dead as the 15.9 per cent of the glorious but grim Nineteenth Indiana of the "Iron Brigade" thirty-three years earlier. A war is a war is a war.

What happened in Indiana in the next two wars was not much different from all that happened in the other states of the Union, except that before the country entered World War I there was probably more pro-German sentiment in Indiana than there was in most states. This sentiment was the result of the large German–American population in Indiana, although many of Irish descent were pro-German too, at first, if only because they were anti-English. But as long as the United States remained neutral, being pro-German was not being unpatriotic, in spite of the accusations bandied about by those who favored the Allies in the war. The German–American vote in large part accounted for Woodrow Wilson's failure to carry the state when he ran for reelection. Wilson defeated Taft by 130,000 votes and Roosevelt by 120,000 in Indiana in 1912, but he lost to Hughes by 7,000 in 1916. After the United States finally entered the war, there was little manifestation of disloyalty in the state.

To those on the home front, World War I meant anxiety about relatives in training camps and in France and the knitting of socks and sweaters for the Doughboys; "service flags" in the windows of homes, with a blue star for each man of the household in uniform and gold stars for those who had given their lives; war-savings stamps and Liberty bond drives and a final Victory bond drive; kids wearing spiked German helmets picked up on the battlefields and sent home by relatives; "wheatless Mondays" and "meatless Tuesdays"; "Hooverizing"; daylight-saving; the closing of some factories not engaged in war industries and pressure on farmers to produce more food; restricted use of grain in distilled and malt liquors, then Prohibition and "near beer"; and finally the joyous frenzy of not one, but two Armistice Days, the false and the real.

Indiana had a Democrat for governor—Samuel M. Ralston—during the first three years of World War I, and a Republican—James P. Goodrich—during the year and a half that the nation took part in the conflict. Party differences, however, did not divide the state nor affect the war effort. It was "a war to end wars," and everyone subscribed to that slogan. One of the first three American soldiers killed in action was an Indianan, James Bethel Gresham of Evansville; after the war was over, Evansville built a memorial home for his mother at the edge of one of its parks. Altogether, 3,354 Indiana men and 15 Indiana women (nurses) lost their lives in World War I.

By the time the Japanese bombed Pearl Harbor on December 7, 1941, Indiana had lost its first enthusiasm for Franklin Delano Roosevelt, who carried the state in 1932 and 1936. In 1940, the state gave its electoral votes by a narrow margin to a native son, Wendell L. Willkie, and in 1944 it overwhelmingly supported Thomas E. Dewey. A Democrat sat in the governor's chair throughout the war, however—Henry F. Schricker—although the Republicans controlled both houses of the General Assembly. Indiana's senators during the war were Raymond E. Willis, Republican; Samuel D. Jackson, Democrat; William E. Jenner, Republican; and Homer E. Capehart, Republican. But again the war effort was not seriously affected by politics in Indiana. There were sharp criticisms of the Federal administration, but this war, everyone knew, was a struggle for survival.

In fact, World War II, unlike the preceding wars, was very much the same for Indiana as it was for all the other states. There was little that set Indiana's role apart from the role played by the rest of the nation; in World War II, all Americans were in the same boat. As was the case elsewhere, food, clothing, gasoline, tires, and other goods were rationed. Some articles became unobtainable. Prices were fixed, and in most counties rents, too. Farmers were placed under strict control and supervision. For a while, at the beginning, civilian defense seemed almost as important as the strategy in the Pacific, in Africa, and in Europe. While LST's and LCI's grimly plied their way down the Ohio River, en route from shipyards to the Gulf and to the sea, men in uniform were everywhere. Military installations, too, in the state became ubiquitous—Camp Atterbury in Bartholomew, Johnson, and Brown counties, Crane Naval Ammunition Depot in Martin, Daviess, and Greene, the Bunker Hill Naval Air Station south of Peru, the Charlestown Ordnance Plant, and the Jeffersonville Proving Ground, to name only a few. All in all, during World War II, Indiana received over seven billion dollars worth of war contracts, about 340,000 Indiana men and women were in uniform, and more than 10,000 lost their lives.

Chapter Eight

☆

O Pioneers!

IN THE autumn of 1816, Thomas Lincoln came to Indiana from Kentucky to look for land. He crossed the river at what is now Troy, Indiana, and made his way up Anderson's Creek about as far as the present village of Huffman to Francis Posey's farm before he set off through the woods on his quest. A few months before, at Corydon, about forty miles east of Posey's farm as the crow flies, Jonathan Jennings and others had drawn up the state's first constitution. Seventy miles to the west, George Rapp's Germans had been industriously building Harmonie on the Wabash for more than two years. About the same distance in a direct line to the northwest was Vincennes, where George Rogers Clark had defeated the British forty years earlier and where William Henry Harrison had recently relinquished his authority of a dozen years as governor of Indiana Territory.

Tom Lincoln was more or less typical of the 64,000 people who already inhabited Indiana in 1816. At least, he resembled the majority of them, the ones who cleared the forests and cultivated small farms. He was of Southern origin, of good yeoman stock, but uneducated and poor. Had he been an ambitious man, it might be believed that he came to Indiana to better his condition in life, which had been deplorable in Kentucky, but his stolid and yet restless nature makes it seem more than likely that he was impelled to make the move only by quiet desperation and an itching foot. Although he may have been vaguely aware that it was futile for him to compete any longer in a Southern society where a man without money or talents was hardly better off than a Negro slave, it cannot be idealistically argued that he disliked slavery, for in Hardin County, Kentucky, he had been a member of the Patrollers, whose duty was to capture and whip any slaves found "strolling" without permits. Aged thirty-eight in 1816, Tom Lincoln was a hunter by preference, a carpenter by trade, and a farmer by necessity.

Having lost all his tools and some of his whiskey overboard from his flatboat on the Salt River in Kentucky, Lincoln left the Posey farm equipped with only a gun, an ax, and a hunting knife and plunged afoot into the deep gloom of the Indiana forest in a region where there lived at that time but one white man for every four square miles. Hacking his way through the undergrowth of sumac, dogwood, and grapevines, which were matted so thick that the ax or the knife slipping from his hands might easily have been lost in them, he followed his instinct for direction instead of a compass, which he lacked, or the fall of shadows, which did not exist in a forest where all was shadow, or the guidance of stars, which were hard to distinguish through the interlacing branches of one-hundred-foot sycamore, oak, hackberry, poplar, sweet gum, and hickory. When at last he found a place that suited his fancy, a mile from Little Pigeon Creek and some sixteen miles north of the settlement of Rockport on the Ohio, he marked out a claim with blazes and brush heaps and returned to Kentucky for his wife, Nancy, and his two children, nine-year-old Sally and seven-year-old Abe.

In late November, 1816, this family of four rode on two horses from their Knob Creek farm in Kentucky to the Ohio River. They were ferried across the river and taken up Anderson's Creek to Posey's farm, where they borrowed a sled and two oxen. From Posey's farm they then "packed through" the woods with all their worldly possessions, making a path for the oxen and sled by chopping away underbrush, felling small trees, and turning aside when their way was blocked by trees too big for them to cut down. Of these there were many. Tom Lincoln paused once in the journey to measure one of them, an oak. Four feet above the ground its trunk was twenty-four feet in circumference.

When Tom Lincoln marked off his claim in the Indiana woods, he made one serious mistake; he never once thought of water. A mile and a half from the spot where he built his first half-faced camp there was a spring, and a slightly shorter distance away, though less accessible, there was Little Pigeon Creek; but that first winter in Indiana and for the next thirteen years thereafter, his family's only source of supply for drinking and washing was melted snow, rainwater in puddles and barrels, and seepage in holes dug for that purpose. Otherwise, one of the Lincolns had to walk two or three miles, round trip, to the spring or the creek with a bucket. Tom Lincoln was never able to dig a successful well on the place, and he had no faith in the Yankees who came by from time to time with forked hazel wands and offered to find water for five dollars. Indeed, in his fourteen years in Indiana, Tom Lincoln seldom had five dollars to spare, and the currency in circulation at that time—"shinplasters," or notes on local Indiana banks, and "cut money," wedges or "bits" cut from silver, eight to a dollar— was usually not worth its face value. Lincoln waited a whole year before he journeyed through the woods to Vincennes and entered his claim at the land office, paying the preliminary installment of sixteen dollars for one hundred and sixty acres. By the time he left Indiana he had paid for only half the land he entered.

The half-faced camp in which the Lincoln family spent their first winter was only fourteen feet wide and open on one side, with a roof of poles, slabs, and leaves sloping down to a back wall that was a single log lying on the ground. No one could stand upright at the back, not even seven-year-old Abe. The floor was the earth strewn with leaves, and the beds were heaps of brush covered with skins and possibly a blanket or two brought from Kentucky. Day and night a fire burned at the open front, not only for warmth and cooking but also to frighten off the wolves and panthers that howled and wailed round the camp all the time. When the wind was wrong, the structure filled with smoke; when it was right, the heat was greater outside the camp than it was within. The family's food that winter consisted almost entirely of game, which was plentiful in the thickets only a few yards from the camp: turkeys, deer, squirrels, and rabbits. They had no vegetables and they soon ran out of meal. No one could bathe, of course, until spring came and the sun warmed the waters of Little Pigeon Creek sufficiently for venturing in.

In the spring and summer of 1817, Lincoln cleared a few acres and built a cabin about forty rods from the half-faced camp. The clearing was accomplished by girdling the largest trees and letting them die and felling others and setting fire to them where they lay. After the great butts had smoldered into charred pieces small enough to be broken into chunks and snaked away with an ox and chain, Nancy and her children planted corn and pumpkins between the stumps and trunks wherever they could grub out roots and sprouts with an ax and hoe. All that spring their faces were black with soot and their eyes smarted until the smoldering logs were removed. The cabin Tom built was the largest the Lincolns had ever lived in, eighteen feet wide and twenty feet long, with a loft beneath the roof, reached by pegs driven into the walls. The bark was left on the round logs, and the roof was made of poles and slabs. There were no windows, and a bearskin draped across the entrance served as a door. The "cats-and-clay" chimney, made of twigs and clay, frequently caught fire and crumbled in dirt and ashes down upon the hearth. Life was lonely as well as arduous at first, but soon after the Lincolns moved into the cabin, Nancy Hanks Lincoln's aunt and uncle, Thomas and Betsy Sparrow, came up from Kentucky with Abe's cousin, Dennis Hanks, and occupied what Dennis, then aged eighteen, would describe later as "that Darne little half face camp."

So the Lincolns lived the second winter in Indiana, their windowless cabin illuminated only by the fire on the hearth unless they burned smoking bear's grease in a metal, dipper-shaped lamp hung from the wall. Again their food was mainly birds and animals, usually fried. They had a little corn that winter, but never enough, and the only mill, a tread-horse affair, was seventeen miles away. Going to the mill was as time-consuming as pounding out the kernels of corn in a hollow hardwood stump with a stone or an axhead. Eventually they would grow enough wheat for the luxury of a cake on Sundays and would acquire hogs and a cow along with a household cat to catch rats and mice; but that second winter they had no domestic animals, and the breast meat of the wild turkey was their substitute for bread when there was no cornmeal for baking into hoecake on a hoe blade at the fireplace.

That was the last winter that Nancy Hanks had to endure in the Indiana woods, for the next October she became ill with a mysterious disease which the settlers called "the milk sick," and after seven days of suffering she died. Previously Nancy Lincoln had taken care of Thomas and Betsy Sparrow and the wife of Peter Brooner, a hunter on Little Pigeon Creek, all of whom had died before the summer's end. When her own turn came, such neighbors as were left from the epidemic, maybe a dozen in all in the settlement of Gentryville nearby, spared their womenfolk to spell Tom and Dennis and Sally and Abe in looking after her. There was no doctor within thirty miles of the cabin, and even if they could have summoned him, he could have done nothing. No one knew how to cure "the milk sick"; no one knew then even what it was, a disease derived from the milk of the forest-ranging cows of those days that had eaten white snakeroot and become sick themselves; in 1818, the pioneers only knew that cows and human beings became ill at the same time.

People lived intimately with death in those days. Neither young nor old were spared its tedious and obscene drama. In an eighteen-by-twenty-foot cabin everyone in the family was in death's presence day and night, eating with it only a few feet from their table and sleeping with it in the same bed; and when at last it was gone, they had to live on in the same shameless intimacy with what it had left behind and perform all the duties that are today performed by someone who is hired to do them professionally.

Tom Lincoln made the box they buried his wife in, and Abe, nine years old, whittled out the pegs that held the whipsawed planks together. They put Nancy's body in the box, fastened the lid with Abe's pegs, and carried it to a knoll near the cabin where they had dug a hole for it in the hard earth with an ax and a wooden shovel. There was no preacher to read the service or say a prayer, and almost a year would pass before one came by the Little Pigeon Creek neighborhood and conducted a funeral ceremony. Nor was any marker put on Nancy Lincoln's grave then, nor in

Tom Lincoln's lifetime or Abraham Lincoln's. The stone that is there now, in the woods of southern Indiana in the Lincoln Boyhood National Memorial, is only a memorial of the approximate place where the Civil War President's mother was buried.

The winter that came thereafter was, if anything, worse than the first and second winters that the Lincolns spent in Indiana, and the following summer and fall were little better. Twelve-year-old Sally did all the cooking, and with no grown woman to supervise the family, the two men, Tom and Dennis, lived unrestrained in their passion for the semi-vagrant life of the hunter while ten-year-old Abe, unwashed and unkempt, simply existed. His one principal chore was to keep the fire on the hearth supplied with wood. It was an important chore, for there were no matches— matches did not come into general use until 1830—and relighting a dead fire with flint and steel was a painstaking and tedious process. But the chore was hardly enough to keep a boy busy all the time. It is little wonder that Tom Lincoln overcame his contempt for "book-larnin' " and let the boy go to school for a short time that year.

In the winter of 1819, Tom Lincoln went back to Kentucky and returned with a second wife, Sarah Bush Johnston, a widow with three small children, two girls and a boy. There were now eight people in the cabin. (At a later date, thirteen men, women, and children would occupy the eighteen-by-twenty-foot home.) But Sarah Lincoln, the new wife, could manage indolent Tom Lincoln and harum-scarum Dennis Hanks in a way that Nancy Hanks Lincoln had failed to do, and within a short time after her arrival, the cabin had a window, covered with greased paper, a puncheon floor, and chairs instead of tree stumps to sit on. From Kentucky Sarah Lincoln had brought a bureau and a bed and cooking utensils and, among other niceties, knives and forks, which Abe and Sally had to learn to use.

Abraham Lincoln's schooling—a few months when he was ten and another month or two when he was fourteen—was no better and no worse than the schooling of most backwoods boys in Indiana in that period. The schools he attended—Andrew Crawford's and then Azel Dorsey's and William Sweeney's—were "blab schools," where the children studied aloud. Abe learned "manners," simple arithmetic, and how to read and write, from Pike's *Arithmetic* and Dilworth's *Spelling Book,* and by studying and memorizing the speeches of famous men he mastered a kind of oratory. Most of his learning, however, he got for himself from books and newspapers borrowed from neighbors, like Josiah Crawford, who lent him Weems's *Life of Washington,* and Judge John Pitcher, a graduate of Yale College who lived in Rockport sixteen miles away. Lincoln also walked to Boonville to listen to the courtroom oratory of John A. Brackenridge, the Warrick County prosecuting attorney.

But periods free for formal schooling and time for reading were rare, because Abe, like other boys, had to work for his father, and when his skill with an ax and a hoe were not needed at home, he hired out to other farmers who could afford to employ labor outside their own families. He cleared fields for planting, daubed cabins, split rails, ploughed and cultivated the land, and for a short period, while in the employ of James Taylor on a farm on the Ohio River, operated a ferry at Anderson's Creek in his spare time, carrying passengers to and from passing steamboats. In April, 1828, in the company of another youth of his age, he took a flatboat laden with produce to New Orleans, returning upriver on a steamboat. In February, 1830, when Abe was twenty-one, the Lincolns left Indiana and moved to Illinois, conveying their belongings in a wagon drawn by four oxen from Gentryville to Vincennes. At Vincennes they crossed the Wabash, and Abraham Lincoln would not set foot on Indiana soil again until 1844, when he came to make campaign speeches for Henry Clay. But Indiana left its mark on him.

Like the Lincolns, most of the early pioneers of Indiana made or grew almost everything they used, for manufactured articles were at a premium in the early days of the state. The goods sold in stores, shipped down the river from Pittsburgh and Cincinnati or up from New Orleans, were costly for people who had to depend chiefly upon barter instead of money. Their cloth of wool and flax they spun in their own homes. In summer, adults as well as children went barefooted most of the time, and in winter, those who could not afford to buy boots and were incapable of making them wore shoepacks and moccasins and leggings. Corn, game, and pork were the principal items of diet; whiskey, made in stills in the woods, was the universal drink, imbibed straight by the men and in diluted toddies by the women. Tobacco was grown, cured, and consumed on the farm. Soap was made with the lye from wood ashes. Such items as knives, axes, chains, guns, gunpowder, pins and needles could not be manufactured at home, but because roads were few and poor and distances were great, trips to village stores and artisans were occasions to be long postponed and prepared for.

The legendary Johnny Appleseed, who signed his name as John Chapman, "by occupation a gatherer and planter of apple seeds," came to the Fort Wayne region in the 1830's. He died near that city in 1845.

In those days, living in towns and villages differed very little from living in the woods, except that stores were more conveniently at hand and neighbors could be quickly called upon in emergencies. In some respects, because townspeople lived closer together, town life was worse than farm life, for there were no sewage systems and no community removal of trash and garbage, and animals in towns ran at large just as they roamed unrestrained in the country. Consequently sanitation was a problem, and the lack of it was a constant threat to comfort as well as health. Cholera, smallpox, and typhoid epidemics were frequent, and there were no hospitals where the sick could be isolated and cared for. Stumps and mudholes obstructed the streets, which were unpaved except occasionally in the centers of towns, where cobblestones and wooden blocks were sometimes used; sidewalks were cowpaths, sometimes boarded but generally not; liquid mud made both street and walk impassable after heavy rains. Yet such rains were often welcomed if only because they washed away collected offal and the carcasses of dead animals. A "gully-washer" was better than a "sod-soaker," but best of all was a "trash-mover."

No public lighting systems illuminated the streets of towns, although sometimes merchants and tavern keepers hung lamps outside their establishments, and no water systems served the inhabitants, except in a few of the more enterprising places such as Brookville, where in 1820 a three-inch pipeline of green sycamore saplings was laid to a spring in the hills nearby. Cisterns, open wells, rain barrels, and town pumps supplied communities with water for washing and drinking; fire departments were no more than neighborhood bucket brigades. Each house had its outdoor privy, but men generally scorned the use of such facilities as effeminate and betook themselves to the alleys and bushes. In summer, townspeople lived with swarms of flies on their food at table and on their faces at night and accepted gnats and mosquitoes as inescapable evils in their houses, window screens not yet being invented.

Like the countryman, the village dweller usually raised his own food, in a kitchen garden, and kept a cow and pigs and a horse. Many supported themselves by farming tracts of land near their villages, unless they happened to be lawyers, bankers, preachers, tradesmen, or craftsmen such as tanners, coopers, cobblers, and blacksmiths; for none of the towns of that era was large enough to support commerce of any significance. Vincennes, for example, had a population of only three thousand when the Lincolns came to Indiana, and New Albany and Madison and Jeffersonville were even smaller. As late as the outbreak of the Civil War, Indiana's largest community, Indianapolis, was inhabited by less than 20,000 people.

But life in Indiana during the years the Lincolns lived in the state, was not all primitive log-cabin dwelling and subsistence living such as theirs. A privileged few with fortunes to start with, with education, with exceptional talents to exploit, or with a native shrewdness at making money, enjoyed a degree of luxury comparable to the best that life could offer in the East or the South. Many of the houses remaining from the first three decades of the nineteenth century bear witness to a grace and ease in the daily routine that people like the Lincolns never dreamed of.

William Henry Harrison, for example, built his "Grouseland" a dozen years before the Lincolns came to Indiana. An imposing, two-storied, brick house of graceful design inside and out, its Federal style of architecture was the mode for the more pretentious homes of the state for the next forty years. Before the end of the 1820's, Corydon, Lawrenceburg, Madison, and other towns could boast of several such buildings, public and private. Corydon took pride not only in its blue-limestone courthouse, which was also the statehouse for a while, but also in the severely classic dwelling of Davis Floyd; Lawrenceburg was ornamented by the presence of Samuel Vance's home, more elaborate than Floyd's, with a Palladian window and a fanlight over the door; Governor James Brown Ray's Palladian window in Brookville, a symbol of luxury, almost cost him an election in 1824; and in Madison, by 1820, the substantial and well-proportioned dwellings of James Allison, Thomas Robinson, and Jeremiah Sullivan had all been built and for some time lived in. People who occupied such houses dined and dressed well, owned libraries, and enjoyed luxuries imported from New Orleans and the East.

In the decade following the Lincolns' departure for Illinois, the construction of fine houses, known as "mansions," flourished all along the Ohio and Wabash rivers and also "inland," in towns farther north and through the center of the state. Among those that still remain to delight the eye and recall the decade of the 1830's are the homes of James McKee and James F. D. Lanier in Madison and Gaines H. Roberts of Newburgh, who was among the first to build paired chimneys at the ends of impressive brick structures; of Jeffersonville's David Grisamore, who added to the practical ornament of paired chimneys the elegance of two-storied Doric columns and iron balconies to decorate his fanlighted twin doorways; of Isaac Elston and Caleb Mills in Crawfordsville, the one using brick, the other a frame construction; of Daniel Stout, who made good use of the native stone, and Andrew Wylie, first president of Indiana University, in Bloomington; and of Oliver H. Smith, near Connersville, whose two-storied, flat-roofed, colonnaded porch is reminiscent of George Washington's Mount Vernon. In the 1840's, the town of Madison was further enriched by the work of Francis Costigan, the architect who designed the second Lanier home and the Charles L. Shrewsbury house. By the end of that decade, there were architectural ornaments everywhere in Indiana—in Brookville, Rob Roy, Centerville, Rising Sun,

Lafayette, Terre Haute, Goshen, Fort Wayne, Attica, Peru, Delphi, Dublin, Cambridge City, and other towns—and many of these fine old homes are still confortably lived in.

Before the building of railroads, rivers were the principal routes of travel and transportation in early Indiana, and flatboats of the kind that Abe Lincoln and Allen Gentry built and navigated from Rockport to New Orleans in 1828 were the most common vessels used for many years. They ranged in size from craft that were hardly more than scows with covered superstructures to the large commercial vessels of a later date that measured as much as one hundred feet in length and twenty feet in width and carried 400,000 pounds of cargo. Most of them, however, were somewhere between ten-by-forty and sixteen-by-sixty feet and were the ventures of individual farmers or small groups of farmers who pooled their labor in construction and navigation as well as their produce for transportation to markets.

The gunwales of these flatboats stood three or four feet above the waterline, and their draught was only a foot or two. Flat-topped cabins ran the length of the boats, rising four or five feet above the gunwales, with doors at each end and windows or portholes cut in the sides. Their passengers and cargoes were thus secure against the weather and, in the earliest days, against attacks by Indians. Kept on their courses in the rivers' currents by stern sweeps, side sweeps or poles, which the crews manned by standing atop the cabins, and by "gougers," or short oars, at the bows, flatboats were not designed for upstream travel and could be moved against the current only with the greatest difficulty. Downstream, however, when the wind and current were right, they could average as much as five or six miles an hour with little effort on the part of their navigators. The practice was to sell these boats for lumber, if possible, when they reached their destinations and for the crewmen to return to their starting points overland or by keelboat or steamboat.

From the beginning, the chief cargo of the flatboat was pork and whiskey. As the land opened up and farms grew larger, they carried also corn, cornmeal, oats, beeswax, live cattle and hogs, chickens, beans, fruits, and lumber. They also brought manufactured goods down the Ohio from the more populated centers of the East. In the first years of the century, some flatboats carried paying passengers, housed in separate cabins for ladies and gentlemen, but this trade fell off after the price of steamboat passage dropped within range of the emigrants' purses, although travelers who were both timorous and unhurried continued to patronize flatboats for a while thereafter because of the steamboat's propensity for exploding or catching fire. As time passed and population along the riverbanks increased, flatboats began to serve as floating stores, drifting from Pittsburgh or Cincinnati down the Ohio and stopping at villages and farms enroute. Even after the railroads were built and roads were improved, the flatboat-store remained for a while the remote settler's best contact with the outside world of little luxuries. As late as the decade after the Civil War, people along the Ohio River watched every spring for the "glass boat" from Pittsburgh or others of its kind to come round the bend, cheering the boatman-merchant as he blew his horn in greeting. Isolated settlers stood on shore and shouted, "Hello, the boat!" and the boatman would turn toward the bank and tie up for them to look over the goods he carried.

For upstream travel and transportation the pioneer depended upon the keelboat until the steamboat took its place. Keelboats were generally manned by professional crews, men whose lives were lived on the rivers, and they were a rough, tough, and merry lot, hard drinkers, ready fighters, and given to boisterous boasting and profanity. Their boats, as the name suggests, had keels and pointed prows, and they were propelled usually by the boatmen walking the length of the boat from stem to stern with long poles stabbed into the river's bottom. When water was too deep or current too swift for this method of progressing upstream, bushwhacking was resorted to, which meant pulling the boat along the water's edge by the branches of overhanging trees and bushes, or the boat was moved by cordelling, which was the process of tying a long rope to the top of the mast and dragging the vessel along from the shore if the shoreline was clear enough of underbrush, or looping the rope round a tree upstream and kedging the boat forward by a hand-over-hand operation. Keelboats were of necessity smaller than flatboats. Their speed against the current was seldom more than five miles a day.

The first steamboat appeared on the Ohio River in 1811, and after the War of 1812 such vessels increased in numbers so that by the 1820's keelboats became outmoded on the larger rivers. The first steamboat in the West was the *New Orleans,* which made a run from Cincinnati to Louisville and back in October, 1811, and then, with the winter freshets of 1811–12, was able to run the Falls at Louisville and steam all the way down to New Orleans. It never attempted the return journey. Within the next three years, the *Comet,* the *Vesuvius,* and the *Enterprise* were on the river, the last-named being one of Captain Henry M. Shreve's boats in competition with the Roosevelt endeavor in steam navigation that had originated in the East. In 1815, the *Enterprise* made the trip from Pittsburgh to Cincinnati in four days and could run from Cincinnati down to Louisville, unload and reload, and return within six days. A year later, the *Indiana Republican* of Madison reported that a steamboat named the *Harriet* passed the Madison waterfront "at the rate of twelve miles an hour!" These later boats, unlike the *New Orleans,* which carried the engine in the hold, were of shallow draft, sometimes less than three feet, with the engine on the deck. When, later, each sidewheel had a separate engine and when paddles were set back to catch the second swell and floats slanted to dip with less resistance into the water, both speed and maneuverability were increased. Soon low-pressure boats were designed to attract the fearful away from their continued patronage of keelboats, and at last the steamboat ruled the rivers unchallenged. Many steamboats, including the famous *Robert E. Lee,* were built at New Albany and Jeffersonville and in other Indiana towns along the Ohio River.

Steamboats plied the smaller rivers into Indiana too, up the Wabash and the White especially, and in a short while thereafter they were appearing on the Great Lakes. In 1823, the *Florence* was the first steamboat to reach Vincennes, but it paddled past that town and went all the way to Terre Haute. After the *Florence* came the *Ploughboy,* and by 1827 the first steamboat was at Lafayette. In 1829, the *Victory* reached Spencer on the White

River, and two years later the *General Hanna* made it to Indianapolis. But she did not make it back to the Wabash for the whole population of Indianapolis, somewhat less than a thousand people, were on shore to greet her, and the welcoming ceremony took so long that she was caught by low water on her return trip and went aground. The Hoosier capital never became a successful riverport.

Meanwhile, in the northern part of the state, steamboats began to probe along the rivers, especially the St. Joseph, but the waterways there were smaller than those of the south and when people of that region finally caught "steam fever," they turned their attention to Lake Michigan, "the Mediterranean of North America." Steam vessels plied Lake Erie first, but by 1836 forty-nine of the 456 boat arrivals at Chicago were steam-propelled. In the next decade, Michigan City, Indiana, became a greater lake port than Chicago and dreamed for a while of becoming the major junction of lake and overland traffic in the West, for the town stood in an ideal location, at the southern bend of the lake and at the head of the Michigan Road, which ran the full length of Indiana down to Madison on the Ohio River. But Chicago soon outdistanced the Indiana town when the railroads changed the transportation pattern of the lake area. One of the sights of Michigan City today is its old lighthouse, built in 1856.

A major obstacle to river traffic for a long time was the Falls of the Ohio at Louisville, a drop of twenty-three feet in three miles. Large vessels could not pass the Falls at all, and small vessels could run them only in high water. Even for the smallest boats and under the most favorable conditions upstream navigation of the Falls was all but impossible. Consequently keelboats and flatboats and, later, steamboats usually plied between Pittsburgh or Cincinnati and Louisville while another fleet connected Louisville with downriver ports. Cargo and passengers were transferred at Shippingport. These exchanges from boat to boat at Shippingport were profitable for teamsters but detrimental to river traffic in general. As early as 1805, the territorial legislature of Indiana authorized a charter for an Indiana Canal Company, but the United States Government refused to allow a land grant and the project failed.

Five years later the U. S. Government and the commonwealth of Kentucky became interested in building a canal at the Falls, but this time Kentucky neglected to act and again nothing happened. In 1817, the Indiana General Assembly in the first year of its existence authorized capital stock of a million dollars for the Ohio Canal Company, and a two-and-a-half-mile ditch was dug before funds and enthusiasm for the project were exhausted. In 1825, private promoters in Louisville took up the matter, as the Louisville and Portland Canal Company, and finally, in December, 1829, a canal on the Kentucky side opened the way to through traffic on the river. In the first year, 406 steamboats and 421 keelboats and flatboats passed through the canal and paid over $12,000 in tolls.

By this time, within the state of Indiana and in collaboration with both Illinois and Ohio, the clearing of passageway for boats on the rivers had become an important concern. In 1820, Indiana declared most of its navigable rivers free public highways and began fining millers who failed to provide adequate locks at their dams. In some instances, in smaller streams, milldams marked the end of free navigation, as in the case of the Patoka River, which was declared a public thoroughfare only from its mouth to Mosley's mill. Man-made obstacles in the rivers, however, were not the only problem that confronted the legislators; sandbars, snags, sawyers, planters, and towheads had to be cleared. On the Ohio the Federal government assisted in the removal and correction of such obstacles, but within the state, dwellers in the river valleys had to be paid out of state funds for labor at such tasks, in the same way that citizens were paid for work on the roads.

In 1818, the U.S. Engineers reported that a canal could be built at the portage at Fort Wayne between the headwaters of the Wabash and Maumee rivers, thus connecting Lake Erie with the Ohio. In 1824, the U.S. Engineers began at Brookville a survey for a canal along the course of the Whitewater River that would link the Ohio with the National Road when finally that highway reached Cambridge City, Indiana. Thereafter, these two canals were some thirty-odd years a-building, the only ones completed of the many that were conceived for the state in a mammoth project known as "the system." The events that intervened in those three decades of planning, financing, and construction compose a paradoxical medley of testimony to man's vision and his shortsightedness, his determination and his foolhardiness, his enterprise and his helplessness before the whims of circumstance, his honorable compulsion to keep his promises and his shameless corruptibility. No historian who has become entangled in the intricacies of facts and figures related to the building of Indiana's canals has ever emerged from his studies with either a denunciation or an exoneration of Indiana and Indianans that is wholly convincing. Today, surviving from the original dream are a few sentimentally cherished remnants and reminders of the system, which ornament a residential section of Indianapolis, lend an additional charm to the beautiful countryside west of Fort Wayne, around Metamora, Laurel, Brookville, and elsewhere in the state, turn an occasional millwheel, and give a name to at least one street, in Evansville.

The principal reason for transferring the seat of government from Corydon to Indianapolis was that Corydon was inaccessible to settlers who were moving into the north and central areas of the state. Legislators and people who had to do business with the government came to Corydon from the Wabash country by traveling on horseback over a trail from Vincennes to New Albany that led through Washington, Paoli, and Fredericksburg; from the hills along the lower Ohio they traveled up the Ohio to New Albany and then overland to the capital; from the Whitewater Valley they came down the Ohio to New Albany and then overland. But as the central and northern counties developed, travel to and from those new regions was not eased, and more and more legislators were put to inconvenience.

Establishing Indianapolis as the new capital did not immediately solve the problem. For a while the new seat of government was as inaccessible as the old. In 1825 only two stage lines led to the town, one from Centerville and one from Madison. The only other main overland routes in the state were the Vincennes–New Albany trail, already mentioned, and another from New Albany by way of Salem, Bedford, and Bloomington to Lafayette. Neither of these directly served the new capital. All roads were bad, fre-

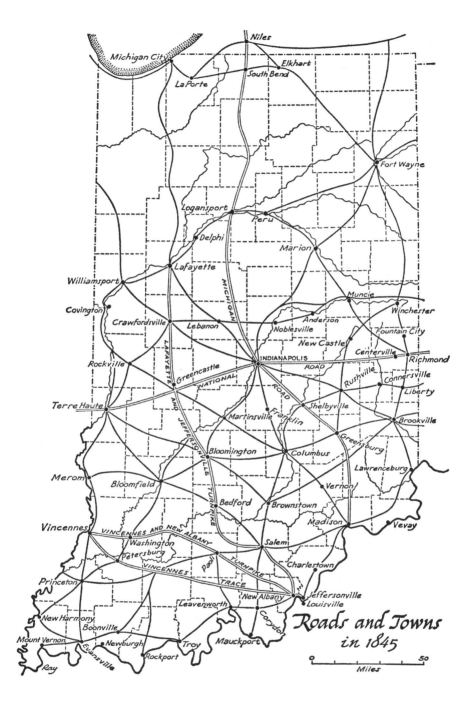

Roads and Towns in 1845

quently impassable; there were no railroads and no canals; and the rivers and creeks, in spite of the law of 1820 that made them free public highways, were seldom navigable. The consequence was a universal clamor for internal improvements. Not only were residents of the south eager for more traversable routes to the north that would facilitate migration and keep them in touch with their state government, those who had already moved into the north demanded easier access to the Ohio River for shipment of their produce. A bushel of corn worth less than twenty cents at Indianapolis would bring fifty cents if it could be transported to the river. At the same time, salt hauled by ox team from Michigan City to the center of the state cost the farmer twelve dollars, and two weeks were required for its transportation.

The enabling act by which Congress admitted Indiana to the Union allowed three per cent of the funds from the sale of public lands to be used for roads and canals within the boundaries of the state. On March 2, 1827, Congress granted the state additional assistance by offering a parcel of land one half of five sections wide along the course of a proposed canal between the Wabash and the Maumee, and on January 5, 1828, the state accepted this Federal gift and thus committed itself to the business of canal building. Construction of the canal at Fort Wayne was delayed, however, for another four years, and this and other canal projects were thereafter obstructed for a while in spite of the general enthusiasm for internal improvements. Some of the state's leaders, like Governor Ray, foresaw the importance of railroads in the state's future and opposed the whole idea of a canal system, while those who favored such waterways over railroads were divided by regional and selfish interests. The Whitewater Canal people, for instance, saw no profit for themselves in supporting a Wabash and Erie Canal; the Wabash and Erie people demanded that their project have precedence over the Whitewater project; and citizens who had no access to either route were reluctant to provide tax money for a program that would be of no apparent benefit to them. It soon became evident that nothing could be accomplished until a compromise was arrived at, and the compromise that eventually developed was inevitably a gigantic, all-inclusive affair. On January 27, 1836,

Governor Noah Noble signed a bill appropriately named the Mammoth Internal Improvement Bill and created what was later called simply "the system."

A canal board of three men was already functioning at that time, and the Mammoth Internal Improvement Bill authorized the governor to add six members to the group. The board was then "to adopt such measures as may be necessary to commence, construct and complete, within a reasonable time" eight major public works. These eight projects were:

1. The Whitewater Canal, to commence at the point near Cambridge City where the National Road crossed the West Fork of the Whitewater River and to follow the West Fork and then the river itself southward until it joined the Miami River and subsequently the Ohio. This canal was to be connected with a Central Canal in either Madison or Delaware County "by a canal, if practicable, if not by a Rail Road." For this project the legislature appropriated $1,400,000.

2. The Central Canal, connecting with the Wabash and Erie at a suitable place between Fort Wayne and Logansport so that it served Muncie and Indianapolis and joined the West Fork of the White River and thereafter the White itself and passing through Pike, Gibson, Warrick, and Vanderburgh counties until it joined the Ohio at Evansville. For this project $3,500,000 was appropriated.

3. An extension of the Wabash and Erie Canal, already begun, to follow the Wabash from the mouth of the Tippecanoe as far as Terre Haute and from there to cut southeastward to join the Central Canal. For this extension the legislature appropriated $1,300,-000.

4. A railroad from Madison to Lafayette through Columbus, Indianapolis, and Crawfordsville. Another $1,300,000 was allowed for this purpose.

5. A macadamized turnpike connecting New Albany and Vincennes via Greenville, Fredericksburg, Paoli, and Washington. For this road the legislature allowed $1,150,000.

6. A resurvey of the Jeffersonville–New Albany road to Crawfordsville by way of Salem, Bedford, Bloomington, and Green-

castle for the purpose of building either a railroad or a macadamized road. Here another $1,300,000 could be used.

7. Removal of obstructions in the Wabash River from its mouth to Vincennes. Appropriation: $50,000.

8. A survey and estimates for a canal or railroad connecting the Wabash and Erie near Fort Wayne with Lake Michigan near Michigan City and passing through LaPorte and Goshen. For this project "the faith of the state" was "irrevocably pledged."

The appropriations totaled $10,000,000. To cover them the bill authorized the commissioners of the system to borrow that amount for a period of twenty-five years at interest not to exceed five per cent. To pay this interest the state "pledged and appropriated the Canals, Rail, and Turnpike Roads, with the portions of ground thereunto appertaining and privileges thereby created, and the rents and profits of the water power thereof, together with the net proceeds of tolls collected thereon; the sufficiency of which, for the purposes aforesaid, the State of Indiana doth hereby guarantee."

The designers of the Mammoth Internal Improvement Bill demonstrated a clear and comprehensive view of the future needs of the state. But the bill was overambitious: A new society of less than half a million people with annual revenues averaging less than $75,000 had no business assuming a debt of $10,000,000. It was unrealistic: By undertaking so many projects in one measure, the state had to compete against itself in the bidding for labor and contracts and thus sent its costs upward beyond all reason, and to appease the impatient it had to commence segmented approaches to all its projects at once instead of carrying one project through to completion before it undertook another. The bill failed to provide for proper supervision of the financing of "the system": Agents in the East accepted unfair bids, sold bonds on credit in violation of the law, and neglected to keep systematic accounts and give detailed reports of their operations. Finally, the bill was ill-timed: The very next year after it became law there was a nation-wide financial panic.

By 1839, the state was bankrupt, and the General Assembly that was in session when the blow fell was composed of men whose limited experience in finance gave them no comprehension of the complex problem that confronted them. They did nothing, perhaps wisely. But of their incompetence the *Indianapolis Journal* wrote: "This body . . . has at last adjourned, and may heaven for all time save us from such another." There was general indignation throughout the state and the nation and in Europe as well, for many of the bonds had been sold abroad. In defense of their state's honor Hoosier politicians spoke and wrote high-sounding words, but none of them came up with a workable proposal for extricating "the system" from its predicament. United States Senator Edward A. Hannegan, for example, when he heard that the state's bonds were selling in New York for seventeen cents on the dollar, rejected the idea of repudiating the debt with the remark that he would "rather part with my last cent and divide my last crumb of bread than sully the fame and honor of Indiana or sanction a principle so abhorrent to all ideas of justice or so dishonorable when practiced by men or nations." A few years after this flourish of oratory Senator Hannegan left Indiana and made his home in St. Louis. "I can not believe that Indiana will openly repudiate her debts," Governor Bigger protested. But Governor Bigger spoke these confident words when he was turning over the responsibilities of his office—and responsibility for the state's financial problem—to a successor who belonged to the opposing political party. The General Assembly itself solemnly affirmed that "when any state in this Union shall refuse to recognize her great seal as the sufficient evidence of her obligation, she will have forfeited her station in the sisterhood of States, and will no longer be worthy of their confidence and respect." But in the end the General Assembly did to a large extent the very thing that it deplored doing.

Indiana apparently had no choice when it finally deeded half of its liability over to its creditors and required the remaining bondholders to exchange their bonds for stocks on which dividends might or might not be paid, declaring that "the State will make no provision whatever hereafter, to pay either principal or interest on any internal improvement bond or bonds, until the holder or holders thereof shall have first surrendered said bonds to the agent of the State, and shall have received in lieu thereof, certificates of stock as provided in the first section of this act; any thing in this act to the contrary notwithstanding." This happened in 1847.

What is remarkable—and admirable—about the ultimate solution of the problem is that the state struggled with its conscience for more than ten years before it finally acknowledged defeat and devised a compromise that was just short of repudiation. Perhaps even more remarkable—and equally admirable—is that Indianans learned a lesson from the experience, for men and societies are not often so wise. The second constitution of Indiana, drawn up three years later, denied the General Assembly the power to incur "any debt, except to meet casual deficits in the revenue, to pay the interest on the present state debt, or to repel invasion, or suppress insurrection." It also prohibited the state's being a stockholder in any corporation, association, or bank, although the state banks had preserved an almost miraculous stability throughout the debacle.

What is perhaps most remarkable of all that happened in those trying years is that two of the eight commitments of the mammoth "system" of 1836 were fulfilled. In the end, private enterprise took over and carried the Wabash and Erie Canal and the Whitewater Canal through to completion, in spite of financial chaos, floods, droughts, cave-ins, leakages caused by infestations of muskrats, miscalculations that resulted in early sections of the canals wearing out before final sections were in operation, an outbreak of cholera in one of the labor camps from which the Irish diggers fled in panic and spread the disease throughout the state, and acts of vandalism by citizens who believed the canals were a source of malaria or had other objections to them.

The Whitewater Canal finally connected Lawrenceburg with Cambridge City in 1846 and was later extended to Hagerstown, running a total distance of 76 miles. The Wabash and Erie Canal joined Evansville to Lake Erie by water route in 1853, making its 468-mile course the longest of all the canals in the United States. The first canalboat from Toledo, Ohio, the *Pennsylvania*, reached the Ohio River city in September of 1853. But by 1865 the Whitewater Valley Railroad had built a line parallel to the Whitewater and ended that canal's usefulness, except for waterpower; and at Evansville an English locomotive, shipped up from New Orleans, had already been unloaded at the wharf by the time the *Pennsyl-*

vania came down the Wabash and Erie Canal from Toledo, and six weeks after the *Pennsylvania*'s arrival rail connections between Evansville and Terre Haute were completed. By 1870 both canals were abandoned and a complex of railroads had replaced most of "the system."

This was not yet true, however, on a hot Sunday in June, 1851, when a wagon drawn by two horses pulled off the National Road and into the yard of the Prairie House at the edge of Terre Haute, a half hour before midday, and the driver, an Englishman named Richard Beste, asked the innkeeper if he had accommodations for himself, his wife, and their nine children. Mr. Beste intended to spend only one night in Terre Haute. He had been told that the climate of the Wabash Valley was unhealthful. But he and his family were destined to remain at the Prairie House several months, for the oldest daughter, who was ill, was unable to leave her bed the next morning. When the proprietor of the Prairie House offered the Bestes a suite on the first floor of an ell at the rear of his establishment, Mr. Beste was not altogether pleased with the rooms but he took them. It is fortunate for students of Indiana's past that he did, for he was a keen observer of his surroundings and a proficient diarist and what he wrote during the enforced period of leisure that followed affords a vivid firsthand view of the traveler's lot in that interim period in transportation in the state.

When the Bestes stopped at Terre Haute, Mr. Beste himself was feverish and badly in need of rest. He had spent the three previous days driving his wagon through the heavy traffic of westward-pushing pioneers on the plank and corduroy road from Indianapolis, a distance of seventy miles. Plank roads, for which there was a rage in Indiana at this time, with Robert Dale Owen as their principal advocate, were slippery when wet and yet a pleasure to travel on when they were new. The elastic boards rose and sank under a wagon like the springs of a fine carriage. But already in 1851 the planking of the National Road was wearing out west of Indianapolis and it was full of holes and dangerous traps. Where the planks had been replaced by corduroy—the unhewn trunks of trees laid side by side and held together by slips nailed across the ends—the sensation of a wagon driver was something like the modern sensation of driving with a flat tire. Along the way, the Bestes had suffered sleepless nights, too, and lean rations, for they had not yet learned that in Indiana the signboard of an inn was no guarantee that a house was a genuine inn. Many Hoosier farmers, especially along the busier turnpikes, put up inn signs to protect themselves from their own hospitable natures. They did not know how to turn away strangers who were hungry and in need of beds, but times had changed since pioneer days and they could no longer afford to play the Good Samaritan to everyone who knocked at their doors.

Conditions at the Prairie House, one of two hotels in Terre Haute at that time, were not much better than those of the private houses in which the Bestes had stayed. At least, so Mr. Beste thought at night. He wrote:

> You go into your bedroom and find it swarming with bats, locusts, beetles, mosquitoes, etc. You send as many of these out as you can; and shutting the window, you undress and throw yourself on your bed, in the vain hope that you will soon be asleep. Before many minutes you feel as if you were in a well-heated oven. You jump off the bed, take off the bottom sheet, and then lie down on the bare mattress; from the beginning, the pillow has been discarded. In a few minutes, the heat obliges you to change from place to place on the mattress at least twenty times; and, at last, you throw it on the ground after the pillow, and lie upon the straw paliasse. But the straw paliasse is not much cooler than the wool or hair mattress; and, as a last resource, you open the window, quite convinced that you would rather be eaten alive by insects than suffocated. You open the window, and in rush all your old enemies again, thicker than ever. You resign yourself to the mosquitoes, and listen to them,—buz! buz! buz! But presently a new enemy appears in the shape of an enormous stag beetle, and flies round and round the room; but being too heavy to remain long on the wing, every two or three minutes it tumbles down. . . .

Nevertheless, the size and prosperity of the Prairie House impressed Mr. Beste. There were many rooms, and they were all occupied. Some of the roomers were transients like the Bestes, but many of them were local people who had taken up permanent residence in the Prairie House because of the servant problem.

Mr. Beste discovered that Indiana women, having just emerged from the pioneer era, were reluctant to do their own housework for fear they would not be recognized as ladies. Indeed, Mr. Beste found them much too "ladylike" for his taste; they spent their days in idle gossip, constantly rocking in the hotel's rocking chairs. The American rocking chair fascinated Mr. Beste's daughters, and by the time they left Terre Haute they were addicts of the rocker themselves. Mr. Beste was only pleased that they did not also adopt the Hoosier women's habit of chewing burgundy pitch. As for his sons, they were soon affected by the Western male's custom of sprawling when they sat down, throwing their legs over the arms and even the backs of chairs; and Mr. Beste himself confessed a secret pleasure in putting his feet on a desk or table, Indiana style. The universal Western practice of spitting tobacco juice, however, offended him, as it offended so many travelers from the East and from Europe in those days, especially after they had been the victims of careless aim.

Housewives in Terre Haute may have suffered for want of domestics in 1851, but the hotel knew no servant problem. Mr. Beste thought the place was overrun with servants. The first to appear each day came through the passages at six, ringing a handbell to awaken the guests. At six-thirty, he came around again, announcing breakfast. But the one who annoyed the Englishman most was the waiter whom the proprietor sent around to the rooms twice a week. Without knocking, this servant poked his head in at the door unexpectedly and asked if any spoons had been carried away from the dining room.

But Richard Beste's diary records no complaint about the fare at the Prairie House. At breakfast,

> there were ranged down the table and cut into slices hot and cold bread of different sorts, including cornbread (a little of which was rather nice with plenty of molasses and butter), little seed cakes, pancakes, and fritters, milk, butter buried in large lumps of ice, molasses, preserves, and blackberry syrup in large soup toureens. Besides these things, there were hot beefsteaks, roast and boiled chickens, and various sorts of cold meat. To drink we had tea, coffee, and, occasionally, chocolate, with hot, cold, and iced milk, and white and brown sugar.

At dinner, there was roast beef always, and, in general, the following dishes:—chicken pie, veal pie, beefsteaks, roast veal, lamb, veal and mutton cutlets, boiled ham, pigeons, roast veal or roast pork. As vegetables, we had generally elderly peas and beans, hominy (a sort of dry bean resembling haricots), and potatoes. Once, we had sweet potatoes, which were red and tasted like common potatoes diseased; and another time we had a vegetable called squash; and always boiled ears of green Indian corn. Several times, we had soup made of land turtles, which was good. Our sweets were generally custard pie (there are no tarts in the United States, everything there is "pie"), or sometimes cherry pie, squash pie, apple pie, and occasionally blackberry pie. Sometimes, too, we had stewed pears or roast apples. Then followed cheese and dessert; at which, latterly, there were large bowls of iced cream and watermelons, which they called "cholera bomb shells"; and, in spite of their terrific name, they were eaten with avidity. Nuts and almonds were, also, always on the table.

For this fare, plus lodging, the charge per person was five dollars a week.

Finally, Richard Beste left his horses and wagon with a grandson of William Henry Harrison to sell, if he could, and started back to the East with his family on the Wabash and Erie Canal. The boat on which they traveled was of shallow draught, like a steamboat, and all baggage was stowed on the roof of the deckhouse. At the stern of the boat were the kitchen or galley, stewards' rooms, and offices. Forward was a large saloon that was a sitting room during the day and the male passengers' sleeping room at night. Aft of it was the ladies' saloon, also used as a dormitory at night; and farther aft was a small cabin composed of four small staterooms. The boat was drawn by three horses plodding along a path about fifty yards ahead.

Again Mr. Beste and his family were miserable because of the heat and the mosquitoes, and Mrs. Beste reported that the "lady" passengers bickered constantly over their rights in the crowded dormitory. Another source of annoyance was a male passenger who shot at birds from the roof of the deckhouse all day long. But as they progressed northeastward, the constant change of scenery prevented their being bored. Above Covington they found the sandstone country especially attractive; and although Lafayette at first disappointed them because it was neither so large nor so prosperous as they had expected, they were delighted when an elegant lady and gentleman came aboard at the last minute, giving promise of more congenial company than they had so far enjoyed on their journey. From Lafayette on, the countryside was wilder and sparsely settled, and Mr. Beste, believing that such a country was more salubrious, began to feel better than he had felt for a long time.

"I never saw more magnificent timber than shaded the valleys through which we passed," he wrote at this time. "Great sticks of plank oak shot up straight from the bottoms without a knot or branch, until their heads spread out some scores of feet above, like the tufted summits of the Italian pine."

At Fort Wayne, the Englishman was fascinated by an old blockhouse on the bank of the canal, the first that he had seen in America. But here he began to lose interest in his surroundings, for soon he was to part with his two sons. In spite of his annoyance with the American climate and manners, Mr. Beste was going to send his sons to college in the new land, believing that as Americans they would have a better chance of prospering and improving themselves.

Chapter Nine

☆

Bridge to Maturity

RICHARD BESTE'S journal makes no mention of shadowy figures moving along the canal's towpath at night, and it is unlikely that the Englishman saw any such mysterious activity or heard of the possibility of its existence; for the furtive men who used the towpaths avoided passing canalboats, and even American travelers on the boats were generally unaware of the nocturnal activity that sometimes went on round them. If any such activity was in progress during Richard Beste's journey, the men at work under cover of darkness were "conductors" of the Underground Railroad leading groups of Negro "passengers" to freedom. They chose the towpaths of canals as trunk lines of their railroad because the paths were direct and convenient and were less frequented than turnpikes, which could be used only when wagons were available with loads that would conceal the runaway slaves. Sometimes, when captains and crews were sympathetic and dependable, the Underground stowed its charges aboard the boats, but more often the night "trains" ran along the towpaths without the knowledge of canal authorities. From the paths more easily than from the boats, fugitives could vanish into the surrounding woods and thickets if their presence was detected.

Although Hoosier Abolitionists were guiding slaves to Canada and freedom as early as the 1820's, the Underground Railroad was not efficiently organized until after the passage by Congress of the Fugitive Slave Law of 1850. The harsh terms of the law won sympathy for slaves among many residents of southern Indiana who

180

had previously accepted the institution of slavery below the Ohio River as right because it was legal. Toward the middle of the century, an Anti-Slavery League established a network of agents throughout Indiana and other states, in the South as well as the North. These agents were either permanent residents who maintained "stations" like Dr. John W. Posey's coal mine near Petersburg and Levi Coffin's home in Fountain City or men who moved about the country in the guise of geologists, peddlers, teachers, and land agents persuading slaves to flee from bondage, gathering groups of them together, and conducting them northward. According to William M. Cockrum of Oakland City, who was involved in this work, the superintendent of the secret organization in the state was John T. Hanover, alias John Hansen, a naturalist. Hansen's work and that of his assistants, who were identified by numbers like those of townships, ranges, and sections, was extremely hazardous, for legality was all on the side of the slaveowners and of slave hunters eager for rewards. A man detected harboring or assisting escaping slaves was subject to heavy fines and imprisonment under the Federal Fugitive Slave Law.

The Underground Railroad got its name from the remark of a frustrated slave hunter from Kentucky who surmised there must be a railroad under the Ohio River and onward, underground, to Canada, because a slave who vanished from his home in the South was always hard to find. Actually, there were several crossing points along the Ohio where slaves were helped over the river. Evansville and the Louisville–New Albany region offered the safest crossings, because slaves could be easily "lost" for a time in concentrated urban populations of free Negroes. At Evansville, two white men who fished on the river at night performed the work of the Underground Railroad. In the daytime, they sold their catch of fish in the city's public market after passing along their night's "catch" of slaves to "conductors" who would take them north to Lake Michigan. On the lake, a lumber bark awaited the fugitives at ports in Lake, Porter, and LaPorte counties.

Other points of crossing for slaves who had made their way safely as far north as the Ohio River were Diamond Island near West Franklin in Posey County, the mouth of Little Pigeon Creek in Warrick County, a point near Rockport in Spencer County, the mouth of Indian Creek in Harrison County, and Madison, seat of Jefferson County. Slaves who crossed the Ohio at Rockport and downriver from that town usually reached Canada by way of Lake Michigan; those who crossed above Rockport headed for Lake Erie via Fountain City, which was the junction point of numerous routes through the eastern and central parts of the state. Sometimes, along the way, the Negroes were kept in "stations" long enough for them to learn to read and write, enough so that they could send word back to their benefactors when they reached safety in Canada.

Slaveowners in the South knew that if runaways reached Wayne County, Indiana, there was little chance of recovering them; for Wayne County was largely populated by Quakers opposed to slavery, and at Fountain City in Wayne County lived Levi Coffin, a Yankee Quaker with ingenuity, determination, and courage, whose interest in a runaway insured his making the rest of his journey in safety. Coffin's activities in the Underground Railroad were frequently investigated, but no legal action was ever taken against him. Estimates of the number of runaway slaves who were sheltered in his house range between 2,000 and 10,000 over a period of twenty years. Today the Levi Coffin house on the east side of North Main Street in Fountain City is one of several National Historic Sites in Indiana that include New Harmony, the Benjamin Harrison home in Indianapolis, and the William Henry Harrison house in Vincennes.

Concerning his part in the activities of the Underground Railroad, Coffin wrote in his memoirs: "The roads were always in running order, the connections were good, the conductors active and zealous, and there was no lack of passengers. Seldom a week passed without our receiving passengers by this mysterious road. We found it necessary to always be prepared to receive such company and properly care for them. . . . Frequently wagon loads of passengers from the different lines have met at our house, having no previous knowledge of each other. The companies varied in number from two or three to seventeen."

The English traveler Richard Beste makes no mention of the

Underground Railroad, but he did have firsthand knowledge of a more conventional railroad in Indiana, the first in the state, in fact, to use steam locomotives. A few weeks before he arrived at the Prairie House in Terre Haute, Mr. Beste was at Madison, writing in his journal early in June, 1851:

> I did not like Maddison [*sic*]. I heard that cholera was in the town: and the hotel, the Maddison House, was uncomfortable and exorbitant in its charges. . . . We slept there one night; and on the following morning, at seven o'clock, took our seats in the railway cars for Indianapolis. I had had much discussion in the office to induce them to take my luggage, which they insisted ought to follow by goods train, as there was some wonderful hill to be ascended, and great weight would be trying to the engine. However, the matter was settled as last in consideration of four and a half dollars being paid for the extra luggage.
>
> After leaving Maddison, we soon came to this hill up the banks of the Ohio to the table land above. It was a very steep inclined plain—steeper than any I have ever seen in England or Wales; but a magnificent engine, made in England, drew us slowly to the top. We then passed a country that was very pleasant. Forests of oak and beech trees covered the land; except where, here and there, they had been removed from some small clearing, some farmhouse, village or rising town. The cars rattled through many of these, in the very streets of which the stumps of the recent forest yet stood, two or three feet above ground, and obliged all wayfarers to turn aside. Hence the origin of the American expression "to be stumped". . . . At two o'clock we arrived at Indianapolis . . . a distance of eighty-six miles in seven hours. . . . We had paid two dollars and a half per grown up person for our places.

Previous to the building of the Madison and Indianapolis railroad, which was chartered in 1832 and for which ground was broken in 1835, a Lawrenceburg–Indianapolis line had laid track, but the single car used by this railroad, projected through Greensburg and Shelbyville, was drawn by horses. The steam line out of Madison was slow in building. It reached Vernon in 1839, Columbus in 1844, and in 1846, when it was badly needed for the transportation of volunteers at the outbreak of the Mexican War, it had gone only as far as Edinburg. The Madison line arrived at Indianapolis in the fall of the following year, but it failed to connect with Lafayette, its originally projected destination, until 1852. For many years the ascent and descent of the grade at Madison that Richard Beste described was achieved by taking passengers up and down in an omnibus; later, eight horses hitched tandem to each car hauled the trains up through the cut and returning trains were lowered by cable; but by the time the Englishman made his journey, an engine with a pinion working on a cog-rail in the center of the track had been in service for several years. This "magnetic engine," as it was called, was one of the wonders of transportation in the Middle West at the time Beste took his trip.

Indiana came by its railroads somewhat later than some states west of the Alleghenies because of its involvement in building the system of canals legislated by the Mammoth Improvement Bill of 1836. Early proponents of railroads, like Governor Ray, argued that railroads would be cheaper than canals, would run twelve months of the year instead of eight or ten, and would not endanger public health with stagnant water such as canals would create; but the advocates of railroads lost the debate to those who contended that canals would be safer and, in the end, cheaper, because they would be less subject to repairs and would be capable of hauling heavier loads. Perhaps the most persuasive argument of the canal people was that canal-building would circulate money within the state whereas the building of railroads would benefit "foreign" interests. The iron rails, for example, would have to be imported from England, and locomotives would come from England or, at best, Philadelphia.

For many years, rails were no more than strips of bar iron along which the carriages and locomotives bumped precariously. Vibration loosened the flatheaded nails that held the rails to the ties, and ends of bar, called "snakeheads," sprang up from time to time and endangered the lives of crews and passengers. When a snakehead was sighted ahead of a locomotive, the train was stopped and the engineer, brakeman, and conductor got out and nailed the rail down, but sometimes snakeheads broke loose directly under moving trains and ripped through the wooden floors of coaches. The iron rails wore out quickly but were often used until they were hardly more than streaks of rust in the weeds that grew along the untended rights of way. Farfetched and derisive stories were told of engineers who had to stop and ask farmers in the fields to direct them to their destinations because they had lost sight of the track. Finally the railroads adopted T rails, and soon steel was substituted for iron.

Early locomotives burned wood and had to stop frequently for refueling, the firemen buying single cords at a time from woodchoppers who worked independently along the lines. Similarly the firemen bailed water for the engine from ponds and streams along their routes. This operation was called "jerking water," and hence the term "jerkwater railroad." Stops were made at all towns and villages through which the train passed, for every train was a "local." Often imposing stations were built out of proportion to the traffic they accommodated. The railroad companies would promise to build these crenelated, pretentious castles in return for grants of rights of way through the main streets of towns, in the hope that if dividends were not forthcoming, stockholders would console themselves by pointing with pride at their local "depots." Originally trains stopped on signal as well as at these stations, and people along the way had no conscience about abusing the privilege of flagging down the cars. Small boys stopped them just for the fun of it, with the same zest with which a later generation jerked the trolleys of streetcars, and lonely wives of farmers ran out and hailed engineers with the excuse of needing change for five-dollar bills, so that they could chat a while with crews and passengers. Life being more leisurely in those days than it is now, trainmen and passengers were seldom seriously annoyed by these diversions in their journeys.

Indiana, incidentally, was the scene of the world's first train robbery when the Reno Gang of Jackson County set the pattern for the James boys of later years by springing aboard an Ohio & Mississippi train at Seymour on the night of October 6, 1866, and taking $15,000 from the Adams Express Agency man. Two years later, by capturing a one-car train, they got $96,000 in gold and government bonds at Marshfield in Scott County. Of another order of romance in the history of Indiana's railroads was the establish-

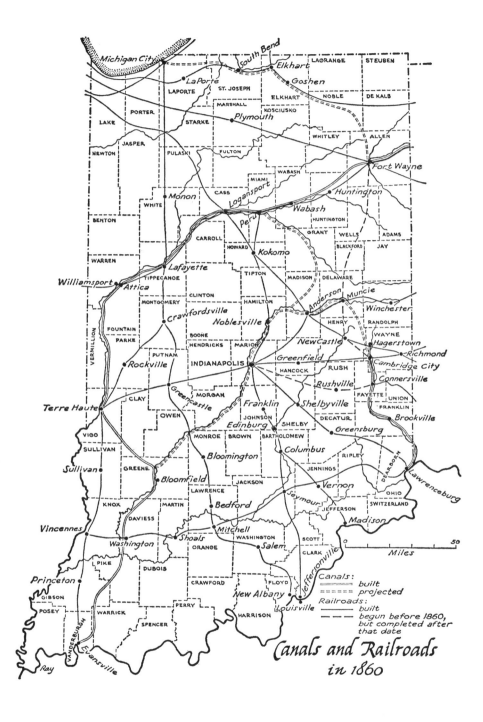

Canals and Railroads in 1860

Canals:
= built
≡ projected

Railroads:
— built
- - begun before 1860, but completed after that date

ment of winter headquarters by three circuses at Peru, which had good rail connections with the rest of the country and was therefore an ideal location for the American circus corporation.

Early railroads took very few precautions to protect passengers and trainmen from injury, although all cars carried posted warnings of things not to do, such as standing in the aisles and walking from one car to another while the train was in motion. In the 1860's, men with only one arm or one leg were almost as likely to be retired trainmen or quondam passengers as Civil War veterans. In May, 1862, one of the early state superintendents of public education, Miles J. Fletcher, was decapitated while riding down to Shiloh battlefield in the same seat with Governor Morton on an Evansville and Terre Haute train. When the cars were suddenly jolted at Sullivan, Fletcher ignored the posted warning in the car and put his head out the window to see what had happened just as the train passed a freight car on the next track. Damage suits were numerous, brought not only by injured passengers but also by residents along rights of way whose unfenced fowls and animals wandered on to the tracks. Cowcatchers were necessary on the front of locomotives to protect such livestock and to prevent derailments.

It was during the pre-Civil War period that the most Hoosier of Hoosier railroads was built, the New Albany and Salem line, which ultimately connected Jeffersonville and Michigan City and today joins Chicago, Indianapolis, and Louisville, with many Indiana way stations along its route. This line is commonly called the Monon, and no one has ever written about it without pointing out that while its Jeffersonville–Michigan City trains serve many educational institutions along the way—Purdue, DePauw, Wabash, and Indiana University, to name a few—it once led to a state penitentiary at one end and a state reformatory at the other. Surveyed and built before modern machinery simplified the problems of cutting through hills and spanning ravines, the Monon is a railroad of many curves, tortuous but picturesque. A former employee, Thomas Carter Perring, writing in the *Indiana Magazine of History* in 1919, observed that "if a lake steamer was hitched on to the Michigan City end and were to pull the kinks and curves out of it to a straight line, it would make a track across the south end of Lake Michigan to Chicago." Legend has it that when a Monon official was asked what he thought of the line after he had made an inspection trip along its 288 miles of meandering from the lake to the river, he replied laconically that he had noticed one straight stretch of track where the builders had neglected to make a curve. Such remarks are of course "family" jokes, cherished among Hoosiers as people cherish anecdotes about their favorite relatives, for almost every Indianan has ridden on the Monon at one time or another in his life and regards its century-old tradition with a kind of possessive affection.

Although the 1850's were the years of the railroads' most rapid growth in Indiana, few Indianans in those early times became rich by investing in them, either executives like Oliver H. Smith, for example, who was president of the Indianapolis and Bellefontaine Line and first president of the Evansville and Indianapolis Straight Line, or the more modest owners of stock in rail ventures; and yet the enterprise and courage of such men first promoted the economic growth of the state and brought it out of its pioneer period into a position comparable to that of any state in the nation. At the beginning of the pre-Civil War decade, there were 228 miles of track in the state; at the end of it, there were 2,163 miles. Twenty years would pass before another 2,000 miles would be added, and only 2,000 miles more of main track have been added since 1880. In 1855, eight lines were using the new union depot at Indianapolis, and the dream of Governor Ray of thirty years before was at last being realized. The governor had envisioned Indianapolis as the railroad hub of the state, with lines radiating from the city in all directions like spokes of a wheel.

After 1855, railroad builders became more preoccupied with construction of east-west lines than with the north-south routes that were originally essential when the movement of passengers and goods to and from the Ohio River was the Hoosier's first consideration. Soon after the first east-west tracks were laid, the story of railroads in Indiana became a story of absorption of local companies by the big corporations that were uniting the East with the West. Today the sixth largest concentration of railroad lines in the nation spreads east and west across northern Indiana out of Chicago. Fifteen Class I roads own 6,600 miles of first main track in the state, and Indianapolis, with one of the most up-to-date electronic freight classification yards in the United States, is one of the country's major railroad centers, and other centers like those at Elkhart and Terre Haute, for example, are of great importance in the railroad network of the state.

As cities grew in Indiana, thanks in part to the railroads that joined them together, public transportation on their streets began to interest their citizens. At first, tracks were laid for cars to be drawn by mules, steam engines being impractical in urban areas and the mule having supplanted the horse that once drew the early trains. Then came electrification. In Indiana, the first attempt to move a streetcar by electricity was made in South Bend in 1882. The experiment was a failure because the current was grounded faster than the powerhouse could supply it, but three years later the South Bend Street Railway had the distinction of operating the first successful electrically propelled car in the state. Three years after that, in 1888, Lafayette installed a completely electrified system, and by 1895 fourteen cities in Indiana had electric railway lines in operation on their streets.

The next step was both logical and inevitable. If electricity would operate trolley lines within a city, why could it not be used for interurban transportation? The first attempt to answer the question in the affirmative was made by a group of Marion businessmen in 1889, and while they were at work connecting the "gas towns" of their area, other groups in New Albany, Brazil, and Anderson attacked the problem. On January 1, 1900, the first electric car entered Indianapolis, arriving from shops in Greenwood twelve miles away, and rapidly thereafter Indianapolis became the hub of such "traction" lines as it was already the hub of railroads. In 1904, the Indianapolis Traction Terminal, now the bus station, was opened, and by 1910 four hundred electric trains were moving in and out of the capital. By the summer of 1914, there were 2,137 miles of first main track in Indiana for electric railroads. They carried 1,229 passenger cars, 363 cars for freight, and 78 for mail and baggage. Sixty-seven of the state's 92 counties were then served by electric lines, and Bedford, Bicknell, and Bloomington were the only towns of more than 5,000 population without them. After World War I, the electric railroad companies went into a decline, but it was not until December 31, 1946, that the last of the interurban lines, the Evansville and Ohio Valley, converted entirely to trucks and buses. At that point, the era of the traction car speeding across the Indiana countryside came to an end, although the South Shore Line, serving the heavy commuter traffic of Gary, Chicago, and the Indiana Dunes area, still thrives and is, in a sense, a survivor of the once far-flung electric system.

As much as anything else the failure of electric interurban transportation may be attributed to the development of the automobile and the resulting improvement of roads. By the 1920's, the old turnpikes of plank, corduroy, and just plain mud had been graveled, and today they are modern hard-surfaced highways. Indiana has now, in fact, more interstate highways than any other state of comparable size in the Union, and it ranks seventh in the percentage of surfaced miles of state highway. Because of the provisions of the second constitution, the state highways are all paid for as they are built.

As in other states, increasing traffic on the public highways has caused a concomitant rise in accidents and casualties. A return to the old electric interurban system is one of the solutions of the traffic problem that are frequently proposed. However, air travel in the state is now almost as common as electric railways travel used to be and is easing the situation somewhat, although it cannot keep up with the proliferation of the automobile. There are commercial airports at Indianapolis, Bloomington, Columbus, Evansville, Fort Wayne, Kokomo, Lafayette, Marion, Muncie, Richmond, South Bend, and Terre Haute, and at least a hundred additional airports in the state provide facilities for commercial as well as private planes, among them 150,000 registered in the state for executive travel. The first airmail flight in the United States was undertaken at Lafayette on August 17, 1859, when 23 circulars and 123 letters addressed to New York City were locked in a bag attached to a balloon. The balloon came down after only 27 miles, however, and the mail shipment was completed from neighboring Crawfordsville by rail.

In the past one hundred years, exploitation of waterways has not advanced with the progress of transportation on land and in the air. Since the steamboat era of the 1850's, 1860's, and 1870's, rivers in the interior of the state, like the Wabash, Whitewater, and St. Joseph, have fallen into disuse. Nevertheless, the Ohio River is still a busy avenue of freight traffic, carrying more low-cost goods than the Panama Canal; there is one large passenger steamboat out of Cincinnati in operation every spring, summer, and fall; and in recent years, the Department of Speech and Theatre at Indiana University has revived one romantic aspect of the old river days with a showboat, the *Majestic*. In the spring of 1966, the Army Corps of Engineers and the Wabash Valley Interstate Commission aroused public interest in reviving the old canal system by proposals to make the Wabash River once more navigable from Terre Haute to its mouth and to connect Evansville and Toledo, Ohio, by water routes. On Lake Michigan, a deep water port will soon make possible direct transportation of Indiana products through the Great Lakes and via the St. Lawrence River to Europe.

The industrial growth of Indiana resulting from improvements in transportation that began with the canals and railroads more than a century ago has exhibited two major characteristics: first, there has been a trend from direct use of the state's natural resources in its manufactures to the fabrication of products from materials not indigenous to the state; and second, industrial concentration in the state has shifted from the south to the north. In 1860, the four leading Hoosier industries were flour and grist milling, lumber, meat, and liquor; today, they are primary metal products, transportation equipment, electrical machinery, and blast furnaces and steel mills. In 1860, the ten counties leading in the value of manufactured products were Dearborn, Floyd, Jefferson, and Vanderburgh in southern Indiana, Madison, Marion, Tippecanoe, Vigo, and Wayne in central Indiana, and only Allen in northern Indiana; today, Vanderburgh is the only southern county to remain in this category, while Lake, St. Joseph, and

LaPorte have joined Allen in the northern area. The total effect of the growth of industry has been to convert Indiana from an agricultural to an industrial state.

Indiana took the first step out of the pioneer way of life when settlers began to buy some of the essentials that they had previously made at home. More and more often they carried their corn to the mill instead of pounding it out, Indian fashion, in hollow stumps or stones. By mid-century, for every county there were seven or eight flour or grist mills, operated by water, steam, or horse power, and the farmer, preoccupied with the cultivation of more cleared land, found it cheaper and more convenient to sell and buy at the neighborhood mill than to be his own middleman. The same was true of disposal of the timber that he cut down; the commercial saw and plane replaced the ax and the adz.

From the beginning, pork packing was a universal Hoosier industry, it being necessary to prepare meat for shipment down the rivers; but gradually neighborhood slaughtering for home consumption was supplanted by the neighborhood slaughterhouse, although it is still common for farmers in southern Indiana to do their own killing and preparing of meat. Finally, "home brew" and native "red-eye" whiskey gave way to the manufactured products, although again unlicensed stills continue to perfume the wooded hills of southern Indiana today in remote places. In 1850, there were sixty-one commercial breweries and thirty-seven commercial distilleries in Indiana, supplementing if not entirely supplanting the labors of individuals who preferred their own private blends. These statistics do not prove, however, that the newly arrived Germans were outdrinking the native and newly arrived Irish residents of the state, for the smaller number of distilleries produced five times the quantity of beverage barreled by the larger number of breweries. Further down the list of leading industrial products before the Civil War were manufactured "luxuries," of which many were formerly homemade: machinery, textiles, carriages and wagons, shoes, and furniture. James Oliver, for instance, began manufacturing the chilled-steel plow in South Bend in 1855, after his discovery of the annealing process.

Bituminous coal was mined primarily in southern Indiana, but coal could be transported easily by rail to all parts of the state, whereas the natural gas discovered in the Muncie area gave that region a local "boom" in the 1880's that helped to draw industry northward. Although milling, meat packing, lumber, and liquor remained the four top industries of Indiana as late as 1900, the manufacture of iron and steel, foundry and machine-shop products, and glass moved ahead of the old pioneer luxuries and suggested the beginnings of what might be called "heavy industries." Today, milling, lumber, meat, and liquor no longer appear among the ten leading industries of the state, and stone, clay, glass, petroleum and coal products have taken their place as Indiana's indigenous output.

In 1850, New Albany, Indianapolis, Madison, Terre Haute, and Evansville, in that order, were the largest towns in the state, three of them Ohio River communities and the other two located in central Indiana; but by 1900, the order was Indianapolis, Evansville, Fort Wayne, Terre Haute, and South Bend, only one of them, Evansville, representing the south. Today, Indianapolis still ranks first in population, but Gary and Fort Wayne have outstripped Evansville, and South Bend edges close to Evansville for position in fourth place. The greatest increase of population in Indiana between 1950 and 1960 took place in Lake, Porter, Miami, Hamilton, Hendricks, Hancock, Morgan, Johnson, and Bartholomew counties. Three of these are northern counties; the rest are central. Of the eighteen counties that lost population in that decade, all but three lie below the Old National Road.

A phenomenal change in the industrial aspect of Indiana took place in the development of the Calumet region at the turn of the nineteenth century. An area of less than one hundred square miles, the Calumet has developed in about half a century from an almost unpopulated expanse of sand, reeds, and sluggish rivers to one of the greatest concentrations of diversified industry in the nation, which includes not only steel mills but also cement plants, oil refineries, soap factories, electrical generating units, and many other enterprises. Gary was "created" in 1905 by the decision of the United States Steel Corporation to construct new steel mills in the Middle West and the corporation's choice of a township at the southern end of Lake Michigan that had a population of only 1,500 people. The steel company's requirements for the venture were a compact and reasonably priced tract of land adjacent to the lake, with adequate rail facilities and near enough to Chicago for an immediately available supply of labor. Already established in the region were the Buffington plant of the Universal Portland Cement Company, the Illinois Steel Company's mills in South Chicago, and the Aetna Powder plant, but it was the coming of U.S. Steel's subsidiary, organized as the Indiana Steel Company in 1906, that initiated the vast industrial complex that is known today in Indiana as "The Calumet." The city of Gary got its name from Judge Elbert H. Gary, chairman of the board of directors of U.S. Steel, who not only consented to the christening and the use of his likeness on the municipal seal but also presented the town with a seal created on his order by Tiffany of New York.

In contrast to the quiet natural beauties of the hills in southern Indiana, the Calumet's panorama of steel cable-towers, cranes, collieries, tanks, gas reservoirs, and giant factories strung along the edge of Lake Michigan competes for the attention of tourists in Indiana as well as attracting investors in future industries. By day it is a forest of stacks pouring out white, black, and yellow smoke; by night, flames from its furnaces leap into the sky illuminating the countryside for miles around and set off the gleaming outlines of shafts and stacks against clouds of belching smoke. But in creating and sustaining its man-made magnificence the producers of the Calumet's dramatic spectacle have threatened the existence of another of the scenic attractions of northern Indiana: the Indiana Dunes. The construction of a port at Burns Harbor on Lake Michigan that will connect the industries of the Calumet directly with the Atlantic Ocean and Europe endangers the survival of the last of the region's natural beauties. Over this threat, the politicians, industrialists, and people of Indiana have been in hot dispute throughout the 1960's as to whether a park region in the area can and should be preserved.

Until the end of World War I, most of the automobiles that traveled Indiana's roads—indeed most of the automobiles on all the roads of the United States—were made in Indiana. The

Hoosier automobile industry began in 1893 with Elwood Haynes at work in the Apperson brothers' machine shop in Kokomo. By 1894, Haynes had put together the first mechanically successful spark-ignition automobile, and on July 4 of that year he drove it a mile and a half out Pumpkin Vine Pike at a speed of seven miles an hour. It was then turned around and ran all the way back to the city without stopping. On the return trip, Haynes later recalled, he encountered "a bevy of girls on wheels" who separated "like a flock of swans and gazed wonder-eyed at the uncouth and utterly unexpected little machine." Three years before, in Indianapolis, Charles Black had invented a car that had to be started by igniting it with a kerosene torch, but this creation would not budge against the wind and was regarded as unsuccessful. Haynes's automobile started by push and had no reverse gear, but once it got under way, it ran.

Haynes and the Appersons made automobiles for seven years and thereafter operated separately in Kokomo until the middle of the 1920's, the Appersons manufacturing the popular Apperson Jack Rabbit. Haynes made the first use of aluminum and discovered stainless steel, which led to the invention of stellite, which much later made possible the Mercury Capsule because of the alloy's resistance to heat. The Kokomo Union Carbide Stellite Division carries on Haynes's original work today, and aluminum castings and all of Chrysler's automatic transmissions are still manufactured in Kokomo.

Indianapolis soon became the heart of the automobile industry in the nation as well as the state, and cars were manufactured there until 1937. Early in the history of auto making, however, Detroit moved into the ascendancy with the organization of General Motors and the birth of Ford's Model T in 1908. The next year, to combat the competition of Detroit, the Speedway opened at Indianapolis and the annual 500-mile Memorial Day races began, giving car makers an opportunity to test their cars for speed and improvements in engineering. But while Indianapolis and other Indiana cities concentrated on quality, Detroit dedicated itself to mass production and soon won the competition for first place in the automotive industry.

Among the automobiles made in Indianapolis were the National (1900–24), one of the first cars to have a push-button electric gearshift; the Premier (1902–27); the Waverly Electric (1896–1915), favorite of ladies in veils and linen dusters in the years before World War I because of its elegance, comfort, quietness, cleanliness, and easy manipulation; the Empire (1898–1919); the Marion (1904–14), named for Marion County; the Cole (1909–25), a pioneer with the V-8 engine; the Henderson (1912–15); the Parry (1910–12); and the Pathfinder (1911–18). Indianapolis also produced the Lafayette (1920–24), which, like the Lincoln and the Pierce Arrow, was a competitor of the Cadillac, and three of the world's most famous cars for luxury and engineering: the Marmon (1902–33); Stutz's American Underslung (1905–14) and Stutz (1913–35), and Duesenberg (1920–37). These three cars had two Hoosier rivals among the world's great automobiles: the Cord (1929–37), famous for front-wheel drive, and the Auburn (1900–37), which buffs compare with the modern Jaguar for its excellent engineering and designing at a reasonable price. Both of these latter cars were produced in Auburn.

Other Indiana towns and cities played roles in the state's unique place in the history of automobile manufacture. In fact, since Haynes's invention in 1893, fifty-six Indiana communities have turned out 246 different makes of cars. Although Portland was one of the few towns that made no automobiles, it has a place in the automobile story as the birthplace of Haynes in 1857 and as a producer of overalls, once essential to the ownership and operation of automobiles in early days, and steering wheels, still necessary. Union City, which made the little known Union for one year (1920), became the birthplace of Harry C. Stutz in 1876 and, for a while, produced the internationally famous Le Grande custom bodies. Connersville was the home of eight makes of cars, including the Lexington and the McFarlan, the McFarlan being Indiana's equivalent of the Rolls Royce if only because it cost $10,000 in the 1920's. Columbus created the unique and impractical Reeves Octoauto from 1908 to 1912, inspiring Elbert Hubbard to describe its "four additional carrying wheels" as "a shock-absorber beyond the dreams of the neurotic." The Octoauto company afterwards simplified this oddity to the Sextoauto, but it was equally impractical. Evansville had its Simplicity from 1907 to 1910 and the McCurdy in 1919, although the latter never reached the market, but the Ohio River city was better known in the automobile industry as the home of the three Graham brothers who made Graham Brothers trucks and later became executives of the Dodge Company. Logansport made the Revere, Brazil the Brazil, and Elkhart turned out some two dozen makes of cars, among them the popular Elcar. Mishawaka had the Simplex and, more ambitiously, the Amplex.

Most famous of Indiana cities in the history of auto making, however, is South Bend, for more than a century the headquarters of Studebaker products. In 1852, Henry and Clement Studebaker opened a blacksmith and wagon shop in South Bend and during the latter half of the nineteenth century built many of the wagons that carried pioneers to the West. The Union army used Studebaker wagons at Gettysburg, and Studebaker carriages occupied the stables of the White House. The Studebaker Company moved into the automobile business in 1902 with an electric, although they continued to make wagons until 1920. By that time they had been manufacturing gasoline automobiles for a number of years—the Garford in 1904 and the EMF in 1908—and had formed the Studebaker Corporation in 1911. Late in 1963, the Studebaker factory closed its doors and moved to Hamilton, Ontario, where it continued for a while a limited production, keeping its corporation headquarters in South Bend. Cummins Engine Company, with headquarters in Columbus, Kaiser-Jeep Corporation, Allied Products Corporation, and other companies have taken over its buildings in the Indiana city, and today Bendix Corporation is South Bend's largest employer, with 12,000 workers. Vincent Bendix, inventor of the Bendix drive for self-starters, was building "gas buggies" in Logansport in 1907. Although Michigan eventually took the automotive industry away from Indiana, the "Big Three" of the industry in Detroit today operate sixteen plants within the Hoosier state.

It was the arrival of the Monon Railroad in Bloomington in the fall of 1853 that saved Indiana University from extinction as much as any other event in that discouraging decade of the institution's history; and so, in some degree, education, like industry in Indiana, owes a debt to expansion of internal improvements, although the cost of that expansion before the Civil War long delayed the state's attention to the intellectual needs of the young. Today education is an important part of Hoosier living.

Founded in 1820 as a county seminary, the school at Bloomington had become Indiana College in 1827 and began conferring degrees in 1831, but Bloomington was an isolated and primitive pioneer village before the coming of the railroad and the state's institution of higher learning could in no sense be called a university. Even more deleterious to its welfare than its location in its first thirty years of existence was the opposition of church-going Hoosiers who not only preferred to send their children to denominational colleges but also protested against paying taxes to support a state college. In 1860, the total enrollment in Bloomington was less than 200, and this enrollment included pupils who were attending the preparatory school of the institution. The Constitution of 1851 ignored the existence of the college, and in the General Assembly of the following year there was a strong sentiment for abandoning it altogether. About the same time, Vincennes University almost succeeded in the courts in taking away the land that had been granted for the state-supported college by the original constitution-makers at Corydon, and the one and only college building in Bloomington burned to the ground.

After the Monon connected Bloomington with the rest of Indiana and the travel of students to and from the college became less onerous, the institution began to stir with new life. By 1873, President Lemuel Moss had reorganized Indiana's somewhat haphazard college courses into three curricula: ancient classics, modern classics, and a scientific course. With the administration of President David Starr Jordan, beginning in 1885, the offerings of the curricula were expanded and the school for the first time achieved the status of a university.

In recent times, during the twenty-five-year presidency of Herman B Wells from 1937 to 1962, the institution in Bloomington moved forward rapidly into the first ranks of the major universities in the nation, expanding and modernizing its building facilities as well as its undergraduate and graduate programs and enlarging and improving its faculty. Elvis J. Stahr, assuming the presidency in 1962, has further directed the growth of the university, while Wells has served as its first chancellor. Today, there are 23,000 students on the Bloomington campus, and another 19,000 are enrolled at the Fort Wayne, Gary, Indianapolis, Kokomo, South Bend–Mishawaka, and Jeffersonville centers that are operated by the university. Indiana University has become one of the major centers for the study of foreign languages in the United States, and its work in the natural sciences is among the best in the country. Undergraduate and graduate courses attract students from every part of the world as well as the nation, and exchange programs for both students and faculty have been established with several foreign countries. At Indianapolis, a large campus is in prospect for the combined units of Indiana and Purdue in the capital city. In addition to the foregoing branches of the Bloomington institution, there are cooperative centers at Vincennes University and Earlham College.

The two major barriers to the progress of higher learning in Indiana before 1850 were the state's rate of illiteracy, the highest of all the Northern states in that period, and the failure of the state, until the second constitution was drawn up, ever to levy a tax or spend money for educational purposes. In the 1830's and 1840's the rage for internal improvements drained the public treasury and left no funds for education. Furthermore, free schools in early days were regarded as pauper schools, and local interests opposed their support by the state. It was Caleb Mills, professor of Greek at Wabash, who was responsible for eventually creating a public school system in Indiana. Through the efforts of Mills, with the support of Robert Dale Owen, the second constitutional convention was persuaded to require the General Assembly "to provide for a general and uniform system of common schools, wherein tuition shall be without charge and equally open to all." The convention created the office of Superintendent of Public Education to examine and license teachers, and although this was an elective office, it was not, in its early years at least, afflicted with the taint of politics. William C. Larrabee, a graduate of Bowdoin College and a professor of mathematics at Indiana Asbury University (now DePauw), was the first superintendent, and Mills of Wabash, a graduate of Dartmouth College, was the second.

The General Assembly enacted the first public school law in 1852, and in that year and the two following years free schools were opened in Richmond, Madison, Indianapolis, Fort Wayne, and Evansville. But in 1854 the Supreme Court of Indiana invalidated the section of the law that authorized townships to levy school taxes, and four years later the court ruled that cities could not levy such taxes because in so doing they would destroy "uniformity" among the state's schools. This ruling was a blow that only Evansville survived, because it was able to operate under an old town charter that gave it a certain immunity to state intervention. In Indianapolis, all public schools closed and two thirds of the children of the city were deprived of instruction. After that, there was no general free public school system in the state until the end of the Civil War, and it was 1870 before the primitive log schoolhouse of the type Abraham Lincoln attended completely disappeared from the Hoosier scene. Annual school terms in this period ran as short as 22 days, and in 1870 seven and a half per cent of the population of Indiana still could not read or write.

In the trying period of the restoration of the public school system after the close of the Civil War, Abram C. Shortridge served as superintendent of public education. In the office from 1863 until 1874, when he became president of Purdue, Shortridge established a program of graded schools through a twelve-year period, in defiance of the Supreme Court's rulings. Fort Wayne, with James H. Smart as its superintendent of schools, was the first to adopt the program, although Evansville had graded schools without the twelve-year plan as early as 1853. In 1869, schools for Negroes were first opened in Indiana, and after 1877 Negroes were admitted to some white schools in the north. By the time desegregation of public schools was required by law in Indiana in 1949, many public schools throughout the state were already completely integrated. During the period of the creation of a public school system, private academies continued to thrive. They were supported mainly by Catholics, Quakers, and Presbyterians, and in much smaller numbers by Baptists and Methodists, who were the most numerous church members in the state. By the 1870's, most of the Protestant academies had disappeared, but the Catholic institutions continued to increase in numbers and enrollment. No compulsory education law was passed in Indiana until 1897. By that time, a test case regarding local taxation had finally reached the Supreme Court, in 1885, and the Court reversed its earlier decisions, legalizing the progress that had been made.

At the beginning of the decade of the 1850's, in which Indiana University passed its crisis, there were four other institutions of higher learning in Indiana that were granting degrees. Hanover, a Presbyterian institution, was founded in 1833, as was Wabash, another Presbyterian college; Indiana Asbury, Methodist, founded in 1837, became DePauw in 1884; and Franklin, Baptist, came into being as a college in 1845, although it had originated in 1834 as the Indiana Baptist Manual Labor Institute. Notre Dame, a Catholic institution, was founded in 1842 and authorized to give degrees in 1844, but in its early years in the remote and thinly populated area where it was established, most of its students were enrolled in its preparatory school. The oldest of the institutions of higher learning in the state, Vincennes University, founded in 1806, was struggling at that time to survive and was not a degree-granting institution. Earlham, founded in 1847, was known as the Friends' Boarding School in 1850 and did not grant degrees until 1859, when it acquired its present name. Soon after 1850, the Northwestern Christian University came into being in Indianapolis and was christened Butler University in 1877, and the Lutherans established Concordia at Fort Wayne in 1861. There are today more than thirty colleges and universities in the state, and in 1952 the Associated Colleges of Indiana were incorporated, with Anderson, DePauw, Earlham, Evansville, Franklin, Hanover, Indiana Central, Manchester, Rose Polytechnic, St. Joseph's, and Wabash as charter members.

In Indiana, there are three state-supported institutions besides Indiana University—Ball State University at Muncie, Indiana State University at Terre Haute, and Purdue University at West

Lafayette. The first two originated as state normal schools, Indiana State opening its doors in 1870 and Ball State coming into being in 1918 as a result of a gift by the Ball brothers, glassmakers of Muncie. Purdue University, by far the largest of the three and the traditional rival of Indiana University on the football field and basketball court, evolved out of a vote by the General Assembly in 1869 to create a state agricultural college under the terms of the Federal Morrill Land Grant Act of 1862.

Various sites were considered for what is now Purdue until the year 1869, when John Purdue, formerly a merchant in Lafayette but at the time the owner of a commission house in New York City, offered to give money in addition to other offers if the school were established in Tippecanoe County and bore his name. In 1872, Richard Owen, professor of natural history at Indiana University, was elected as the first president of the institution, but he continued to teach at Bloomington and spend his summers in New Harmony, never taking up residence in Lafayette or drawing a salary, and in 1874 Abram C. Shortridge succeeded him. With a Federal land grant and a later start in more propitious times, Purdue has endured little of the struggle for survival that characterized her sister institution's early years in Bloomington, and from its inception, it has been recognized as one of the nation's leading agricultural and engineering institutions. In addition to its technical courses, it offers students opportunities for work in the humanities. In the so-called "Golden Age" of Hoosier writing, it had a stronger literary tradition than the state university, where the humanities and sciences form the *pièce de resistance* of the curricula. Receiving the same biennial appropriation from the state legislature, Purdue, like Indiana, has expanded phenomenally since World War II and operates centers in the state as does Indiana University. Frederick L. Hovde, like Elvis J. Stahr of Indiana University, is a former Rhodes Scholar. Hovde has been president of Purdue since 1946.

Chapter Ten

☆

Reflections

CORN, hogs, politics, and literature have long been regarded as the principal products of Indiana; but only in a discussion of the first two is a writer of the state's history on safe and uncontroversial ground, for corn and hogs can be reduced to statistics, whereas politics is a matter of opinion and literature a matter of taste. That is why corn and hogs—along with their modern rival, steel—have been treated briefly in this book while politics filled two chapters. Now, before Indiana's literary output is considered in these final pages, another last brief look at Hoosier politics is necessary in order to point out certain similarities between the state's politicians and the writers who most commonly wear the brand "Hoosier."

As already noted, Indiana has given the nation eight vice-presidential candidates, four of them successful, but no native Hoosier has yet occupied the White House. Irvin S. Cobb once attributed the frequent appearance of Hoosier names in second place on national ballots to what he called "the nationalistic normalcy of Indiana." Cobb was, of course, a Kentuckian and a humorist, with the limitations of a neighbor who finds it profitable to make jocular remarks about the people next door, but there is an element of truth in his observation that "Indiana gives us our vice-presidents and vice-presidential candidates because she is the average American state." If Indianans were subaverage, he argued, they could not get the nomination; if they were superaverage, they would not take it. Perhaps, however, this is true only when Indianans are content with thinking of themselves simply as Indianans.

With baseball offering a better metaphor than the state pastime of basketball, it must be admitted that Indiana politics has been largely a sandlot game and those few players reaching the big leagues have enjoyed no more than a moderate success. For example, Indiana's eight vice-presidential candidates may be said to have got as far as the benches in the majors, but none of them ever left the dugout for a turn at the plate. Indeed Indiana owes its latter-day reputation for political genius to four men who never ran for the vice presidency, men noted more for their managerial skill than for occasional listings as players on the big league scorecards. Two of these men were Republicans: James E. Watson and Will H. Hays. Two were Democrats: Thomas Taggart and Paul V. McNutt. If to their names is added that of Charles A. Halleck, twice majority leader in the House of Representatives and later minority leader, Indiana's major-league participation in the national game of politics in this century is just about covered; for Albert J. Beveridge's political genius was best demonstrated before 1900, few Hoosiers are willing to acknowledge Eugene V. Debs as a Hoosier politician, and Wendell L. Willkie was not a professional.

Throughout the first third of this century, James E. Watson weathered many changes of climate within his own party in the state and nation, presiding over seven Republican state conventions and attending nine Republican national conventions as a delegate, in addition to serving ten years in the U.S. House of Representatives and seventeen in the U.S. Senate. Of Will H. Hays, during a somewhat shorter period, it was said that his faintest whisper in Indianapolis was the law in Indiana—until the Klansman Stephenson moved in from Texas and took over. Thomas Taggart, a delegate to all the Democratic national conventions from 1900 to 1924, ruled the "Tammany of the Middle West" from French Lick Springs in those years. Following him in the 1930's, Paul V. McNutt was briefly in power and gave the Democratic Party a "new look" in Indiana.

And yet these four shrewd Hoosier politicians accomplished

very little in the national arena. For all of Jim Watson's "public service," he made no permanent contribution to the Republican Party and hardly affected the course of American history. Will Hays rose to the office of Postmaster General in Warren G. Harding's Cabinet, but after a year-minus-a-day in that dubious company he retired from politics to become the "Czar of Hollywood" as president of the Motion Picture Producers and Distributors of America. On the Democratic side, while Tom Taggart was attending all those national conventions, his party was successful in only two of the seven presidential contests that took place, and when he was chairman of the Democratic National Committee, from 1900 to 1908, Republicans McKinley, Roosevelt, and Taft won handily. Even back home on the sandlot, Taggart was a loser; during his regime as Democratic boss of the state, six of Indiana's eight governors were Republicans. As for McNutt, it has already been seen how the man from Hyde Park, New York, outwitted the boy from Indianapolis, Indiana, as soon as the Indianan emerged from his local Two Percent Clubhouse and announced that he wanted to be captain of the national team.

What has been said about Indiana's reputation in politics cannot be said about Indiana's renown for literary production. Many of Indiana's authors moved from the sandlot to positions in the big leagues such as Indiana's politicians never achieved. There has never been the equivalent of a president of the United States among Indiana's writers, but there have been many players in the national literary field far more active and spectacular than those Hoosier political figures who warmed the vice-presidential bench or the Taggarts and Hayses who coached from the sidelines. A librarian at Purdue, after an assiduous examination of statistics, has determined that between the turn of the century and the beginning of World War II Indiana ranked second only to New York in the production of national best sellers, and a close second at that, with a score of 213 to New York's 218, while Pennsylvania, in third place, could claim only 125. In the early years of that period and a few years preceding it, many Hoosiers earned large sums of money with their pens, established national reputations, and created what Indiana's literary historians have called "The Golden

Age." In spite of the Hoosier writers' greater success, however, there are similarities between them and Hoosier politicians that are significant.

First of all, in a glow of Indianamania it can be too easily forgotten that statistics are not literary criticism and best sellers are not always enduring literature. In the light of time's passing, it must be admitted that the gold the writers of "The Golden Age" earned in royalties now shines brighter than anything that can be panned out of the millions of words that flowed from their pens. They were all competent writers; some of them were more than merely talented; they made the big leagues; but none of the men and women associated with Indiana's "Golden Age" has a very large niche in the nation's literary Hall of Fame today. For some reason, even at the height of their careers, these men and women always played to a little knot of the folks from back home gathered in the grandstand to watch them; they seemed to regard literature as their Hoosier counterparts in politics regarded affairs of state, as a game only, a show, not a profession or an art; they seemed always concerned about the opinions of the folks from back home, who were suspicious, even a little afraid, of art.

A professor of art at Indiana University once remarked that he would enjoy the beautiful scenery of Brown County more if it did not look so much like all those paintings. What he was really saying was that the Brown County "school" of painters would do better if they stopped trying to make their paintings look so much like Brown County. Perhaps real eminence and an effort to live up to a provincial or regional expectation are mutually exclusive in any endeavor, artistic or otherwise. It is not as a native of Kentucky, a resident of Indiana, or a politician from Illinois that the world remembers Abraham Lincoln. He transcended his origins, as he could not have done if he had accepted their limitations. So, in literature, a regional view can be a serious handicap to artistic performance. It can also seriously distort judgments of artistic performances. If there were no such category as that of the Indiana Author, many Hoosier writers could be forgotten and the state's literary reputation would be the better for their oblivion; conversely, without such a label upon them some so-called Indiana

Authors might have achieved a taller stature as literary figures in their own right.

Appraising an Indiana author is much more difficult than assessing an Indiana politician, and not only because the one judgment is a matter of opinion and the other a matter of taste. A complex problem lies in the appellation itself and in the inevitable limits, at once restrictive and elastic, of such an appellation; it lies in the very concept of an Indiana Author, the belief that such a creature exists distinct from other authors, just as it sometimes lies in the effects of the concept upon an author's work. But the legend of Indiana as a literary state has been so long established and so widely accepted that it is impossible to ignore the subject in a history of Indiana. If there are Indiana Authors, one must ask, who are they and what are they worth? Fortunately, the answers reflect areas beyond the narrow boundaries of the subject and reveal something about Indiana itself.

R. E. Banta of Crawfordsville set up a definition of the Indiana Author when he compiled his *Indiana Authors and Their Books, 1816–1916,* which was published in 1949. In this collection of biographical sketches and bibliographies, Banta included writers "who (a) were born in Indiana, (b) were reared and educated in Indiana, (c) whose literary work began during residence in Indiana and was obviously influenced by Indiana residence, or (d) who chose Indiana as a place in which to spend the major portion of their lives." The definition is a canny one if only because it is all-encompassing in its Hoosier hospitality; Mr. Banta cannot be accused of any sins of omission except by oversight, and there are few, if any, oversights. With irreproachable fairness and regardless of his preferences, although he includes them, too, the Crawfordsville bibliographer accepts almost anyone who ever drew a whiff of Hoosier air into his lungs and published a pamphlet or a book at his own or another's expense. There are about a thousand entries in the Banta volume.

In it one will find Noah J. Clodfelter, author of *Snatched from the Poorhouse,* along with Booth Tarkington, who seldom strayed off fashionable North Meridian Street for his subjects, and James B. Elmore, "The Bard of the Alamo," who plummeted to the nadir of poetic underachievement with his line, "Cut, Oh cut my leg away," in "The Monon Wreck," in the company of William Vaughn Moody, who, although he lived for a while in Spencer and New Albany along the Monon's route, never reflected any awareness of that Hoosier institution's existence in his poetry. Here too are Isaac Heller, murderer first of a young girl in Pennsylvania and later, with an ax, of his wife and three children in Liberty, Indiana, and, a few pages away, Theodore Dreiser, whose moral concern ninety years later in *An American Tragedy* over the causes of a murder not unlike Heller's first venture into crime is, in Mr. Banta's opinion, "sensational." The book also includes Cincinnatus Hiner (Joaquin) Miller, who was born in Liberty about the time that Heller was writing his *Confessions* but whose parents soon whisked him away to the Sierras and the Sun-lands that later inspired him, and James Whitcomb Riley, who was born and lived all his life in Indiana and wrote about the state almost exclusively.

Reading Mr. Banta's spicy and compendious book to find out what constitutes an Indiana Author is like attending a Hoosier barbecue to learn the flavor of the Hoosier hog; there are too many side dishes, not to mention the sauce and the smoke, for the essence of the *pièce de resistance* to assert itself. But in reading the book one does learn something about the Hoosier character; and if one keeps in mind Mr. Banta's view of literature when one takes up Arthur W. Shumaker's *A History of Indiana Literature* and observes how Professor Shumaker manipulates Banta's basic definition to suit his own view, one emerges from the confusion with at least a concept of the Indiana Author, if not with a sharp image of the creature himself.

Shumaker, whose book was published in 1962, edges twenty-three years closer to modernity than Banta; that is, he is willing to examine the credentials of any candidate for the Hoosier Pantheon who published prior to 1939. He then goes on to define the kind of author he is looking for within the period he will explore. Indiana Authors, by Shumaker's standards, are (1) writers born in Indiana who spent all or most of their lives in the state; (2) writers not born in Indiana who spent all or most of their lives in the state (Shumaker does not explain how it would be possible for a writer not born in Indiana to spend *all* his life in the state); (3) writers not born in Indiana who spent a few years here which were very productive in their literary careers; and (4) writers "whose Indiana backgrounds influenced strongly" their later writings. At the same time, Professor Shumaker excludes (1) writers born in Indiana but "who moved elsewhere before producing any significant writing"; (2) writers "who spent only a few years in the state and whose literary work seems not to have been particularly affected by residence here"; and (3) writers who, though they otherwise fulfilled his definition, did not publish at least one book. By these exclusions and others, such as authors of books for children, whom he regarded as "tangential to this study," Professor Shumaker reduced a list of 1,563 names of "possible Hoosier creative writers" to a still sizable 142.

Closely examined, the DePauw professor's criteria reveal a flexibility that makes it possible for him to include and exclude writers in a way that Banta does not permit himelf to do. While Banta expressed his preferences in Indiana literature in no uncertain terms, he left no one out deliberately, whereas Shumaker, ostensibly more catholic in his tastes than Banta, quietly chose and omitted as he wished. For example, William Vaughn Moody, who was born in Indiana and lived in Indiana until he was eighteen, is the subject of twelve pages in *A History of Indiana Literature,* although Moody was surely one of those "who moved elsewhere before producing any significant writing" and his "literary work seems not to have been particularly affected by residence here"; but Theodore Dreiser and David Graham Phillips, who were also born in Indiana and lived in Indiana until they were eighteen, are left out "because of insufficient residence and Indiana influence on their works." These exclusions also ignore the fact that Phillips had already begun to write when he was a student at DePauw and seem not to take into account Dreiser's *Jennie Gerhardt,* in which the early scenes strongly suggest that the author was recalling the Terre Haute House, where his mother worked as a scrubwoman, *Dawn,* which describes Dreiser's childhood and youth in Indiana, and *A Hoosier Holiday,* whose very title Shumaker apparently overlooked. (In passing, it might be mentioned that Dreiser took that Hoosier holiday in 1915 in a Hoosier-built Pathfinder, the "King of Twelves," a fact which should have made some amends to those who were offended by his "cavalier treatment" of his Indiana friends.)

In the light of Shumaker's selections and omissions, Banta's opinions, and other approaches to the subject like those of Meredith Nicholson, Logan Esarey, and Jacob Piatt Dunn, a strong suspicion arises that the only true definition of an Indiana Author is that he or she is any man or woman with pen in hand whom any Hoosier who wishes to define the term would be willing to accept as a next-door neighbor (it should be noted that the murderer Heller was executed and safely dead by the time his *Confessions* became available and that Noah J. Clodfelter, who must have been an unconscionable bore, did, after all, according to his autobiography, live in "a beautiful home erected at a cost of over $20,000"), any writer, in other words, whose writings do not offend the moral or aesthetic sense or the local pride of the Hoosier who is doing the defining.

Thus, Jessamyn West, for example, might be included in one study of Indiana Authors because her beautiful book, *The Friendly Persuasion,* is about Hoosiers and depicts the Quakers of Indiana as very admirable people by anybody's standards; but she might be omitted from another study because she herself disclaims the title of Indiana Author, pointing out that she spent very few years of her childhood in the state and has written more about Californians than about Hoosiers. Thus, also, one bibliographer might include Max Ehrmann, poet, playwright, and essayist, in a list of Indiana Authors because Ehrmann lived and died in Terre Haute and must certainly have thought of himself as a Hoosier, while another might willfully exclude him because Ehrmann supplemented his DePauw education with a term or two at Harvard, or because he took an un-Rotarian view of the causes of prostitution, attributing the scarlet woman's fall, in part at least, to the low wages paid by businessmen.

To define an Indiana Author in terms that are universally acceptable is then, apparently, a vain endeavor, but to conclude therefore that Indiana has no real tradition of literary accomplishment is to ignore facts. For more than a hundred years, Indianans have written a remarkable number of books, many of them about Indiana, some of them simply for Indianans. Perhaps there is no other state in the Union that has produced the printed word in so large a quantity. Although the product may not always be literature, it is often of a distinct Hoosier flavor, either in the person of the writer or the nature of his writing, and this flavor is readily recognizable, whether it can de defined or no.

John Finley is an early case in point. Finley was born in Virginia, in 1797, but his poem "The Hoosier's Nest," published in the Indianapolis *Journal* in 1833, places him at the beginnings of the Indiana tradition. In this poem, Finley described the Hoosier's pioneer cabin realistically enough:

> One side was lined with divers garments,
> The other spread with skins of varmints;
> Dried pumpkins overhead were strung,
> Where venison hams in plenty hung;
> Two rifles placed above the door;
> Three dogs lay stretched upon the floor,—
> In short, the domicile was rife
> With specimens of Hoosier life.

But he also defended the simple virtues of his adopted state against the adverse judgments of outsiders:

> Blest Indiana! in thy soil
> Are found the sure rewards of toil,
> Where honest poverty and worth
> May make a Paradise on earth.
> With feelings proud we contemplate
> The rising glory of our state;
> Nor take offense by application
> Of its good-natured appellation.
> Our hardy yeomanry can smile
> At tourists of "the sea-girt isle,"
> Or wits who travel at the gallop,
> Like Basil Hall or Mrs. Trollope.

In other words, Finley not only put the seal of the already currently accepted word *Hoosier* on the state of Indiana, he also formalized the Hoosier attitude toward writing about Indiana, a genial acceptance of homeliness—and "hominess"—as the Hoosier trademark and a gentle scorn for anyone who does not wholeheartedly admire the state's virtues, a scorn that can sometimes become vituperative, as was later demonstrated when Baynard Rush Hall, a professor at the Indiana State Seminary in Bloomington, published *The New Purchase.* Describing the life of that town when he lived there as crude and harsh and deploring the materialism of the natives and their determination to "larn" at the seminary only "what they most like best," Hall touched a sore spot in Hoosier pride that was still sore in 1859 when Mrs. Henry Ward Beecher, in similar caustic tones, wrote, in *From Dawn to Daylight,* about her ten unhappy years in Indianapolis when her husband was pastor of the Second Presbyterian Church on the Circle. Mrs. Beecher's book was banned in Indianapolis and remained for thirty years a subject of controversy in the City Library.

Twelve years after *From Dawn to Daylight,* Edward Eggleston's *The Hoosier School-Master* drew attention again to Indiana as a rude pioneer society; but Eggleston, unlike Hall and Mrs. Beecher, was a native Hoosier, born in Vevay, and his book was a best seller, and those two facts made some difference in the degree of his acceptance in Indiana. A fellow Hoosier who gets ahead in the world, especially if, like Eggleston, he leaves the state, always wins a grudging admiration from Indianans. However, in some areas, *The Hoosier School-Master* was bitterly resented. Fifty years after the appearance of the book, a local historian of Evansville was protesting in the *Indiana Magazine of History* that it was an unjust portrait of southern Indiana, and Professor Shumaker, writing his history of Indiana literature in 1962, feels called upon to protest that Eggleston was writing about a "relatively small segment of population" and to explain, with more Hoosier loyalty than scholarly accuracy, that "such people . . . either moved on or lost their identity through an improved educational system."

Since Eggleston's day, novel writing has been a major pursuit of Indiana's authors, and it was the novel that produced "The Golden Age." But never again would Indiana be described so harshly by its own.

In "The Golden Age," Lew Wallace, the most unliterary of the group, was the most successful financially. That brisk little man, son of a Hoosier governor, himself a political figure, and veteran of two wars, wrote *Ben-Hur* before he had seen the Holy Land and from it and *The Fair God* and *The Prince of India* made a fortune. Wallace was territorial governor of New Mexico and, afterwards, minister to Turkey and then finally settled down in Crawfordsville to enjoy his literary eminence in a home that today is one of the tourist sights of the town. With his royalties he made many investments, among them the first apartment house in Indianapolis, which he named The Blacherne after the palace of the Emperor of Constantinople in *The Prince of India*. Born in Brookville in 1827, Wallace died in Crawfordsville in 1905. He is still the most widely read of the authors of "The Golden Age."

Other writers of that period were Maurice Thompson, Charles Major, Meredith Nicholson, George Barr McCutcheon, Gene Stratton Porter, George Ade, and Booth Tarkington, Tarkington becoming "dean" of the novelists after Wallace's death. Thompson, like Lew Wallace, preferred the long-ago and far-away to the contemporary Indiana scene. His best-known book is *Alice of Old Vincennes,* a best seller that rivaled Wallace's *Ben-Hur* for a short while at the turn of the century. Charles Major, who lived in Shelbyville, also wrote romantically of distant places, making the best-seller lists immediately with his *When Knighthood Was in Flower* in 1898 and following it with another best seller, *Dorothy Vernon of Haddon Hall,* in 1902. His *The Bears of Blue River,* however, a more realistic book and set against an Indiana background, is the one that most Indianans read with pleasure today. George Barr McCutcheon went still further afield from the here and now in his *Graustark,* a story of a kingdom that never was, and in all the Graustark sequels that followed it. Gene Stratton Porter (*Freckles,* 1904; *A Girl of the Limberlost,* 1909; *Laddie,* 1913) celebrated the swampy forests round her home in Geneva, until she moved to California in 1914, when she began to write more about the problems of childhood and less about its delights. To George Ade, playwright and short-story writer, author of *Fables in Slang,* is attributed the oft-told story of the lecturer from the East who came to Indiana in "The Golden Age" and invited any writers in his audience to join him on the platform and found himself immediately surrounded there by the entire gathering. Meredith Nicholson, 1866–1947, made greater use of his native scene than any of the other novelists of this school except Tarkington. The action of his thriller, *The House of a Thousand Candles,* though highly romantic, moves toward its denouement in a very real and recognizable setting near Lake Maxinkuckee, and *A Hoosier Chronicle,* probably Nicholson's best book, is a serious novel about Hoosier politics, autobiographical, and with vivid scenes on the campus of Wabash College. Booth Tarkington was the most literary and the most distinguished novelist of the group and will be discussed at some length later; however, even he was overshadowed in "The Golden Age" by a member who was not a novelist but a poet, James Whitcomb Riley.

Riley was born in Greenfield in 1849, in a house by the side of the National Road, and he attended a school on the National Road where the traffic distracted him from his studies but gave him an early view of the variety and vagaries of human nature. For a time following his schooldays, he read law in his father's office, but after his mother's death he left home and became a traveling sign painter with the Wizard Oil Company. Riding beside "Doctor" McCrillus on a medicine-wagon across the Indiana countryside, stopping in villages to play the guitar, recite, or paint signs, and, afterward, writing late into the night the beginnings of verses that he would keep and polish later in his successful days, Riley filled his storehouse of Hoosier impressions and at the same time developed the "iron mask" that makes his photographs look more like those of a judge or a doctor than a poet, a sharp and stern expression that concealed his sensitiveness to his surroundings. He developed, too, in those days the skill as a showman that was to serve him well, years later, on the lecture platform.

At the age of twenty-four, Riley quit the road for newspaper work and began to appear in the columns of the Indianapolis *Saturday Mirror* under the pseudonym "Jay Whit"; but he attracted little attention until he published a literary hoax in the Kokomo *Dispatch,* a poem that purported to be an undiscovered work by

Edgar Allan Poe. For this prank, Riley's own newspaper, the Anderson *Democrat*, fired him, but he was promptly hired by the Indianapolis *Journal*, where his writing career finally began to flourish. Under the signature "Benj. F. Johnson of Boone," he published the first of his famous verses, "When the Frost Is on the Punkin." When he died in 1916, volumes of his poems were a part of the furnishings of almost every Indiana home, and "Riley Day" is still an annual event in Indiana schools.

Riley's verse was Indiana, at least that Indiana that Indianans love to believe they remember from their childhood. It carried the scent of Indiana's woods and fields, echoed the voices of its country people, stirred memories of years never to be relived, painted rich and mellow Hoosier scenery, and captured the tempo of easy, comfortable Hoosier manners. Riley knew the appetizing flavor of the Hoosier air when the frost was on the "punkin," the scent of clover and the pagan delights of boyhood in "wortermelon time," and the simple pleasure of seeing the sunshine spread on country roads "as thick as butter on country bread." His head was full of stories of the kind that delighted small children and their parents as well, tales of griffins and elves and giants and "Squidgicum-Squees 'at swallers theirselves." He pulled out all the stops when he wrote about "The Happy Little Cripple" who had "Curv'ture of the Spine," but kept them under control in poems like "Old Aunt Mary's" and "Little Orphant Annie," and struck a responsive chord in the hearts of Indiana's many dwellers by a riverside when he wrote of "noon-time and June-time, down around the river."

Whether Riley knew the Hoosier dialect is debatable. R. E. Banta credits him with an infallible ear, but Jeannette Covert Nolan, in the most sensible essay that has ever been written about Riley, suggests that Riley's "dialect" was his own invention and that Hoosiers have been imitating it ever since it was first conceived, just as they have tried to be typical Hoosiers in the Riley image. "Our contention," Mrs. Nolan writes, "is that Riley came first; the typical Hoosier has come afterward." Be that as it may, whether indeed the so-called "Hoosier accent" is anything more than a combination of faulty grammar and nasal resonance that

can be heard anywhere in the Middle West, James Whitcomb
Riley is, for better or for worse, the Hoosier writer universally
accepted, in the state and out, as an Indiana Author.

But after Riley and "The Golden Age" how does one proceed
in the search for the Indiana Author? With Riley's ineradicable
stamp upon the state's literary image, does one include in the
Pantheon only those who modeled themselves after him, the Clod-
felters, the Elmores, and the hundreds of other little Rileys who
scribbled and recited Hoosieresque doggerel in every community
in Indiana from Point Township in Posey County to Clear Lake
in Steuben? Or does one call Kenneth Rexroth and Samuel Yellen
Hoosier poets, writers as unlike Riley and, at the same time, as unlike each other as any two poets could be, the one a native of South
Bend but better known as the pundit of the beat generation in San
Francisco, the other a native of Lithuania but all his many peda-
gogic years a teacher at Indiana University? Ezra Pound once
taught for a term at Wabash College; is *he* a Hoosier poet? Hein-
rich Schliemann *(Ithaca)* lived for a few months in Indianapolis
and his will and probate record are on file in a Marion County
court; were those ravished Trojan treasures, therefore, a Hoosier
trove?

In recent years, Ross F. Lockridge, Jr., came very close to the
tradition of "The Golden Age" with his best-selling novel, *Rain-
tree County*; but what of other novelists of modern Indiana: Nel-
son Algren *(The Man with the Golden Arm)*, Lloyd C. Douglas
(Magnificent Obsession), George P. Elliott *(Among the Dangs)*,
A. B. Guthrie *(The Big Sky)*, Joseph Hayes *(The Desperate
Hours)*, Rex Stout (the Nero Wolfe stories), Kurt Vonnegut
(God Bless You, Mr. Rosewater), Jessamyn West *(The Friendly
Persuasion)*, William E. Wilson *(Crescent City)*, Marguerite
Young *(Miss MacIntosh, My Darling)*? All have associations
with Indiana of one degree or another, some have written about
Indiana, but they hardly compose a "school." What of the many
writers of stories for children, whom Professor Shumaker excludes
from his history as "tangential" but who have proved that they
possess as clear an understanding as Riley's of what children like to
read, although there is nothing Rileyesque about them: Jeannette

Covert Nolan, Miriam Mason Swain, Mabel Leigh Hunt, Ann Weil, Ellen Wilson, Augusta Stevenson, Frances Cavanah, Beatrice Schenk de Regniers, Elizabeth Friermood, and many others?

How does one classify two historians living in Indiana in modern times—R. Carlyle Buley (*The Old Northwest, 1815–1840*) and Herbert J. Muller (*The Uses of the Past*)—one a native, the other a resident since 1935? Because of their divergent political opinions and the disparity in scope of their views of history, they make strange literary bedfellows; and yet they are both writers that the state can claim as its own. John Clark Ridpath was an Indiana historian and so were Charles and Mary Beard, but all they had in common was their association with DePauw University. And where does one place those writers with Indiana associations who are just to one side of the ranks of historians? Claude G. Bowers, for example, was ambassador to Spain and Chile as well as the author of numerous books. Robert and Helen Merrill Lynd gave a dubious immortality to the city of Muncie in two books, *Middletown* and *Middletown in Transition,* but their labors brought a happier renown to themselves and to Columbia University, where they were members of the faculty, than to the state of Indiana. (Incidentally, does the fifteen-year residence in Muncie of *Saturday Evening Post* writer C. E. Scoggins, although he was born in Mexico and died in Colorado, make him an Indiana Author and restore to that city some of the cultural dignity that it lost at the hands of the Lynds?) Ernie Pyle of Dana was a "boy from back home" all his life, but the same cannot be said of Elmer Davis of Aurora, who was an eminent journalist of a different order of recent times; and yet Professor Shumaker's *A History of Indiana Literature* gives Elmer Davis several pages and mentions Ernie Pyle only in passing. Might not a reversal of this emphasis be more appropriate? Was Alfred C. Kinsey, native of Hoboken but for forty years a resident of Bloomington, indeed an "author" at all in any literary sense, or was his book, *Sexual Behavior in the Human Male,* a best seller only because of its subject matter and its statistics?

More than a century ago, Stendhal wrote in *Le Rouge et le Noir*: "A novel is a mirror carried along a highway. Now it reflects the blue of the sky, now the mud puddles of the road. Have you a right to say the man who carries the mirror in his basket is immoral? His mirror reflects mud and you accuse the mirror! Accuse, instead, the highway where the puddles are, or, rather, the highway inspector who allows the water to stagnate and the puddles to form."

In this metaphor, Stendhal was defending realism in fiction. But the truth about a place and its people is not found only in the reflections of realism nor in fiction alone; it can be found in all the kinds of writing that a place and its people encourage and in those that they reject as well. Through their highway inspector, the people who live along a road are indeed responsible for the mud puddles, but they are also responsible for the degree of welcome they extend to writers traveling along their road and for the angles at which they insist the mirrors in those writers' baskets must be tilted. Along Indiana's literary highway, Hoosiers have usually preferred mirrors that reflect only the blue sky, rejecting as false those that show the mud puddles. Such a prejudice is natural and not characteristic of Indianans alone, but Indianans too often deny the existence of mud puddles and refuse to recognize anyone on their highway whose mirror is not tilted always upward. Witness, for example, the contrasting receptions given to two novelists who were born in Indiana within two years and within seventy miles of each other and whose deaths occurred less than four months apart: Booth Tarkington and Theodore Dreiser.

Newton Booth Tarkington was born July 29, 1869, on North Meridian Street in Indianapolis, in the best residential district of that city. His father, a prosperous lawyer, was of Southern ancestry. His mother, who was of New England stock and counted Thomas Hooker among her forebears, was born in Salem, Indiana. Booth Tarkington was named for his mother's brother, Newton Booth, who was a governor of California and later a senator from that state. The boy had one sister, eleven years his senior.

Herman Theodore Dreiser was born August 27, 1871, on Ninth Street in Terre Haute and in his early years moved from one shabby neighborhood to another in that city. His father, a weaver by trade, had fled from Germany in 1844 to escape conscription.

For a while he prospered in America; but by the time Theodore was born—the twelfth of John Paul Dreiser's children—Dreiser Senior was a broken man of fifty, whom his son remembered as a religious fanatic and morose disciplinarian, withdrawn from the circle of the family, poring over the *Lives of the Saints* or a German newspaper, "a thin grasshopper of a man, brooding wearily." John Paul Dreiser was a Catholic; his wife was the daughter of a Mennonite farmer in Ohio. Sarah Schanab Dreiser was almost illiterate and was unable to write until her son Theodore was old enough to teach her. By Dreiser's own later accounts, his sisters were none too careful about their morals.

The two boys, Tarkington and Dreiser, grew up in Indiana in the 1870's and early 1880's seldom more than a hundred miles from each other; but the one lived always in the same city in a well-established social group in a family of comfortable, cultivated, and gentle people, while the other drifted from rented house to rented house—in Terre Haute and Vincennes and Sullivan and Evansville and Warsaw—learning early in his childhood how to steal coal from railroad yards for a family that was poor and disunited. From time to time, brother Paul, who had changed his name to Dresser and who was a dandified songwriter and actor thirteen years Theodore's senior, came home and introduced into the Dreisers' life its only spark of gaiety, its only semblance of cultural stimulus —the false, tawdry, sentimental splendor of the vaudeville circuit.

It was Paul Dresser, the oldest brother, who moved a remnant of the family, including Theodore and his mother, from Sullivan to Evansville in 1882 and established them in that city in a comfortable brick cottage on East Franklin Street. This cottage was owned by Paul's mistress, Annie Brace, who was the madam of the most sumptuous house of prostitution on Evansville's waterfront. It was in Annie Brace's house of prostitution that Theodore, at the age of eleven or twelve, had his first glimpse of luxury, when he visited his brother Paul in Paul's suite overlooking the river. Theodore Dreiser wrote later, in *Dawn,* that he found the suite "rich and wonderful" and admired especially its striped awnings, its piano, and its private bathroom.

In the late 1930's, the author of these pages visited the brick cottage on East Franklin Street in which Theodore Dreiser with his mother had lived fifty years before and in which Dreiser's brother, Paul Dresser, never lived. On the front lawn at that time there was a large sign that read, "Home of Paul Dresser, Composer of 'On the Banks of the Wabash.'" The author of these pages told the woman who showed him through the house that it was Theodore Dreiser and not Paul Dresser who had lived in the house. "Who," the woman asked, "is Theodore Dreiser?" The sign on the lawn has since disappeared, but over the door in more recent years there has been a sign that reads "The Dresser." Under often-changing management, Annie Brace's sumptuous and notorious establishment on the Evansville waterfront continued to flourish until the 1930's, but it never bore a marker to commemorate either the Hoosier songwriter who once lived in it, although he has been shown great honor elsewhere in Indiana, nor the novel-writing brother who innocently visited it when he was a boy, although he has been variously excoriated by Hoosier critics for an interest in such places in his fiction.

About the same time that Theodore Dreiser was having his first glimpse of the rewards of sin in Evansville, Booth Tarkington, aged thirteen, was making the acquaintance of the wages of virtue in Indianapolis. "These last two months have been very sad," young Tarkington was recording in his diary. "Fritz [his dog], poor little Fritz has died. . . . So have President Garfield and Mrs. Holoway. Fritz . . . died while I was at the grocery."

Tarkington was educated at home in his father's library, in the public schools of Indianapolis, at Phillips Exeter Academy, for one year at Purdue University and two years at Princeton University. At Purdue, he excelled in zoology, botany, and literature but probably worked hardest at his art course. At Princeton, as a special student, he edited the *Nassau Literary Magazine,* the *Tiger,* and *Bric-a-brac,* was soloist in the Glee Club, wrote the book for the first play of the Triangle Club, enjoyed a full social life, and was still able to maintain respectable grades in his courses. He was not graduated from either Purdue or Princeton, but Princeton gave him an honorary M.A. before he was thirty and a Litt.D. before he was fifty, and in his old age, after he had refused to make any more public appearances, Purdue organized a special academic procession and delivered an honorary degree to his home in Indianapolis.

Dreiser, from his seventh year to his fourteenth, attended parochial schools, which he found as bleak and almost as bare of books as his numerous homes, and where, according to his own report, he was frightened by the black habits of the priests and nuns and by the ritual in which he participated as an altar boy. In Warsaw, Indiana, he attended a public high school and there impressed one of his teachers so favorably that she gave him the money for a year at Indiana University. In that year in Bloomington, 1889–90, the year before Tarkington entered Purdue, Dreiser passed Elementary Latin, was conditioned in Geometry, passed Philosophy, and received a grade of "Good" in a course called "The Study of Words." He also took part in spelunking expeditions to the caves of Monroe County, and in a relationship with a girl student he failed so miserably that his attitude toward sex was conditioned by the experience for years afterward. In Indiana University's Lilly Library there is a portrait of Dreiser and there are numerous manuscripts, including his courtship letters to his wife, Sallie White Dreiser, whom he called "Jug," but not until a year or two ago was there ever a tablet or marker on the campus commemorating Dreiser's year of residence, nor was there ever any serious movement to give him an honorary degree after he became famous.

At the close of Booth Tarkington's formal education, the young writer had the privilege of a five-year apprenticeship in Indianapolis supported by an inheritance from his uncle and encouraged by the admiration and sympathy of his sister. For a long time after Theodore Dreiser left Bloomington, his principal concern was to earn a living in any way that he could. He worked in Chicago as a shipping clerk, a collector for a milk company, and then for an installment company, losing one of these jobs because he embezzled. He was a newspaperman in Chicago and in St. Louis, Toledo, Pittsburgh, and finally New York, losing a job in St. Louis when he wrote a review of a dramatic performance that did not take place and losing another in New York, with the Butterick

Company, because of his pursuit of the seventeen-year-old daughter of one of his assistant editors. Dreiser began to write short fiction in the summer of 1899, the year that Tarkington published his first novel.

Both Dreiser and Tarkington wrote their first novels in their late twenties, and these novels were accepted for publication when each author was twenty-nine. Tarkington's notice of acceptance came from a young writer named Hamlin Garland, who was the editor of the publishing house of S. S. McClure. Hamlin Garland's letter began: "Mr. McClure had given me your manuscript, *The Gentleman from Indiana,* to read. You are a novelist. . . ." The acceptance of Dreiser's manuscript came from a young writer named Frank Norris, who was a reader for the firm of Doubleday, Page and Company. Frank Norris's report was that *Sister Carrie* was "a masterpiece . . . the best novel I have read since I have been reading for this firm."

Booth Tarkington was summoned to New York by his publisher, put up at the Players Club, entertained at the Century Club in the company of Frank Stockton and Paul Leicester Ford, and invited to the home of Frank Doubleday, who was at that time a member of the McClure firm. When S. S. McClure introduced young Tarkington to Ida Tarbell, he said, "This is to be the most famous young man in America."

In the offices of Doubleday, Page, and Company, Theodore Dreiser was accorded a different kind of reception. Unfortunately, the house had accepted *Sister Carrie* during the absence of Frank Doubleday—the same Frank Doubleday who previously, as a member of the S. S. McClure Company, had welcomed Tarkington into his home. However, Doubleday read the proofs of *Sister Carrie* before Dreiser appeared in person in the Doubleday, Page offices. Worse still for the young novelist's reception was the fact that Mrs. Doubleday also read the proofs. Mrs. Doubleday, a social worker, was a very high-minded woman. *Sister Carrie* horrified her. She persuaded her husband to cancel the contract for the book, and he tried to do so, but Dreiser insisted that the agreement be kept.

The agreement was kept, but not in spirit. A mere thousand copies of the novel were printed, bound in dull red cloth, and no attempt was made to sell them. Frank Norris did send out one hundred review copies, and some of the notices were favorable; but the novel was not available in the bookstores when readers of the reviews came in to purchase the book. Only four hundred and sixty-five copies were sold, netting the author less than one hundred dollars. *Sister Carrie* was not reissued for seven years, and it was eleven years after this initial fiasco before Dreiser was able to publish his second novel, *Jennie Gerhardt.* Meantime, *The Gentleman from Indiana* was an immediate success, and twenty years after its appearance, with a score of published books to his credit, Tarkington's first novel was still selling 18,000 copies a year.

As a result of the *Sister Carrie* disaster, Dreiser had a nervous breakdown and was on the verge of suicide when his brother Paul discovered him in a Brooklyn rooming house and sent him off to a sanitarium. By the time Dreiser published his second novel, Booth Tarkington had written twelve more successful books and was well on his way toward the first of his two Pulitzer Prizes. Measured in terms of money, the only novel of Dreiser's that had any real success was *An American Tragedy,* published in 1925 when he was fifty-four, and the returns from it came largely from a motion picture that Dreiser tried, unsuccessfully, in the courts to suppress because he thought it reduced the book to a sex-murder film. In terms of money, Tarkington never had a failure.

What damaged Dreiser most in *Sister Carrie* was that he violated the Genteel Tradition and wrote about poverty and sex as if they really existed in America, as indeed he had seen them exist in Indiana when he was a boy. But he was also damaged by the fact that he did not measure up to any of the current popular concepts of a literary person of his day. He was neither a polished gentleman nor an exotic. True, he was a Hoosier, and in those days it was expected of every Hoosier that he be a writer, for "The Golden Age" was at its meridian. But it was also expected of Hoosiers that they write uplifting stories about just plain folks or romantic tales of never-never lands, and Dreiser did neither.

In 1915, Stuart Sherman, a professor of English at the University of Illinois and a prominent critic in the first quarter of this century, complained that Dreiser's "field seems curiously outside

American society," although Dreiser's Terre Haute was less than a hundred miles away from Sherman's Champaign-Urbana study. Professor Sherman then pointed out that Dreiser was born of German–American parents, as if that fact were darkly significant, and went on to say that he could not find any moral value in Dreiser's novels nor any memorable beauty. He professed to be "greatly impressed by them as serious representatives of a new note in American literature, coming from that 'ethnic' element of our mixed population which, as we are assured by competent authorities, is to redeem us from Puritanism and insure our artistic salvation." He accused Dreiser of sinking "supinely back into the law of the jungle" and complained that he failed to motivate characters as George Eliot, Thackeray, Trollope, and Meredith motivated theirs. He did not go on to explain how he thought Trollope would have told the story of Jennie Gerhardt or what George Meredith would have done with an American business titan like Cowperwood.

In 1922, Professor Logan Esarey of Indiana University published a *History of Indiana* in which he stated: "From Crawfordsville also came Meredith Nicholson, one of the most widely known literary men at present. Like *all* literary men of Indiana, he comes of good stock and enjoyed a first class education." The italics are not Esarey's but are implied in Esarey's text by the omission of Theodore Dreiser from the Hoosier professor's chapter on Hoosier literary men, although by 1922, the date of the professor's history, Dreiser had published eleven books, including *A Hoosier Holiday*.

As late as 1949, R. E. Banta, including Dreiser in his *Indiana Authors and Their Books 1816–1916*, condemned him as "a writer who could find a rotten spot in every apple." Mr. Banta explained that *"Sister Carrie* was startlingly frank in its treatment of delicate subject matter." By "delicate subject matter" Mr. Banta undoubtedly meant sex, and here he was echoing a notion held by many people who have never read Dreiser. Any one who does read *Sister Carrie* may indeed be startled by Dreiser's treatment of that subject, but it will be because of Dreiser's delicacy and not because of his frankness. Only by interpreting Carrie's sister's dream that Carrie is descending into an abandoned coal mine in a basket are we able to determine that Carrie that same night was seduced by the flashy drummer Drouet.

What benefited Tarkington most in *The Gentleman from Indiana* was that, while the novel seems to paint small-town life in Indiana realistically and the Whitecaps, forerunners of Indiana's Ku Klux Klan, are depicted as an evil force, virtue triumphs completely in the end and the crusading country editor wins, as his reward, a beautiful wife. Professor Esarey, the Hoosier historian who ignored Dreiser and preferred gentility and a first-class education, found Tarkington's story "well told" and predicted that it would "preserve for all time a picture of the time when the 'fellers' gathered on Saturdays or Sundays at the old mill, or the neighborhood store." R. E. Banta, so easily disturbed by "delicate subject matter," felt safe with a book by Tarkington in his hands. Of Tarkington's characters Banta wrote in his *Indiana Authors:* "They were by no means all nice people; there was always the leavening of Alice Adams' bootlegging brother, the nastiness of some of the Magnificent Ambersons, but the proportion of good, near-good, wistfully good and pure bad was about right. There was neither the high romance of George Barr McCutcheon nor the grimy realism of Theodore Dreiser: Tarkington's people lived." As for Stuart Sherman, if he ever gave Booth Tarkington's work any serious thought, he could certainly have found nothing objectionable in a novelist whose ancestry included Thomas Hooker; in Tarkington there would have been no "ethnic" problem to upset him.

The contrast between the two novelists persisted to the ends of their lives as striking as it was at the beginnings. In all that they did as well as wrote, they remained on opposite sides of the tracks. Dreiser seemed at times to choose the wrong side deliberately; as a man he was erratic, cantankerous, equivocal, and usually his own worst enemy. For example, when the Muckrakers were in their heyday, exposing the evil ways of the rich and powerful, during Theodore Roosevelt's trust-busting regime, Dreiser was busy in the editors' chairs of popular magazines deleting sex and cigarettes from articles entitled "The Serious Side of Burlesque" and "The Funny Side of Woman Suffrage" and soliciting articles like one

written by H. L. Mencken—incredible as it may seem—entitled
"When Baby Has Diphtheria." A few years later, when the literary
tide had turned away from the novel with a social conscience and
American writers were dedicating themselves to art for art's sake,
Dreiser published *The Financier,* a novel based on the life of
Charles Yerkes, a buccaneer of big business such as the Muckrakers
had formerly loved to expose. It was characteristic of Dreiser that
he publicly hated the British in World War I and got himself
accused of anti-Semitism at the beginning of Hitler's tyranny, that
he praised the Communists in the booming 1920's when "Bolshe-
vik" was a dirty word, shied away from them in the depressed
1930's when Party-joining and "fellow-traveling" were not only
acceptable but fashionable among the intelligentsia, and finally
became a member of the Party in 1945, the year of his death, when
American ex-Communists were beginning to scurry for cover behind constitutional amendments.

Meantime, Tarkington never left the respectable side of the
tracks. In public issues, he moved neither to the right nor the left
but stalled in the posture of a conservative Democrat. This was
more or less his position in letters, too. Once he had abandoned his
early romanticism and found his most profitable vein in gentle
satire and quiet realism, he never experimented. In his private
life, there were divorce and remarriage and a period of threatened
alcoholism, but there was never a public scandal as there was in
Dreiser's, who drank moderately but was a satyr to the end of his
days and whose wife would not give him a divorce. Tarkington
and Dreiser both traveled extensively, but Tarkington always as a
tourist; he never got himself involved with unwashed foreigners
by trying to look behind the scenes or saying anything about them
—or about Americans either, for that matter—that would rile the
"fellers" in the neighborhood store, as Dreiser was forever doing
in his often inept and bumbling way. Of Tarkington's *The Tur-
moil* Dreiser once said, "It's not real life," commenting further
that Tarkington did not know reality, life, work, the average
human being, or sex. On the other hand, Tarkington disapproved
of Dreiser, whose literary motto seemed to be that of a newspaper

reporter in one of his short stories: "I'll get it all in!" That is what Dreiser tried to do in his novels, whereas Tarkington always left something out, even when he was dealing with people like Alice Adam's bootlegging brother or the nastiness of some of the Magnificent Ambersons.

Today Tarkington is all but ignored by serious critics of American literature while Dreiser is recognized as a powerful force in the twentieth-century novel even by those who find him prolix, unliterary, and sometimes absurd. Except in Indiana! Perhaps the difference of opinions can best be pointed up by quoting two critics, both of them Hoosiers. George Jean Nathan, better known in his day as a sophisticated New Yorker than as a native of Fort Wayne, called Dreiser "the most important American author." Jacob Piatt Dunn, in his day more widely read in Indiana than George Jean Nathan, accused Dreiser of being "afflicted with the . . . idea that it is fine to bare your soul to the world, unconscious of the fact that the average soul is more presentable in a figleaf—much more so in pajamas." Both men were wrong.

In a final judgment of the two novelists, no one should dismiss the gentleman, Tarkington, because he wrote no books like Dreiser's *The Titan* or *An American Tragedy,* but neither should anyone dismiss the titan, Dreiser, because he wrote no books like *The Gentleman from Indiana* or *Seventeen.* There have been times in the past when the art of leaving something out was more highly regarded than the feat of getting it all in. Even in our own day, no less a writer than Hemingway has insisted that what a writer knows but does not say can be more important than what he says. A time may come again in the changing vogues of fiction when suggestion will be more appreciated than full statement. If it does, Tarkington may assume a larger place in American literature than he holds at present. It is unlikely, however, that Dreiser's place will ever be much diminished by comparison.

The point of this chapter—and of this book—is that Indiana, like any other state, has been the home of all kinds of men and women —average, subaverage, superaverage, good and bad—and that the only danger Indianans should ever concern themselves about is the danger of accepting only one category and, in fear, rejecting all others. *No man is an Iland, intire of it selfe.* Neither, any longer, is any place, any state, any region, any nation, any planet. Let Indianans be proud of what they are, but never self-righteous about what they may think they are not, for that too is *a peece of the Continent, a part of the maine.*

Selected Bibliography

CHAPTER ONE: *The Hoosier State*

Barnhart, John D., and Donald F. Carmony. *Indiana: From Frontier to Industrial Commonwealth.* 4 vols.—2 biographical. New York: Lewis Publishing Co., 1954.

Dillon, John B. *History of Indiana, from its Earliest Explorations by Europeans to the Close of Territorial Government in 1816.* Indianapolis: W. Sheets, 1843; revised ed., Indianapolis: Sheets and Braden, 1854; 2nd revised ed., Indianapolis: Bingham and Doughty, 1859.

Dunn, Jacob P. *Indiana and Indianans.* 5 vols.—3 biographical. Chicago and New York: The American Historical Society, 1919.

Esarey, Logan. *History of Indiana.* 2 vols. Indianapolis: Bowen, 1918.

Indiana. Indiana Plant Location Fact Book. Departments of Commerce, Agriculture, Industry, and Public Relations, c. 1961.

Indiana: A Guide to the Hoosier State. Compiled by workers of the Writers' Program of the Work Projects Administration. (American Guide Series.) New York: Oxford University Press, 1941.

Indiana Magazine of History. (1906– .) See indexes.

Leibowitz, Irving. *My Indiana.* Englewood Cliffs, N.J.: Prentice-Hall, 1964.

Martin, John B. *Indiana: An Interpretation.* New York: Knopf, 1947.

Visher, Stephen S. *Economic Geography of Indiana.* New York: Appleton, 1923.

Wilson, William E. *The Wabash.* (The Rivers of America Series.) New York: Farrar and Rinehart, 1940.

CHAPTER TWO: *The Indians*

Black, Glenn A. *Angel Site, Vanderburgh County, Indiana: An Introduction.* (Indiana Prehistory Research Series, Vol. 2, No. 5.) Indianapolis: Indiana Historical Society, 1944.

Dunn, Jacob P. *True Indian Stories.* Indianapolis: Sentinel Printing Co., 1908.

Guernsey, E. Y. (Map) *Indiana: The Influence of the Indian upon its History, with Indian and French Names for Natural and Cultural*

Locations. (Publication No. 122.) Indianapolis: Indiana Department of Conservation, c. 1933.

Lilly, Eli. *Prehistoric Antiquities of Indiana.* Indianapolis: Indiana Historical Society, 1937.

Walam Olum, or Red Score, The Migration Legend of the Lenni Lenape or Delaware Indians, A New Translation, Interpreted by Linguistic, Historical, Archaeological, Ethnological, and Physical Anthropological Studies. Indianapolis: Indiana Historical Society, 1954.

Wilson, William E. *Shooting Star: The Sory of Tecumseh.* New York: Farrar and Rinehart, 1942.

Winger, Otho. *The Lost Sister among the Miamis.* Elgin, Ill.: Elgin Press, 1936.

———. *The Potawatomi Indians.* Elgin, Ill.: Elgin Press, 1939.

CHAPTER THREE: *The March of Empire*

Barnhart, John D. *Valley of Democracy, 1770–1818.* Bloomington: Indiana University Press, 1953.

Bodley, Temple. *George Rogers Clark, His Life and Public Services.* Boston: Houghton Mifflin, 1926.

Cleaves, Freeman. *Old Tippecanoe: William Henry Harrison and his Times.* New York: Scribner's, 1939.

Dillon, John B. *History of Indiana, from its Earliest Explorations . . . to the Close of Territorial Government in 1816.* Indianapolis: Bingham and Doughty, 1859.

English, William E. *Conquest of the Country Northwest of the River Ohio, 1778–1783.* 2 vols. Indianapolis: Bowen-Merrill, 1896.

Goebel, Dorothy B. *William Henry Harrison: A Political Biography.* (Indiana Historical Collections, Vol. 14; Biographical Series, Vol. 2) Indianapolis: Indiana Historical Bureau, 1926.

James, James A. *Life of George Rogers Clark.* Chicago: University of Chicago Press, 1928.

Parkman, Francis. *The Discovery of the Great West: La Salle.* Boston: Little, Brown, 1869; reprinted, New York: Rinehart, 1956.

Thornbrough, Gayle, and Dorothy Riker (eds.). *Readings in Indiana History.* (Indiana Historical Collections, Vol. 36.) Indianapolis: Indiana Historical Bureau, 1956.

CHAPTER FOUR: *Utopia on the Wabash*

Bestor, Arthur E., Jr. *Backwoods Utopias: The Sectarian and Owenite Phases of Communitarian Socialism in America, 1663–1829.* Philadelphia: University of Pennsylvania Press, 1950.

Blair, Don. *Harmonist Construction.* (Indiana Historical Society

Publications, Vol. 23, No. 2.) Indianapolis: Indiana Historical Society, 1964.

Bole, John Archibald. *The Harmony Society*. Philadelphia: Americana Germanica Press, 1904.

Owen, Robert. *The Life of Robert Owen, by himself*. New York: Knopf, 1920.

Owen, Robert Dale. *Threading My Way: Twenty-Seven Years of Autobiography*. London: Trübner, 1874; New York: G. W. Carleton, 1874.

Wilson, William E. *The Angel and the Serpent: The Story of New Harmony*. Bloomington: Indiana University Press, 1964.

CHAPTER FIVE: *Horse-Trading and Logrolling*

Buley, R. Carlyle. *The Old Northwest, 1815–1840*. Indianapolis: Indiana Historical Society, 1950; Bloomington: Indiana University Press, 1951, 1962.

Hawkins, Hubert H. (comp.) *Indiana's Road to Statehood: A Documentary Record*. Indianapolis: Indiana Sesquicentennial Commission, 1964.

Indiana Constitutional Convention: Report of the Debates and Proceedings . . . 1850. 2 vols. Indianapolis: 1850. (Indiana Historical Collections Reprints.) Indianapolis: Indiana Historical Bureau, 1935. *Journal . . . to Amend the Constitution . . . 1850*. Indianapolis: 1851. (Indiana Historical Collections Reprints.) Indianapolis: Indiana Historical Bureau, 1936.

Kettleborough, Charles (ed.). *Constitution Making in Indiana*. 3 vols. (Indiana Historical Collections, Vols. 1, 2, 17.) Indianapolis: Indiana Historical Commission, 1916–30. The editor's introduction to the first volume was also published separately in 1916 under the same title.

Owen, Robert Dale. *Threading My Way: Twenty-Seven Years of Autobiography*. London: Trübner, 1874; New York: G. W. Carleton, 1874.

Pence, George, and Nellie C. Armstrong. *Indiana Boundaries: Territory, State, and County*. (Indiana Historical Collections, Vol. 19.) Indianapolis: Indiana Historical Bureau, 1933.

Report of the Sixteenth Annual Meeting of the State Bar Association of Indiana. (Contains the Journal of the Constitutional Convention of 1816.) Indianapolis: Harrington and Folger, 1912.

CHAPTER SIX: *Into the Twentieth Century*

Bowers, Claude G. *Beveridge and the Progressive Era*. Boston: Houghton Mifflin, 1932.

Clarke, Grace Julian. *George W. Julian*. (Indiana Historical Collections, Vol. 11; Biographical Series, Vol. 1.) Indianapolis: Indiana Historical Commission, 1923.

Ginger, Ray. *The Bending Cross: A Biography of Eugene Victor Debs.* New Brunswick, N.J.: Rutgers University Press, 1949; reprinted as *Eugene V. Debs: A Biography.* New York: Collier Books, 1962.

Julian, George W. *Political Recollections, 1840–1872.* Chicago: Jansen, McClurg, 1884.

Kelly, Sister M. Margaret Jean. *The Career of Joseph Lane, Frontier Politician.* Washington, D.C.: The Catholic University of America, 1942.

Kenworthy, Leonard S. *The Tall Sycamore of the Wabash, Daniel Wolsey Voorhees.* Boston, Bruce Humphries, 1936.

McNutt, Paul V. "An Executive Looks at History," *Indiana History Bulletin,* XIII (February, 1936), 92–102.

Stone, Irving. *Adversary in the House.* Garden City: Doubleday, 1947.

Wallace, Lew. *Life of Gen. Ben Harrison.* Chicago: John W. Iliff, 1888.

Zink, Harold. "Paul V. McNutt," in *The American Politician,* ed. J. T. Salter. Chapel Hill: University of North Carolina Press, 1938.

CHAPTER SEVEN: *Five Wars*

Buley, R. Carlyle. "Indiana in the Mexican War," *Indiana Magazine of History,* XV (September, December, 1919), 260–326; XVI (March, 1920), 46–68.

Cavnes, Max P. *The Hoosier Community at War. (Indiana in World War II,* Vol. 9, Indiana War History Commission; Indiana University Publications: Social Science Series, No. 20.) Bloomington: Indiana University Press, 1961.

Cockrum, William M. *History of the Underground Railroad.* Oakland City, Ind.: J. W. Cockrum Printing Co., 1915.

Cummins, Cedric C. *Indiana Public Opinion and the World War, 1914–1917.* (Indiana Historical Collections, Vol. 28.) Indianapolis: Indiana Historical Bureau, 1945.

Ewbank, Louis B. *Morgan's Raid in Indiana.* (Indiana Historical Society Publications, Vol. 7, No. 2.) Indianapolis: Indiana Historical Society, c. 1918.

Foulke, William Dudley. *Life of Oliver P. Morton.* 2 vols. Indianapolis: Bowen-Merrill, 1899.

Klement, Frank L. *The Copperheads in the Middle West.* Chicago: University of Chicago Press, 1960.

Nolan, Alan T. *The Iron Brigade: A Military History.* New York: Macmillan, 1961.

Stampp, Kenneth. *Indiana Politics during the Civil War.* (Indiana Historical Collections, Vol. 31.) Indianapolis: Indiana Historical Bureau, 1949.

Terrell, W. H. H. *Indiana in the War of the Rebellion: Report of the Adjutant General.* (Reprint of Vol. 1 of an eight-volume report, published in 1869; Indiana Historical Collections, Vol. 41.) Indianapolis: Indiana Historical Society, 1960.

Thornbrough, Emma Lou. *Indiana in the Civil War Era, 1850–1880.* (*The History of Indiana,* Vol. III.) Indianapolis: Indiana Historical Bureau and Indiana Historical Society, 1965.

CHAPTER EIGHT: *O Pioneers!*

Benton, Elbert Jay. *The Wabash Trade Route in the Development of the Old Northwest.* (Johns Hopkins University Studies in Historical and Political Science, Series XXI, Nos. 1–2.) Baltimore: Johns Hopkins Press, 1903.

Beste, J. Richard. *The Wabash: Or Adventures of an English Gentleman's Family in the Interior of America.* 2 vols. London: Hurst and Blackett, 1855.

Beveridge, Albert J. *Abraham Lincoln, 1809–1858.* 2 vols. Boston: Houghton Mifflin, 1928.

Esarey, Logan. *Internal Improvements in Early Indiana.* (Indiana Historical Society Publications, Vol. 5, No. 2.) Indianapolis: Indiana Historical Society, 1912.

Garman, Harry O. *Whitewater Canal, Cambridge City to the Ohio River.* Indianapolis: The Author, 1944. A major portion of this pamphlet, with the same title, is in *Indiana History Bulletin,* 39 (September, 1962), 127–38.

Peat, Wilbur D. *Indiana Houses of the Nineteenth Century.* Indianapolis: Indiana Historical Society, 1962.

Price, Robert. *Johnny Appleseed, Man and Myth.* Bloomington: Indiana University Press, 1954.

CHAPTER NINE: *Bridge to Maturity*

Boone, Richard G. *A History of Education in Indiana.* New York: D. Appleton, 1892. (Indiana Historical Collections Reprints.) Indianapolis: Indiana Historical Bureau, 1941.

Breyfogle, William. *Make Free: The Story of the Underground Railroad.* Philadelphia: J. B. Lippincott, 1958.

Cockrum, William M. *History of the Underground Railroad.* Oakland City, Ind.: J. W. Cockrum Printing Co., 1915.

Huffman, Wallace Spencer. "Indiana's Place in Automobile History," *Indiana History Bulletin,* 38 (September, 1961), 143–44.

Leich, Alexander and Roland. "Cars of Indiana," *Motor Trend*, 17, Nos. 9, 10 (September, October, 1965).

Littell, Harold. "Development of the City School System of Indiana—1851–1880," *Indiana Magazine of History*, XII (September, 1916), 193–213; (December, 1916), 299–325.

Moore, Powell A. *The Calumet Region: Indiana's Last Frontier.* (Indiana Historical Collections, Vol. 39.) Indianapolis: Indiana Historical Bureau, 1959.

Perring, Thomas Carter. "The New Albany–Salem Railroad—Incidents of Road and Men," *Indiana Magazine of History*, XV (December, 1919), 342–62.

Poucher, John. "Social Effects of the Monon Railway in Indiana," *ibid.*, XII (December, 1916), 326–36.

CHAPTER TEN: *Reflections*

Books and authors cited in this chapter.

Index

Centerville, 107–9, 133, 162, 168; *News-Letter*, 108
Central Canal, 171
Chapman, George A., 100
Charlestown, 61, 83–85, 87
Charlestown Ordnance Plant, 152
Chase, Ira, J., 104
Chicago, Ill., 4–5, 27, 166, 187, 189–90, 194, 221; *Tribune*, 16
Cincinnati, Ohio, 31–32, 58, 77, 82, 115, 141, 144, 146–47, 159, 164–66, 191
Civil War, 10; loyalty to Union, 14, 143–44, 147–48; home guards, 14, 137, 144–46; battles, 14, 138–39, 144, 146, 148; Copperheads, 14, 141–44; Indiana's role, 127, 138; recruiting for, 136–37, 139; regiments, 137, 147–48, 150; politics, 139–43; Morgan's Raid, 143–47; casualties, 147–50. *See also* Morton, Oliver P.
Clark, George Rogers, 9; captures Vincennes, 13, 51–55, 82, 153; receives grant, 56–57, 59
Clark, William, 59
Clark County, 56, 83–85, 88
Clarksville, 57
Climate, 7, 10
Clodfelter, Noah J., 207, 210, 216
Coffin, Levi, 181–82
Colfax, Schuyler, 15, 101, 104–5, 114, 135
Columbia City, 104
Columbus, 171, 183, 190, 196–97
Concordia College, 201
Connersville, 162, 196
Constitution, 1816: antislavery article, 93; Article IX, 94–95; amending, 95; General Assembly's power, 97
Constitution, 1851: the governor, 97, 103; bill of rights, 101–2; education, 102; public debt prohibited, 102, 174; amending, 102–3
Constitutional amendments, 103
Constitutional convention, first: delegates, 64, 85, 91–93; enabling act, 88–89; antislavery article, 93; work of, 97
Constitutional convention, second, 95–96, 100–1, 108; delegates, 79, 101; work of, 101–2
Corydon, 87, 162; state capital, 6, 97, 168; territorial capital, 86; constitutional convention at, 91–93, 97, 101, 153, 198; capitol, 92, 108; battle of, 146
Costigan, Francis, 162

Counties, in 1809, 84; in 1816, 85, MAP, 90; ninety-two, MAP, 186
Covington, 98, 112
Craig, George, 123, 126
Crane Naval Ammunition Depot, 152
Crawfordsville, 98, 134, 162, 171, 191, 207, 213, 224
Croghan, George, 29, 48–49

Dana, 217
Danville, 104
Daviess County, 152
Davis, Elmer, 16, 217
Davis, Jefferson C., 137, 139
Dawn, 209, 219
Dearborn County, 23, 84–85, 88, 135, 191
Debs, Eugene V., 15, 104, 106, 120–22
Delaware County, 171
Delaware Indians, 13, 20–21, 23, 26–27, 32, 39; *Walam Olum*, 20, 23, 27
Delphi, 112, 163
Democratic Party, 14–15, 204–5; organization of, 97–98; and McNutt, 97, 124–26; and second constitutional convention, 100–1; campaigns, 103–5, 109–10, 116–17, 121, 129, 133–36, 139, 204–5; during Civil War, 136, 140–42
DePauw, John, 91
DePauw University, 15, 91, 112, 118, 187, 200–1, 209–10, 217
Douglas, Lloyd C., 216
Dreiser, Theodore, 16, 208–9; career of, 218–27; family of, 218–20, 224; education of, 221; wife of, 221, 226; earning a living, 221–22, 225–26; first novel, 222–23; and concepts of day, 223–24; personality of, 225–26; travels of, 226; on Tarkington, 226; literary position of, 227
Dresser (Dreiser), Paul, 219–20, 223
Dublin, 163
Dudley, William W., 116–18
Dunes, Indiana, 8, 41, 190, 194
Dunn, Jacob Piatt, 12, 96, 210, 227
Dunning, Paris, 97, 131
Durbin, Winfield T., 104

Eads, James B., 16
Earlham College, 15, 199, 201
East Chicago, 5
Edinburg, 130, 183
Education: at New Harmony, 15–16, 73; state universities, 15, 102, 197–99, 201–

edge," 72–73; Declaration of Mental Independence, 75–76; contrasted with Rapp, 75–76

Owen, Robert Dale, 77, 175, 199; and Smithsonian Institution, 73, 79; at second constitutional convention, 79, 101; congressman, 79, 132; and Emancipation Proclamation, 79, 139

Owen, William, 70, 76–77, 79–80

Paoli, 59, 87, 142, 168, 171

Parke County, 6

Parks, state, 6

Pennington, Dennis, 92, 108

"People's Party" (Jennings), 96–97; (Republican), 134–35

Perry County, 84, 89

Peru, 39, 152, 163; circuses at, 187

Petersburg, 181

Pioneers, 27, 30, 34, 37–38, 86–89, 153; education, 158–59, 199–200; *farms,* life on, 153–60; self-sufficiency, 159–60; *towns,* life in, 160–61; "mansions" in, 161–63

Plainfield, 100

Plants, native, 7–8, 10

Plymouth, 39; *Democrat,* 141

Politics: today, 14–15, 126–27, 203–5; horse-trading and logrolling, 96–97; Jacksonian Democracy, 97, 98–99, 101, 126, 136; campaigns, 99–100, 103–6, 108–9, 115, 117, 126, 134–36, 150–51; mother of vice presidents, 104–5, 203; during Civil War, 134–36, 139–42, 143. *See also* Democratic Party; Republican Party; Whig Party

Polke, William, 93

Pontiac (Ottawa), 29, 48

Poplar, yellow (state tree), 7

Population: ethnic groups, 10–11, 87, 102, 150; nonwhite, 11; statistics, 61, 87–88, 130; sources of, 87

Porter, Albert G., 104

Porter, Cole, 16

Porter, Gene Stratton, 213

Porter County, 181, 193

Portland, 196

Posey, Thomas, 61, 96

Posey County, 4, 22–23, 62, 80, 85, 89, 92, 181, 216

Potawatomi Indians, 13, 26–27, 38, 42; "Trail of Death," 38–39

Prehistoric Antiquities of Indiana, 20

Princeton, 63; *Union Democrat,* 141

Proctor, Henry, 37

The Prophet (Shawnee), 14, 36, 60

Purdue, John, 202

Purdue University, 15, 187, 199, 201–2, 205

Putnam County, 6

Pyle, Ernie, 217

Quakers. *See* Friends, Society of

Railroads, 170–72; early problems, 184–85; Railroads in 1860, MAP, 186; safety precautions, 187; rapid growth, 188; today, 188–89

—, Madison and Indianapolis, 130, 183–84; Evansville and Terre Haute, 175, 187; Lawrenceburg and Indianapolis, 183; Ohio and Mississippi, 185; Monon (Louisville, New Albany, Chicago), 187–88, 197–98, 208; Indianapolis and Bellefontaine, 188; Evansville and Indianapolis Straight Line, 188

—, electric, 189–90; Evansville and Ohio Valley, 190; South Shore, 190

Raintree County, 216

Ralston, Samuel M., 103–4, 151

Randolph, Thomas, 84–85

Randolph County, 7

Rapp, Frederick: Harmony Society's business manager, 64, 68, 91; at constitutional convention, 64, 92–93; sale of Harmonie, 69–70

Rapp, George: in Byron's *Don Juan,* 62; religious communism of, 64–65; adopts son, 64; Harmonie, 65–69; contrasted with Owen, 75–76; book by, 77

Ray, James, 97, 99, 162, 170, 184, 188

Regniers, Beatrice Schenk de, 217

Reno Gang: first train robbery, 185

Republican Party, 14–15, 204–5; campaigns, 104–6, 109, 115–17, 126, 134–36, 150–51; and Civil War, 134–36, 138–43, 146

Resources, natural, 14, 88, 192–93

Rexroth, Kenneth, 216

Reynolds, David, 129

Richmond, 4, 110, 190, 200; *Jeffersonian,* 141

Ridpath, John Clark, 217

Riley, James Whitcomb, 16, 100, 108, 114, 208, 214–16

Rising Sun, 162